TEACHING FOR PURPOSE

TEACHING FOR PURPOSE

PREPARING STUDENTS FOR LIVES OF MEANING

HEATHER MALIN

HARVARD EDUCATION PRESS
Cambridge, Massachusetts

Paperback ISBN 978-1-68253-257-7
Library Edition ISBN 978-1-68253-258-4

Library of Congress Cataloging-in-Publication Data
Names: Malin, Heather, author.
Title: Teaching for purpose : preparing students for lives of meaning / Heather Malin.
Description: Cambridge, Massachusetts : Harvard Education Press, 2018. | Includes bibliographical references and index.
Identifiers: LCCN 2018023835| ISBN 9781682532577 (pbk.) | ISBN 9781682532584 (library edition)
Subjects: LCSH: Affective education—United States. | Social learning—United States. | Educational psychology—United States. | Education—Aims and objectives—United States. | Educational change—United States. | Education, Humanistic—United States.
Classification: LCC LB1072 .M35 2018 | DDC 370.15/340973—dc23 LC record available at https://lccn.loc.gov/2018023835

Published by Harvard Education Press,
an imprint of the Harvard Education Publishing Group

Harvard Education Press
8 Story Street
Cambridge, MA 02138

Figure 4.1 Design: Katharine Atwood
Cover Design: Endpaper Studio
Cover Image: iStock.com/tatianazaets
The typefaces used in this book are Lunaquete and Isidora

CONTENTS

INTRODUCTION

What matters most to you? What are the things you really care about? If you could change anything in the world, what would you change?

When you were in school, did you have the opportunity to explore these questions and really think about what you value, who you wanted to become, or how you wanted to use your learning to contribute to the world? Did your school assignments connect to the things you thought were most meaningful and help you develop your purpose in life? At the Stanford Center on Adolescence, my colleagues and I have asked hundreds of teenagers these questions, and the majority say, "I want to get good grades so I can go to college, get a good job, and be successful." Students today know the script well, but do they know what it means? Do they have a vision of what success looks like for them? In our interviews, we have found that few students—about 24 percent of high school seniors and fewer in younger grades—have identified and are pursuing a purpose for their life. We do not expect that students have identified their singular life purpose before they leave high school, but we do know that high school students, and even middle school students, are capable of identifying something that matters, that gives them a sense of purpose, and pursuing it. The low levels of purpose seen among middle and high school students is a concern. Purpose is associated with numerous other benefits for young people, including academic benefits. Students who cannot connect their learning to any sense of purpose are less likely to be motivated by or engaged in what they are doing in school. In the bigger picture, they have no purpose to connect their education to as a whole, so even if they learn the skills they will need in college, most students lack the sense of purpose that will get them through college successfully. Students are not actually ready for college if they have no idea how to make good use of the time and resources once they get there.

What if purpose were the purpose of education? Purpose, as it is discussed in this book, is a future-directed goal that is personally meaningful and aimed at contributing to something larger than the self. Purpose is a driving force that motivates and organizes shorter-term goal setting, goal action, and behavior. With a sense of purpose, young people are more inclined to seek out and gain the skills and expertise they need to fulfill their goals, so purpose can drive learning that results in the necessary college and work life skills to succeed. What if we put this highly motivating driver at the center of how, why, and what we teach students, and let that purpose be the primary driver of students' engagement with school? The challenges of doing so are immediately evident. Purpose is different for everyone, so how can a teacher teach to every students' purpose? How can students know their purpose at such a young age? How can purpose motivate students to learn the difficult and boring academic skills that they need but that do not align with their interests? The answer to the last question is it cannot, at least, not always and not for every student. However, there is a lot that purpose can do to engage and motivate students at school, and I believe it can transform schools as well. I wrote this book to interrogate these questions and challenges and explore the role that purpose can play in shaping school climate, relationships, and learning activities. My purpose in writing this book is to share what I have learned from over a decade of conducting research on youth purpose at the Stanford Center on Adolescence, and from investigating current efforts to teach for purpose in K-12 schools, so that educators can help more students make the connection between what they are learning now and the person they want to become in the future.

PURPOSE OF THE BOOK

You might be wondering if this book is about having a purpose for teaching, helping students understand the purpose of what they are learning, or helping students create lives of purpose. The answer, of course, is "yes," and you will find all three woven into these chapters. The goal of this book is to argue for expansive thinking about the direction our schools can take, as we increasingly need students to be educated differently from how they were in the past—students who are creative, critical thinkers, innovative problem finders and solvers, socially and environmentally aware, and self-directed in constructing their lives. Developing these capacities in students requires that they see the purpose of what they are learning for their future, and it requires that students learn to see themselves as people who can and must contribute to bettering the world. At the same time, the goal of this book is not to propose a whole new set of reforms for teachers to take on, or argue for the implementation of cutting-edge educational tools and technology to individualize student learning. Teachers, I believe, have the capacity to adopt and adapt strategies for purposeful teaching from enduring good ideas in educational theory and practice. There are a few new teaching ideas in these pages, but largely there is a call for educators to ask themselves the question posed above: What if purpose were the purpose of education? And with that question as the driving force, reimagine the whole experience of school for our children.

We teach children that they should aspire to academic achievement at all costs, in some cases asking them to sacrifice their childhood for academic gains. When we do look beyond academic skills, it is to focus on "non-cognitive" character strengths and skills that will support their academic achievement, such as grit and growth mindset. We put tremendous value on academic achievement, and we convey that value to students, but what about their lives beyond school, when academic achievement is behind them? What about all of the other domains of life that they live and develop in? The current mantra in schools is "college and career readiness," and it is true that college and career are crucial beacons for guiding students to their future, especially for students who see college as a distant or unrealistic goal for their lives. But when do we ask students to articulate a vision of who they are becoming and the kind of person they want to be? We teach students grit, growth mindset and self-control, hoping that they can use these strengths and mindsets to pursue their goals, but when do they get to think about *what* their goals are, what they want for their future, who they are becoming, and how they want to be in the world? What kind of world do they want to live in, and how will they participate in creating that world? What are their most central values and how are they going to live out those values? We have created such a narrow vision of success for our children and a shortsighted target for their dreams. By focusing on purpose, we can expand that vision of success. Students do not need to know what they want to do with their life when they leave high school, nor do they need to have a single purpose figured out, and that is not the goal of this book. They should, however, know that purpose is accessible to them and worth striving for, and they should have aspirations and expectations of their future that are robust enough to set their sights through and beyond college, even if those aspirations will evolve over time.

ORGANIZATION OF THE BOOK

This book integrates three sources of information to explore the question of making purpose the purpose of school: theory and research on youth purpose development, examination of pedagogy and teaching practices that can support purpose development, and investigation of programs designed to teach students to create purpose in their lives. Part 1 provides an overview of purpose theory and research from the perspective of how it relates to the context of schools and education. If we want to do anything with purpose, we first need to have a sense of what purpose is and what gives us a sense of purpose. Therefore, chapter 1 opens the book with a purpose exploration activity to examine what drives you and why. With an internalized sense of your own purpose in mind, the first chapter then unpacks some popular ideas about purpose, looking at some of the myths and metaphors that tend to shape our beliefs about purpose.

Chapter 2 takes us to the earliest days of purpose formation, investigating play and making activities as the foundation of purpose. This chapter discusses concepts related to purpose—meaning and intention—as aspects of purpose that can be supported through playing and making things at school. Play is presented as an early childhood activity, but the connection between play and purpose should not end in elementary school. The processes involved in playing with ideas and making connections between our inner lives and the outside world are essential to purpose throughout the life span. Chapter 3 relates purpose to social-emotional development and learning, emphasizing that purpose is personally meaningful and also outward looking, and therefore integrates social and psychological development. In this discussion of the social, emotional, and moral aspects of purpose, we also find the advantages teachers might see when their students have a sense of purpose, such as increased motivation and engagement at school. Chapter 4 outlines the theory of purpose as the integration of three dimensions—beyond-the-self motivation, higher-order goal setting, and action—and proposes a set of skills—self-regulation, agency, and values formation—that form an internal engine that can help integrate the three dimensions. This chapter then begins the transition to part 2 by introducing some of the research on social factors that support young people's purpose development.

Part 2 takes us into schools to investigate the pedagogies and practices that can support student purpose. The questions examined in the second half of the book are: How can schools and teachers support student purpose? And, what is the impact on schools when they do? Therefore, this section starts in chapter 5 with an investigation of school climate and student-teacher relationships, how they can be shaped to support purpose, and inversely, how relationships and climate in schools are transformed when purpose is prioritized. Chapter 7 provides a framework for making instruction more purposeful through project-based learning and related pedagogies. This chapter highlights the elements of project-based learning that are believed to support purpose according to theory and research on purpose development. Examples provided in this chapter show how project methods can be made purposeful at different school stages. Chapter 9 introduces content that can be integrated into the curriculum to support purpose development. This chapter looks at four topics—empathy, values, the future, and power—in terms of how they relate to purpose and strategies for including them in the curriculum so that they can support purpose. This chapter also introduces the potential of teaching purpose as a topic with some interventions that were designed to engage students in exploration of their own purpose through short activities.

Woven throughout part 2 are profiles of external organizations that have developed purpose programs for schools. There are six profiles all together, two each in chapters 6, 8, and 10, describing organizations that bring purpose education to K–12 schools throughout the US. The profiles describe the models they use, some of their strategies, and the response from teachers, principals, and students. Each profile demonstrates the innovative approaches these organizations are developing to not just teach purpose, but to transform how we educate young people. Though each organization takes a unique approach, their commonalities point to elements that can make up the core of a purpose education program. Chapter 11 summarizes what was learned from the program profiles and looks back over the entire book to offer a point-by-point list of what educators can do right now to start making their classrooms and schools more purposeful.

Throughout the book, we hear the voices of young people who participated in research interviews conducted by the Stanford Center on Adolescence. Their names are pseudonyms, but their stories and quotes are real and provided here to illustrate the role that adults and schools can play in helping students create purpose in their lives. The young people quoted and described throughout this book are exemplary in their purpose and are not meant to indicate what is normal for adolescents. Rather, they show what is possible when the circumstances and opportunities are right for purpose to flourish.

The goal of this book is not to prescribe a program for teaching purpose. Rather, my goal is to offer purpose as a touchstone for evolving the practice of education, and to suggest strategies and frameworks that might inspire educators to take steps toward creating a culture of purpose in their schools. The ideas in this book are based on longstanding theory and research in youth purpose development, along with conversations with teachers and school leaders, program providers, and students, as well as observations in schools. There are brief interventions for teaching purpose and related concepts included here, which are effective according to the research. However, my hope is to leave readers with encouragement to do more. Rather than asking how little of the school day can be spent on student purpose development, this book ambitiously looks at purpose as a comprehensive approach to addressing some of the biggest challenges schools face today. We have, together and over time, created a school system that does not work for our children or our society today. But we also have the power to change it. Teachers, counselors, administrators, and all the adults in schools who work directly with students are the ones who can make this happen. The aim of this book is to encourage and inspire you to bring purpose to your work with students, to make our schools places of purpose.

PART I

PURPOSE AND EDUCATION

WHAT IS PURPOSE? How do we get it? Why do we want it? In part 1, we examine purpose as a psychological construct and as a developmental path young people can follow to lead a meaningful and fulfilling life. Some of the more complicated theoretical questions about purpose are discussed in this section: Do we have one purpose in life or many? Does purpose have to last my whole life, or can I change purposes? What is the difference between purpose and meaning in life? Do I have to "find my passion" to have purpose in life? After exploring your own purpose in chapter 1, you will read about the developmental precursors of purpose that emerge in childhood and the external supports that adults can provide to help students pursue a life of purpose. The investigation of how purpose might emerge and develop during childhood begins in preschool, when children start to develop their sense of self in relation to the world. Building from that early awareness, this section looks at how children make meaning in their lives, engage their personal intentions as they participate in social activities, and learn how they can contribute to the world beyond themselves, paving the way for purpose to develop. Chapter 4 outlines a model of purpose as a developmental construct made up of three integrated dimensions: beyond-the-self motivation, a meaningful higher-order goal, and action. The model shows how these three dimensions develop independently and integrate, weaving together what is personally meaningful with what is socially consequential, resulting in fully realized purpose. This purpose is beneficial as a positive developmental outcome for students and is associated with other beneficial psychological, social, emotional, and academic outcomes.

The path of early purpose development is examined here through research conducted by developmental scientists and positive psychologists. Purpose is a topic of intense interest to developmental psychologists who study positive youth development and those who study positive psychology at all stages of life. Several have theorized about what purpose is and why it matters, and from this theory have conducted research that shapes our understanding of what it means to have purpose and how it develops. The study of purpose as a distinct psychological construct is a relatively recent development, and research findings that shape our understanding of purpose continue to emerge. The description of purpose development that follows reflects the current science-based knowledge in a growing and evolving field of study. In addition to scientific studies, this section uses interviews with young people to illustrate purpose and its development in childhood and adolescence. Weaving developmental theory, research findings, and quotes from young people, this section provides a model of youth purpose development that can be connected to students' lives in school and begins to reveal the things that educators can do to support students' purpose development. Of note, this section describes how educators can understand and connect with students who come from different backgrounds than their own, by learning about what might give their students a sense of purpose. By looking at the science of youth purpose development through the lens of what it means for teaching and learning, we can envision school as a place where purpose grows.

CHAPTER ONE

What Is Your Purpose?

My hope with this book is to inspire, inform, and encourage educators, school staff, and others to help young people live a life of purpose. Although the primary focus is on how to support students in developing their purpose, it is also about making schools places of purpose, and what would happen to schools if the most desired outcome of education were purposeful lives. We are not only concerned with student lives, but the lives of everyone in the school environment, including you. For one thing, you matter. Your experience and happiness and fulfillment matter. This is something people forget when their career is a service to others. I do not believe you can be truly focused on your students' purpose if you haven't explored your own. To that end, this chapter is an exploration of purpose up close and personal—it is an exploration of your purpose. Through this exploration, you will be more in tune with what really matters to you, in your work and in other areas of your life, and we will have a shared understanding of what I mean when I am talking about purpose throughout this book.

The first step is for you, the reader, to reflect on your purpose. If you work in a school, you might do a lot of reflecting related to your work, but how often do you reflect on what matters to you, fills you up, and energizes you? When do you reflect on the aspects of your life and work that are most meaningful to you? How often do you get to step back and think about your most important values and the role those values play in shaping your teaching practice? Even if you do find opportunities for this kind of deep reflection, I encourage you to do the following activity. The focus of this activity is not on your students' needs or your supervisor's expectations. You are the focus of this chapter, so spend some time with it.

If you have been caught up in the demands of teaching or working in or with schools, it is possible that you have lost sight of why you started working in education in the first place. The outside demands become so important and pressing that they require you to set aside your own purpose again and again. But your purpose is what centers you and drives you forward. It energizes, engages, and motivates. It helps you focus on what matters and provides guidance for setting daily goals that will move you toward accomplishing your big life goals. It keeps you moving forward despite obstacles, challenges, and setbacks. When you are aware of what matters to you and working on what gives you a sense of purpose, you will feel fulfilled by your work more often than you feel drained or defeated by it.

This purpose-exploration activity is based on the definition of purpose that we have used in over a decade of research on youth purpose development. Purpose, as we define it, is a higher-order goal that is general and driving, such as a desire to help others or protect the environment, in contrast with more specific goals that provide avenues for pursuing purpose, such as getting into nursing school or starting a recycling program in your neighborhood. The goal is stable and projected into the future, and therefore it provides direction for setting short-term goals that you can act on in your day-to-day life.[1] A purpose goal is one that is *personally meaningful and connected to what is most central to your identity* and feels like something you must do. Most important to our definition of purpose, it is *motivated by a desire to be of consequence in the world*, to do something positive for the world beyond the self. When this personally meaningful, beyond-the-self–oriented, higher-order goal is *acted on in a way that is sustained*, we call it purpose. This definition is based on intensive investigation of theory from philosophers and psychologists, dating back to Aristotle. It is not the only definition of purpose being used today, and although our research supports our belief that this definition is a valid way to think about purpose, you might have a different way of thinking about purpose in your own life. I encourage you to complete the following exploration based on how we define purpose, then afterward reflect on how this relates to your own ideas about purpose. The more you reflect on this, the better prepared you will be to fully develop your own purpose and engage students in pursuing theirs.

REFLECT ON YOUR PURPOSE

I invite you to spend some time with the following questions, which are adapted from the purpose interview protocol that our team originally created to do research on how purpose develops in adolescence.[2] We have since used these questions to learn about purpose among young entrepreneurs, civic exemplars, and retirees, and versions of this interview have been used with people as young as eleven years old and as old as ninety-two. Members of our team have used this interview not only for research, but also as an intervention with high school students and in professional development with teachers. We learned early in our research program not to ask about purpose directly. It can be intimidating to have a stranger grill you with questions like, "What is your purpose in life?" Aside from not wanting to scare off our participants, we have learned through years of studying purpose that not everyone thinks of it in quite the same way. For example, some people think of purpose as their passion, others think of it as their connection to a higher power, and still others think of it as whatever will give them the greatest happiness in life. In a study that asked teachers to talk about purpose, they did not describe purpose in the same way that we define it.[3] Some did not think of purpose as beyond-the-self oriented, while others did not think of it as personally meaningful. To make sure all our interviewees are answering the same question, we do not ask about purpose at all. Instead, we ask about the things that matter to them, and then ask a lot of follow-up questions to fully understand those things that matter and what role those things play in the person's life. So, that is what I am going to ask you to reflect on now. Below you will find a series of questions to think about, and I ask that you spend a few minutes with each question before moving on to the next one. I encourage you to write your responses, so you can look back at them if needed.

First, spend a few minutes writing down some of the things that are most important to you. What really matters to you? You might only think of one or two things, but I encourage you to come up with a few things that might cover different aspects of your life. If you find yourself thinking about many things, try to categorize them so you have general areas instead of specific things. For example, instead of naming each member of your family, you can think about "family" as something that matters. As you come up with a list of things that are very important to you, see if you can rank them so that you have two or three overarching aspects of your life that are clearly the most important to you, even if you have a long list of other things that are also important.

TABLE 1.1 Three things that matter most

1.
2.
3.

In the next step of this reflection activity, you will walk through some why, when, what, and how questions about the things that matter most to you, which can also be thought of as your most important values. These questions will help to paint a vivid and voluminous portrait of the aspects of your life that might be sources of purpose. First, think about *why* the things you listed in table 1.1 are most important to you. Make a list of the most compelling reasons (for yourself, not for others) that you listed these as the things that matter most to you.

TABLE 1.2 Reasons the important things matter

WHY does it matter to you?
1.
2.
3.

When did each value listed in table 1.1 become important to you? Is it a temporary interest or something that has mattered for a long time? Will it be important long into the future? These questions can help you think about how these values express your enduring identity by examining the connection between the things you value most, events in your past, and expectations of who you will be in the future.

TABLE 1.3 Connection to identity

WHEN did it become important to you? HOW LONG will it be important?
1.
2.
3.

How energizing is each value listed in table 1.1? Does it drive you to set goals, make plans, and take action? These questions can help you think about whether the things that matter most to you are giving drive and direction to how you live your life.

TABLE 1.4 Drive and direction

HOW energizing is it? Does it motivate, drive, or direct your actions?
1.
2.
3.

If you work in education or some other role with young people, did you focus on your work at any point in the reflection activity you just completed? If you did not reflect on your work in education or schools, that's fine because it is important to focus on what really matters to you, but now I am going to ask you to do the same reflection in relation to your work. If you did focus on some aspect of your work in the previous reflection, you can skip this step.

Think about the things that are most important to you in your work. What really matters? What do you really care about in your work? Focus on up to three things that are very important to you about your work. Next, revisit the why, when, what, and how questions, but focused on the aspects of your work that matter to you the most.

TABLE 1.5 Three things that matter most to you at work

1.
2.
3.

Why are the things you listed in table 1.5 most important to you about your work? Make a list of the most compelling reasons (for yourself, not for others) that you listed these as the things that matter most to you

TABLE 1.6. Reasons the important things at work matter

WHY does it matter to you?
1.
2.
3.

When did each value listed in table 1.5 become important to you? Is it a temporary interest or something that has mattered for a long time? Will it be important long into the future? These questions can help you think about how these values express your enduring identity by examining the connection between the things you value most, events in your past, and expectations of who you will be in the future.

TABLE 1.7 Connection to identity

WHEN did it become important to you? HOW LONG will it be important?
1.
2.
3.

How energizing is each work value listed in table 1.5? Does it drive you to set goals, make plans, and take action? These questions can help you think about whether the things that matter most to you are giving drive and direction to how you engage with your work.

TABLE 1.8 Drive and direction

WHAT goals, plans, or activities relate to these important things?
1.
2.
3.

Thinking more broadly now, and not in connection to the important things you just ranked, answer the next two questions about your goals and activities. First, what are your most prominent goals right now? What are you planning for and hoping to accomplish?

TABLE 1.9 Current goals

What are your most prominent goals right now?

Next, think about the activities that you are involved in. How do you spend your time? What are some of the activities you spend most of your time on? When you have unstructured time, how do you use it?

TABLE 1.10 Current activities

What are the activities that you currently spend most of your time and energy on?
1.
2.
3.

Now you can reflect on your responses in tables 1.1 through 1.10 to explore possible areas of purpose in your life. This exploration will guide you through the process we use to determine if our study participants are fully purposeful, have a precursory form of purpose, or are not purposeful at this time in their lives. We do this by looking at their responses for indicators that they have some or all the dimensions that make up the definition of purpose used in this book: at least one personally meaningful goal, driven by a desire to contribute to the world beyond the self, and acted on in a way that shows enduring connection and commitment.

Look back to the values you listed in tables 1.1 and 1.5. These are some of your most important values. Purpose is usually rooted in our most important values, and if we have purpose, it will most likely be revealed in these things that we value most.

When you reflected on your most prominent current goals in table 1.9, were they related to the things that you listed in table 1.1 or 1.5? Are your most prominent goals aligned with your values?

When you reflected on the reasons that those most important things matter to you in tables 1.2 and 1.6, were any of the reasons beyond the self? That is, are any of these important things important because they are a way for you to help others, contribute to society, be connected with something larger than yourself, or somehow have a positive impact in the world, no matter how big or small? Do you ever think about how the things that are important to you impact the world or others? Purpose is not necessarily only motivated by beyond-the-self concerns. In fact, it is more likely that we find both self-oriented and beyond-the-self–oriented motivations driving our purpose. But if there is no—or only very superficial—beyond-the-self motivation, it is not what is defined here as purpose.

When you reflected on how you spend your time in table 1.10, did you find that you regularly spend time doing things to act on the values that matter most to you? "Regularly" means that you find time to commit to those important things, ideally weekly, though the time frame will differ depending on what it is. For example, if visiting new countries is very important to you and you make international trips every summer, that could be considered spending time regularly. On the other end of the time spectrum, if you find staying physically fit to be most important to you, daily or every-other-day exercise might be a better indicator of regular time commitment. Purpose does not have to consume all our time, but if it is purpose, we will be driven to stay at it, return to it, make room for it regardless of whatever else is happening in our lives. It will also be something that has been driving our activities for a while and will continue to be into the future (even if the specific way we act on it evolves).

TABLE 1.11 Reflect and integrate

How do the things that matter most to you relate to your most prominent goals and activities?
1.
2.
3.

Look again at those things you listed in tables 1.1 and 1.5. Do any of those things give you a sense of purpose in life, according to your own definition of purpose? Or would you say that any of those things are, or are related to, your purpose? Earlier, I defined purpose as a higher-order goal that is meaningful and contributes to the world beyond the self, and commitment to doing something about it. Do any of your most important values fit that definition?

After you have taken some time to reflect on the questions above, write about the things that emerged that are potential sources of purpose for your life in table 1.12.

TABLE 1.12 Sources of my purpose

Do You Have Purpose?

The answers that emerged in this exploration should give you an idea of what areas of life might be a source of purpose for you. It also provides the information needed to find out if you are fully purposeful (according to how we define it), and what you can work on if you are not fully purposeful but want to be. As described above, purpose is three things integrated: a broad, higher-order goal that is meaningful to you and energizes you; beyond-the-self motivation driving the goal; and active engagement in pursuing the goal. If each of those things are present and integrated, we would say that you are fully realizing purpose in your life. If any of these aspects of purpose were missing, or not integrated, that suggests you are on your way to full purpose, and working on the missing aspects could help you gain a greater sense of purpose in life.

If you do not quite feel that you have a fully realized sense of purpose in your life, the reflection and exploration you just did can help you identify what is missing, and what you can work on if you do want to move toward a fuller sense of purpose. Our research team, under the direction of William Damon, identified partially-realized forms of purpose based on the presence and absence of each of these aspects of purpose. Borrowing from Damon's terms, I will call these partial purpose forms *dreaming*, *dabbling*, and *success seeking*.[4]

Are You Dreaming?

Do you have intentions and aspirations motivated by a desire to make a positive contribution in the world but have not found an opportunity to act on them? Often, we get stuck on big, abstract problems that seem impossible to solve. If that is you, it will help to identify smaller, more specific and tangible goals that will take you further, step-by-step, toward fulfilling your dream. Purpose is an abstract, higher-order goal, but the way to achieve that goal is to find very specific ways to act on it. The desire to achieve world peace is admirable, but it is impractical as a personal goal. Each of us who aspires to world peace needs to think about the concrete contributions we can make toward that lofty goal, and by doing so we can attain personal purpose. If you are an educator, you might want to see all your students go to college, an admirable dream, but unlikely to be possible unless you establish clear, smaller and more specific goals that will bring you closer to that goal. For example, you might identify two or three students each semester who show the drive to get to college but need support to understand the steps they need to take to get there. The key for dreamers is to take action and stick with it. Having purpose means finding a way to be of consequence, big or small, and that requires doing something. In fact, recent research suggests that acting on goals contributes more to having a sense of purpose in life than the nature or content of our goals and dreams.[5]

Some people become overwhelmed because they see so many problems or issues that are important and have difficulty identifying one to focus their time on. It is true, there are so many issues that need attention, but purpose only happens when we act. If you feel overwhelmed by too many problems in the world, see if you can identify some of the overarching values that unite those problems. If you do not see one, try looking at the domains of the things you identified as most important. Which of the following do you feel a stronger pull to when you think about the things that matter most to you: family, community, society, culture, or environment? If you can see an overarching theme or domain, or identify the set of values that are most important to you right now, you can try following the steps in committing to goal pursuit described by Sonia Lyubomirsky in her book *How of Happiness*.[6] Lyubomirsky suggests a process to use for pursuing important goals: (1) select a goal that is authentic, intrinsically motivated, and most meaningful to you (and to be a purpose goal, that also contributes beyond the self), (2) make a personal or public commitment to the goal, and (3) break that larger goal into a list of concrete baby steps, or sub-goals, that can be completed and checked off before moving on to the next baby step. Those of us who feel overwhelmed by all the problems we see can become paralyzed, and rather than doing something, we fail to act. This is a roadblock to purpose, but it can be overcome when we identify one goal with concrete sub-goals, commit to the goal, and act on it by checking off the small steps taken to accomplish it. The other issues or interests will not go away, but by putting them in the background temporarily, you can make the sustained commitment to action that is needed to feel a full sense of purpose in life.

Are You Dabbling?

Do you engage in a lot of different activities without finding purpose in any of them, and without making any sustained commitments? Those of us who dabble might volunteer occasionally, attend first meetings but not attend follow-up meetings, or take workshops but not act on them afterward. If we are dabbling, we are likely very busy with activity, but none of our activities feel particularly meaningful and do not drive us to develop aspirations or make the activity more central to our identity. If this is you, you will need to think about what your most important values are and go deep. Take time to reflect on two or three things that you identified as most important, and why you identified them as important. Can you find a thread through these things that might represent the values that are most central to your sense of self? If you struggle to come up with some values that feel central to your identity, you can try reflecting on the things you spend your time doing, to uncover and amplify the connections that draw you to those activities. Do you most value working with others to accomplish something? Or helping people in need? Do you value creating a more vibrant community by sharing common interests with your neighbors? Or making a more beautiful world through art and poetry? Is social justice really important to you? These deeper, beyond-the-self values may not lie on the surface of the activities and interests you are drawn to, but reflection can help you discover them. Those who tend to dabble often lack a sense of meaning in the things they do. They might be inspired to try something or be active in a lot of ways, but there is little coherence in the things they do and the goals they set. To find purpose, dabblers need to reflect on what matters, set goals according to the things that matter most, and choose activities that reflect their values.

Are You Success Seeking?

Did you identify one or more important life goals that you are committed to and actively pursuing but that show little or no interest in making a positive contribution to something beyond the self? Many of us are driven to succeed, to make something of our lives by achieving happiness, material wealth, or status in our careers. We might seek to win praise or awards in our work or hobbies so that we have tangible indicators of our accomplishments. We might engage in hobbies purely for the enjoyment they give us. Some argue that these interests and pursuits are ways of finding purpose in life, that those who are dedicated to achieving personal happiness or success, improving in an activity that they are passionate about, or demonstrating their worth by climbing up the ladder at work, are all showing the commitment of someone with purpose. But is this purpose in life? The questions answered with these self-satisfying pursuits is "What do I want my life to be like?" and, "What do I want to accomplish?," not, "Why am I here?" or, "What is the purpose of my life in the world?" When we are motivated to pursue goals for beyond-the-self reasons, we get a greater sense of well-being and satisfaction, decreased loneliness and interpersonal problems, and are likely to experience better health and longer life, compared to purely self-interested reasons. If you are focused on self-oriented aspirations and success, you might experience a sense of accomplishment and happiness, but the research suggests that you will be less likely to feel those accomplishments are meaningful and fulfilling, and will not get the same psychological well-being and physical health benefits you would experience if you thought about how your pursuits might serve others or something larger than yourself.[7]

If you did not identify a beyond-the-self purpose in this activity but you do feel a strong commitment to pursuits that are aimed at your own sense of success or happiness, you do not necessarily need to identify entirely different goals or pursuits to have purpose as defined here. However, if you want to explore the possibility of finding more fulfillment and meaning in those pursuits, and perhaps even gain more psychological benefits from them, you can reflect on how those pursuits can contribute to others or society. Purpose is not entirely beyond-the-self motivated, but is most likely driven by both self-oriented and beyond-the-self reasons, so it might simply be that you have not taken the time to reflect about how acting on the things that matter most to you can also serve others. It might be, however, that the self-focus in your interests and pursuits makes you uncomfortable or dissatisfied, which might suggest that your goals and activities are not well-aligned with your values. In that case, it would be worth examining how you set your goals, how you spend your time, and how both your goals and actions relate to what matters most to you.

PURPOSEFUL TEACHERS

This exercise might suggest that purpose is necessarily found in a single goal or activity, but it is possible, and even likely, that you identified more than one area of life that is a source of purpose or potential purpose. You might also find that you are a dreamer in some aspects of life and a dabbler in others. The goal is not to zero in on your One and Only Purpose, something few people have. Rather, this activity is an opportunity to identify and explore the potential for purpose in your life. Because this book is written primarily for education professionals, I want to take a moment to further examine work-related purpose, and the potential of finding multiple sources of purpose at work, especially for those who work in schools.

People who find purpose in their work do so in different ways. Some people find their work fulfilling because providing for their families gives them an immense sense of purpose. Others do not find anything meaningful about the function of their job but find purpose in making a positive work environment for their colleagues. Some teachers might find purpose in giving children access to the world of ideas through reading. Others might find purpose in contributing to creating a more equal society. Many education professionals will have more than one purpose motivating their work. Yet, many others will struggle with these questions because outside demands have caused them to lose connection with the purpose that drove them to work in education. To make matters more complex, purpose is not necessarily the starting point for a career choice. Rather, it is possible and even common to start a job or career and find purpose in it along the way or start the career with one purpose in mind and shift purpose over time.

A few examples will show how teachers can be doing the same job, and find purpose in their work, yet be purposeful for entirely different reasons. The first example is Dave, a tenth-grade biology teacher. Dave is fascinated by science and energized by sharing the mystifying world of microbes and DNA with his students. He also loves to see the ways that biology is applied in the world. He follows the current research and shares popular science articles with his students so they can make connections between their classroom learning and science discoveries that are having an impact in the real world. Dave's greatest hope for his students is that they will take with them the connection between classroom biology and the real-world study of biology and awareness of how biologists' research increases our understanding of the physical world. He gets his greatest sense of fulfillment when he hears that former students are doing work that applies what they learned in their science classes.[8]

Melissa, also a tenth-grade teacher, works in a school in a high-poverty neighborhood. Many of her students come to school without having breakfast, some have not slept because their homes are noisy around the clock, and several do not have secure housing at all. She chose this school because she wanted to make a difference in the world. She sees education as the best hope for alleviating childhood poverty and became a teacher so she could be part of the solution. Her focus is on getting as many of her students as possible on the path to college. Melissa teaches English, a subject that has never excited her, but she believes strong communication skills are the most valuable thing she can give her students to help them get to college and succeed once they get there. Her greatest sense of accomplishment comes from seeing her students' letters on the college acceptance wall each spring.

If you identified purpose outside your work in education, you might still find ways to connect your purpose with your work. People who work in schools have a unique opportunity in this regard because students benefit from having purpose role models. If you find purpose in something outside your work, bring that to your students and share it with them, and you will be supporting their purpose by doing so. Show them what it is to have purpose, how you pursue it, and how you stay committed to something that gives you purpose on top of your work responsibilities. Share your purpose and open yourself to being a mentor for students who are inspired by your interests. You can be fulfilled at work even if you are not finding a sense of purpose in your job by bringing the thing that energizes you most to work with you. This brings us to our third example, Alex, also a tenth-grade teacher. Alex teaches world history, which he enjoys as a natural storyteller, but he does not get a strong sense of purpose from his work with students. Outside of the school day, Alex makes political documentaries, which does give him a sense of purpose. To make his lessons more interesting, Alex has students create films about a current event that is somehow connected to what they are studying in the history curriculum. He teaches them how to use a video camera and editing software, and he offers tips for using images to tell a compelling story. By doing so, he is a role model of purpose for his students and is introducing them to an activity that might be a purpose spark for some of them. If a student shows a strong interest in filmmaking, Alex might point the student to opportunities outside of school to pursue that interest or mentor that student himself.

PURPOSE MYTHS AND METAPHORS

Now that you have had an opportunity to reflect on purpose in your life, we can use that reflection to make better sense of what purpose is and what it is not. There are some beliefs about purpose—let's call them purpose myths—that can get in the way of having it, and we should examine those so they can be removed as obstacles both for yourself and for supporting students. After examining these myths, we will look at some metaphors often used to describe purpose to consider how they can both expand and limit how we think about purpose.

Myth #1: *I need to find my passion to have purpose.* We often hear the words *purpose* and *passion* used interchangeably. The implication is that you must identify a passion if you want to have purpose. Having explored purpose in your life, do you agree that passion is necessary for purpose? Passion is "strong and barely controllable emotion."[9] Purpose does not require such strong emotion, and it is the opposite of uncontrollable. It is a sustained intention and commitment. The intensity of passion, on the other hand, is rarely sustainable. To have purpose in life, you must stay with something even when it is boring, difficult, or drudgery. The team that teaches a Designing Your Life course at Stanford University has found that 80 percent of people they work with cannot identify a passion, yet they are able to design and pursue a purposeful path for their lives.[10] Don't think that you must find something you are passionate about in order to have purpose in life. Purpose simply implies that you find something important and meaningful to you, that you want to commit to regardless of distractions, challenges, or obstacles. There may be an initial spark of intensity that ignites purpose, along with feeling enthusiastic and energized when pursuing a purpose, and those feelings will help sustain you through the hard times. Your purpose might also be something that you are truly passionate about, and that is great! But it does not have to be experienced as that level of intensity or narrowed to a single, consuming interest. Purpose sometimes means asking, "What is it I need to do?" That is certainly not passionate. The flame of purpose, once ignited, burns steady and acts as a guiding light. It does not flash and burn out quickly, as passions often do.

Myth #2: *I must find my one, single purpose in life.* We also hear people talking about purpose as a single thing, as though we can only have one. It can be easier to talk about purpose as singular—we want to find *a* purpose in life. When we interview adolescents, we look for *a* purpose, so we can determine if they have purpose or not. But purpose is not singular. As we found above, purpose is usually based on a very broad, generalized, and abstract intention, but that abstract intention can be fulfilled by pursuing any number of concrete goals or activities. Someone who is deeply concerned about child welfare might find purpose by tutoring at a low-income school, studying child psychology, and developing a summer art program for a local museum. A student who aspires to be an asset to the community might pursue that goal by learning to play guitar to entertain at local events and studying engineering with plans to one day invent safer cars. Furthermore, it is not even clear that purposeful people have just one broad area of purpose. In our research, we have found that purposeful people are at least as likely to be highly engaged in many different activities as focused on a single activity, with potential for purpose in any of them.[11] We also know that purpose can change over the course of life, and people who have purpose in a specific area at one time may have purpose in something entirely different a few years later.[12] So we do not need to worry about finding the one thing that gives our life purpose. Your purpose might be very broad and abstract, or it might evolve over time, or it might be found in pursuing several goals at once. There is no reason to get stuck on the idea that you cannot have purpose if you do not identify the single important thing that you want to dedicate your life to.

Myth #3: *Purpose is a luxury and only accessible to those who are privileged.* We often hear the complaint that we should not expect people to have purpose when they are struggling to make ends meet or fighting other life challenges. We will go deeper into this question in chapter 3, but for now I want to put this out there as a myth about purpose that we need to dispel. Purpose does not require unusual resources, and it is not out of reach for anyone. Elon Musk finds purpose in trying to get civilians to Mars, and Nelson Mandela went to prison fighting for a purpose, but they are outliers. On a more relatable level, we interviewed a ninth grader who wanted to be a caring person and create more respect in the world, especially for animals. She had several pets she cared for at home, was a member of 4-H, and aspired to be a veterinarian. She is not getting to Mars, but this young person is driven to do something meaningful to make the world a better place, which is just as purposeful as Musk's aspirations. It does not require privilege or expensive resources or prohibitive amounts of time, it simply requires aspiration and enduring commitment. Purpose is not a luxury. Most positive psychologists argue that purpose is an important asset that supports resilience, thriving, and optimal development.[13] If anything, purpose is most useful to those who face hardships, and it should be encouraged as a necessity of life rather than a luxury.

Now we have some idea what purpose *isn't*, are there helpful ways to think about what purpose *is*? Abstract ideas like purpose are often thought of in metaphorical terms, to make them more concrete or relatable. Theorists trying to explain purpose use metaphorical imagery to convey the drive, direction, and transcendence that people feel when they have purpose. The following are some of the common metaphors used for explaining purpose, with some exploration of when they work and where they fall short.

Metaphor #1: *Purpose is an arrow hitting a target.* Some metaphors describe purpose as an ultimate goal that we aim for and hope to achieve. By aiming for a distant goal or target, we set a course to follow in life that will get us there. While it is helpful to think of purpose as a steady path toward an important, distant target, we have already seen that it is limiting to think of purpose as a single goal to aim for. It might also be limiting to assume that we must stay on a straight trajectory through life to have purpose, because it often involves taking an indirect and winding path, exploring potential interests, gaining diverse skills, and trying things that fail. Even if we can find a straight, direct path to a target goal, what happens after we hit the target?

Metaphor #2: *Purpose is a javelin, propelled along a perfect arc to go as far as possible.*[14] Some metaphors see purpose not as a target, but as a trajectory through life. Like an arrow, a javelin soars in a straight and steady path. However, there are a few key differences that make a javelin a better metaphor for understanding purpose. The goal in throwing a javelin is not to hit a target, rather the goal is to find the path that will take the javelin as far as possible. The javelin thrower tilts and aims to find the angle between two extremes. Aiming straight upward—a lofty but unrealistic aspiration—would cause the javelin to fall back down to the ground where it started, whereas aiming straight forward—plowing ahead without aspiring to something meaningful—would drive the javelin into the ground. If the upward thrust is the lofty aspiration to make a difference in the world, and the forward drive is the commitment and actions taken to accomplish life goals, the purposeful individual is the one who finds a path in the balance of these two extremes. More accurately than the arrow metaphor, the javelin describes purpose as an ongoing process, rather than a destination. However, like the arrow, the javelin implies that purpose is a straight path through life, which usually is not true.

Metaphor #3: *Purpose is a boat traveling on water.* The arrow and javelin images accurately capture purpose as a driving force that comes from within the individual, but they imply a straight and steady path. Most purpose paths meander, curve, zigzag, and double back. It is not that purpose lacks direction, but it is a direction that allows for experiencing more of life than a direct path can provide. Another reason the path is not a straight, direct one is that purpose comes from within an individual, but it is necessarily influenced by external forces. The social context we live in, our family, events in our lives, and opportunities we have all alter the course of life purpose. To accommodate the shifting nature of purpose trajectories and the influence of external forces, some theorists envision purpose as a boat on water.[15] For example, Seana Moran of Clark University describes purpose as a light guiding the boat (the individual) over open waters. External conditions, such as the wind, can blow the boat off course, or forge a new course, but a strong guiding light will help keep the boat moving forward. With purpose, there is forward momentum and direction, but the path it creates is not straight. A job taken out of financial necessity might provide experiences that shape one's purpose, or an unexpected move might provide new circumstances that illuminate a new direction for purpose to grow. When we look back over a life of purpose, the wake is curved and shifting, but there is a clear trail connecting one point to the next.

What metaphors help you deepen your understanding of purpose and the role it can play in your life? Do you think of purpose as a target to aim for? Is purpose a trajectory that balances the extremes of lofty dreams and driving effort? Is it a guiding light in your life? Or the driver steering you over the open waters of life? Has your pursuit of purpose always been on a straight line, confidently putting one foot in front of the other, certain of where you are heading? Or were there leaps of faith and diversions involved? This book plays with all of these ideas about purpose, but above all sees purpose as a driver, or an internal force that gives us direction and momentum through life. When it is strong, it keeps us from drifting. The drive is internal, but fired and fueled by our desire to be part of something larger than ourselves.

As a final step in this reflection activity, take a moment to connect what you have been thinking about in your work. If you do not already go to work every day with awareness of your purpose in mind, consider how it could affect your relationship with students and colleagues to do so. This means starting the day mindful of *your* purpose, not someone else's goals or expectations. If you are often overwhelmed by demands pressing on you from many directions or burned out from relentless stress or negativity in your workplace, connecting regularly with the aspects of your work that give you a sense of purpose can be energizing. It is a reminder of why you are tolerating the hardships and pushing through the obstacles. It is a compass that points you to the important things to focus on and away from the things that do not need so much of your attention. It is vital self-care. Imagine a school where all teachers arrive with awareness of their own purpose for being there. They are not only aware of their own purpose, but are more tuned-in to their students as people and are better prepared to prioritize the needs of their students as meaning-making, purpose-seeking people over the demands of the system. They are empowered to create a classroom environment that is compassionate and energetic, where students are heard and learning is meaningful.

By arriving at school with awareness of their purpose, or potential for purpose, educators can be better prepared to see the potential for purpose in their students. Students will not have the same purpose as their teachers. They may be coming from entirely different backgrounds or planning for a very different future. Being tuned-in to purpose will prepare educators to support their students in pursuing what matters at school, to provide a place where they feel safe enough to bring what is personally meaningful into the classroom and explore their potential for purpose. In the following chapters, you will read ideas and inspiration for inviting purpose into your school or classroom. The next two chapters offer an overview of what youth development researchers have learned about how purpose develops, especially in the school context. We will start in the playful years of preschool and follow students' development until they leave for college, or whatever awaits them after high school. The second part of the book investigates purpose at school and in the classroom to offer ideas for how it can be done and what happens when schools make purpose a central outcome, or the purpose of education.

CHAPTER TWO

Play, Meaning, and Intention

"All music is, is understanding somebody else," twenty-two-year-old Sam said to explain why he listed his punk rock band as the second-most important thing in his life (his girlfriend was first), and why he never got into Tupac Shakur, "I couldn't relate." Sam finds purpose in singing with his band because the audience responds, letting him know that they were moved by the songs he wrote. "When people come to you, and they're interested in you for something that you put your heart into and they can relate to it, it just feeds you. I feel the most accomplished I've ever felt in my life." Sam has attained a mature sense of purpose. He has the skill to write moving songs, but more importantly, the social and emotional capacity to recognize how his songs affect other people, and the drive to make music to connect with and understand others. What were the developmental precursors to this mature sense of purpose? When do those developmental precursors emerge? There is no exact science explaining how people develop purpose or when, but there are some ideas taking shape in the developmental research. This chapter begins with the earliest school years to describe what is happening—and what could be happening more—in those early years to create a foundation for purpose development. In this chapter, we will see how children on their way to purpose discover what matters to them, set and act on intentions, make meaning, develop agency, become participants, and learn self-regulation in order to achieve their goals. It is a lot, but it is all part of the most natural activities of childhood: playing and making things.

"WHAT DO YOU WANT TO BE WHEN YOU GROW UP?"

We often think of purpose as an adult accomplishment, or at least something discovered by teens as they face the end of their high school years and ponder what comes next. Purpose, in that sense, is something out there, waiting for them after they leave the structure of school that has up to that point made all their decisions for them. We ask children questions that suggest this is how it works: "What will you be when you grow up?" "What are you going to do with your life?" But life does not begin after school ends, and our research suggests that neither does purpose. We do see more consistent and more fully developed purpose in people as they approach adulthood, but by studying children as young as eleven years old, we have found that purpose is not waiting beyond the school steps. Children are developing purpose throughout childhood, both in and out of school. This is not to say that we should expect students to fully develop purpose before they leave school, but rather that it can be nurtured early. It takes shape over the course of childhood and adolescence, and it can be supported and encouraged by adults who know what to look for. This chapter and the next one will help you be able to identify the early indicators of purpose.

Developmental psychologists can trace the roots of purpose to infancy. We are all born with a drive to connect with the world beyond ourselves, which is the seed of our purpose. In those early years, children act on their drive to connect in increasingly complex ways, exploring and engaging with people and objects around them, cajoling others to give them attention, touching things to know what they are, and seeking ways to leave a mark on the world. This chapter describes how these interactions with the world in early and middle childhood set the stage for mature purpose development, but not by casting the early years as merely preparation for adulthood. One of the wonderful things about putting the focus on purpose development is how it causes us to engage the best practices for giving children happy and meaningful lives from the very beginning. Moreover, by focusing on purpose development from the very beginning, we provide children with an abundance of social, psychological, and academic advantages. When purpose is prioritized in school, a climate of caring, meaning, engagement, and cooperation is a natural outcome.

Purpose is on the developmental trajectory that extends from those early days when babies reach out to tangle fingers in Mom's long hair, or scribble in mud on the sidewalk, or add a block to their sister's construction and then knock it over. As they grow older, they gain empathy, perspective, and moral reasoning, so they can make more positive contributions in the world, which we will examine more in the next chapter. Here, we start in preschool and elementary school to observe the earliest glimmers of purpose in meaning-making activities, as young children develop awareness of what is meaningful to them and connect that meaning to the world outside of themselves. The seeds of purpose are sown in the most important activity of those early years—play.

Infants begin their exploration of self in the world by engaging with objects around them, touching, grabbing, squeezing, and mouthing, to know what things are and how they feel in their hands, taste in their mouths, and sound in their ears. Soon, infants grow from the sensorimotor stage of play to the relational-nonfunctional stage, when they interact with objects by moving them, pushing, stacking, shaking, and banging, to see not just what the objects are, but also what they do—What noises do they make? How do these objects impact each other? How can they be arranged and rearranged?[1] In this stage, babies and toddlers manipulate objects without concern for what the objects are designed to do. Their interest is in discovering the physical and sensory qualities of the things in their world. In the next stage—the functional-conventional stage—toddlers understand that objects have functions, and they play with objects according to their conventional use. A small piece of fabric, previously used for squeezing, rubbing, and swinging, is now a blanket for a doll. This phase is an important social advance, as children demonstrate that they are observing the actions of others and can mimic them. They show that they share understanding of things in the world with other people around them and recognize that objects have a meaning or function, separate from what the child does to them. At this stage, children begin to find coherence with the social world. They learn to act and engage with the world in a way that makes sense to others. This is the first way that children "make meaning," in that they figure out what things mean and align their actions to that meaning. It is also the first indication of agency, when they realize they can act on things in the world, and when they do, those things will move or change or make a sound. Their early explorations with meaning and agency are the first building blocks of the foundation that could someday support a life of purpose.

Beyond the infant and toddler years, children enter the stage of symbolic play, when their interactions with objects are not only physical and sensory, but start to be more abstract. Preschoolers know what scissors are for, but they can also transform a pair of scissors into a duck bill, opening and closing them while saying "quack quack!" Their control over things in the world has gone from simple physical manipulation to transforming the meaning of things using their imaginations. Their exploration of what they can do to things, how they can change things, and what impact they can have on the things in their world intensifies. In a preschool setting, this symbolic play occurs with other children. They create new meaning for objects, but they do so in collaboration with others who also want to create new meaning for the same objects. Playing together, preschoolers gain experience in creating meaning in a social context and in having control over the things in their world that considers the interests of others and not only their own self-interest.

What do children gain through this object play and social play that relates to purpose? They gain the skills and capacities that will ultimately enable them to be like the twenty-two-year-old musician quoted at the start of this chapter, who wrote songs to move others and create shared understanding. The key skills and capacities that connect play to purpose are:

- Meaning making: the ability to make sense of and find coherence in the world, and to contribute to a community of shared meaning
- Self-Regulation: the ability to manage behaviors and emotions in order to accomplish long-term goals
- Agency: awareness of ones' own capacity to have control of one's life and to cause a response or impact in the world; the ability to take action on ideas

Imagine six-year-old Zach, playing with a cardboard box that is big enough to climb in. He decides the box is a boat and sets sail. Across the lawn, he spots a stick. He grabs the stick and hops back into his boat. What should the stick be? Zach already set the boundary of this game: the box is a boat. Therefore, the stick must be something that will go with the boat, such as an oar, a fishing pool, or a pirate's sword. Without guidance or instruction from an adult, he puts limits on his own play. He set the intention for what he wants the game to be, and as he continues this game he gains practice in regulating his decisions and behaviors to act according to that intention. The stick cannot be a light saber unless Zach can justify to himself how it fits with the boat theme.

The importance of this self-inflicted limitation is subtle and not always acknowledged in the noise and tumult of a child's pretend play, but it is vital to early purpose development in several ways. First, he is making connections between his imagination and the external world, giving things new meaning in a way that is coherent and can be understood by anyone else who might want to play with him—he is *making meaning*. Second, he is developing *agency* by controlling and transforming things in the world according to his own ideas, and doing so in a way that can be understood and joined by others. If others join him, he will have to negotiate the game, share the power, and adjust the meaning of the game, which will also teach him about the collective nature of creating meaning in society.

Finally, he is developing *self-regulation*, which will help him to pursue and achieve his goals in the future. Self-regulation is how we monitor and select our own behavior to stay committed to long-term goals.

You might be familiar with the now famous Marshmallow Test, in which preschoolers were observed to see whether and how they controlled their impulse to eat a treat left on a nearby table.[2] Impulse control is just one aspect of self-regulation for goal commitment; it also involves planning and directing one's short-term actions toward an abstract or distant outcome. When children direct their own pretend play, set their own boundaries for the meaning of their games, and act in accordance with those boundaries, they are developing self-regulation and increasing their capacity for long-term goal commitment. With the capacity for long-term goal commitment comes the capacity for the sustained pursuit of purpose.[3]

FROM PLAYING TO MAKING: GLIMMERS OF PURPOSE IN ELEMENTARY SCHOOL

What happens to pretend play after early childhood? By about third grade, in most contemporary school settings, children are increasingly expected to focus on academic work and structured activities, such as sports. Children still play, pretend, experiment, and imagine, but we look less and less to these activities for signs of their successful development. Often, we think of "play" in these years in terms of games and sports, and less in terms of symbolic, imaginative interaction with people, objects, and ideas. What happens to the cognitive and social path they were on when they engaged so intensely in pretend play? In my research on children's art making, I found that it does not disappear, but can be transferred, when possible, to abstract materials and media.[4] As they move through elementary school, children become abstract thinkers, and they increasingly transfer their play activity from concrete objects, such as dolls and toys, to more creative materials that do not have predetermined form or meaning. Making meaning becomes not only *making sense of*, but is also about making and doing things that are *meaningful*, to oneself, to society, or to one's culture. Some educators and psychologists argue that this is what learning is—not just an individual person absorbing knowledge about the world, but people participating together to create socially and culturally meaningful ideas.[5]

School is an important space for children to develop the foundations of purpose in many ways. One of the key ways is that school provides children access to the diverse materials and media needed to develop abstract thinking and meaning making. I use the example of visual art materials, such as paper, clay, paint, and markers, because that is the area I know best. I taught art for several years and then did research on children's art making, observing elementary school students in the art room and interviewing them about their art making. There is another reason I use art to illustrate these ideas about meaning making in school. The arts have a unique advantage in that they are rarely subjected to high-stakes assessment in elementary school. Because of this, the arts are often taught in a way that is more open and less bound by curriculum requirements. However, students will find opportunities for meaning making in school whenever they are given the opportunity, even beyond the arts. Children engage in the same way with words, science materials, numbers, and technology—any materials that can be manipulated and altered with their hands and mind.

When I observed children making art at school, and talked to them about their art making, what stood out most was the very intentional ways they engaged with materials. It is easy to assume that children are spontaneous and unintentional when they make art.[6] However, the six- to eleven-year-olds I observed and spoke with were not at all spontaneous in their self-directed making activities.[7] Even if they could not articulate their intentions directly, they readily revealed the intentions that drive them when they are given opportunities to "play" with materials in school. Intentions are like reasons, but more intrinsically meaningful and compelling. *Reasons* for making something are that you are bored, or a teacher asked you to, or because it is fun. *Intentions* are what motivate you to make something when you could do anything else, and they determine what you will do with the materials, how you will manipulate them, and what you will make. Intentions come from inside, and through their intentional engagement with materials, children connect their inner selves with the world around them. They make sense of the world and assert their inner self in the world by making things with intention. In short, they make meaning and make their mark.

Third grader Stephanie was a prolific artist and admired by her classmates for her creativity.[8] I asked Stephanie why she made art, and she had many things to say. She used art to think about people she cares about: "I really like thinking about certain people, and just drawing something that reminds me about them." She also described art as a way to make her imagination real, share her imagination with others, and experiment with making things different from how they really are:

> I make art to explore my imagination and get my imagination somewhere in reality. It's different from the real world because you can make up anything you want. If I was trying to do the splits, I could just imagine that I did the splits all the way, but I didn't really. [By drawing it], it would be in reality, because on paper something that you draw is in reality. You can paint something that you really liked when you were little and you don't have any more and you want it back, like when I wanted the scooter I had when I was little.

Stephanie eloquently describes what happens when we have opportunities to explore our thoughts and ideas and use materials to put them out into the world. We can make meaning in our own lives, and we can create a new reality. Stephanie is unusually articulate for her age, but the intentions that guide her actions as she puts paintbrush to paper are typical of school-age children. I interviewed dozens of children about their art making and spent time with them as they made art at school, and in doing so I heard about the same intentions again and again. Some were specific to art, such as children who made art because they wanted to make things that look beautiful or interesting. However, the intentions they described most often would be the same for many of their activities at home and at school. These are the intentions children bring to their activities when they play openly with abstract materials. Three of these intentions are described below: experimenting and inventing, storytelling, and relationship building.[9] They are ways that children reach out to make sense of, connect with, participate in, and make a difference to their world, and as such, they are vital to the earliest stages of purpose development. These are not the only intentions that children bring to their making activities, but they are the ones I heard about most often when talking with children, and they are great examples of what we can look for when trying to understand what students are doing when they engage in any kind of activity that involves playing, making, tinkering, or exploring with materials, words, and ideas.

Experimenting and Invention

Some children conduct experiments when they make things, investigating the possibilities in objects, natural materials, words, or anything they can manipulate and use to make a mark or impression in the world. These experiments are the same process as pretend play with toys—children explore what objects and materials can do, and then experiment to see what they can do with the materials and objects. When they use art or tinkering materials, technology, words, and numbers, children's experiments are responsive to their growing cognitive and motor skills. Because the materials are more abstract and open-ended, children have more control over what the materials will become, and what meaning they will take on. An important change is happening for children in this shift from playing to making. From the playful explorations that respond to the question "What does this do?" they are shifting to a process of finding out "What can I, with my imagination and my own hands, make with this?" Along the way, they are learning to see themselves as people with the power to create new things in the world—they gain awareness of their agency.

School-age children are often driven to make things because they want to experiment and investigate what they can create that is new. They experiment with materials to see how they can change them, to come up with new solutions to problems, express an idea in a different way, or invent something that has never seen before. A ten-year-old might experiment with his drawing by turning it upside down to see what else it could be, to create an all new drawing from it, or try to make a landscape painting that uses unexpected colors, such as orange grass and a green sky. When children experiment with materials, they often do so because they want to create something different, that no one has seen before. As this child gets older, he might apply the same way of thinking to more complicated problems or design tasks, such as a teenager who experiments with a car engine, altering it in hopes of inventing a new engine that runs faster or more efficiently.

Children experiment, investigate, and invent by ignoring the constraints of existing materials, words, patterns, or technology, which gives them greater capacity to be meaningful in how they make things. Paper, for example, has basic constraints when it is used for writing or drawing on. It is flat, rectangular, and has edges. Experimenters will let go of those constraints and invent new ways to manipulate paper by bending, crumpling, soaking, twisting, and tearing it. In doing so they find new things that paper can be, and new meanings that they can give to paper. With this experimental activity, children open a vast space in their minds for imagination, and can apply self and personal meaning more freely, unconstrained by the usual limitations. Students who tend to experiment like this in the classroom are often redirected. They seek the boundaries of an assignment and find ways to push past the boundaries, which can look like they misunderstood the lesson or are deliberately challenging the teacher.

Children who continue to develop this capacity become adolescents and adults with strong divergent thinking ability, who can apply these skills to invention and entrepreneurship as ways of solving problems they see in the world. This capacity begins with inventive manipulation of easily accessed materials, but as they get older it can be applied in any field, such as technology, medicine, environmentalism, or product design. The ten-year-old who turned his drawings upside down to invent a new image may someday be the scientist who discovers a new source of renewable energy.

Storytelling

Early storytelling occurs in the dramatic play of preschool, when children pretend to be princesses, superheroes, dragons, and daddies, and use those characters to act out scenes from the stories they love or explore the events of life that they have not yet experienced. As children get older and their stories gain complexity and depth, they increasingly rely on materials that they can manipulate to change the story as it unfolds. Many children are drawn to telling stories as they make objects. They use paint, clay, foil, sand—anything that can be shaped and reshaped with the hands and mind, narrating the events of the story and revising as they go. By following their stories over time, their recurrent and personally meaningful themes emerge. A third grader I spoke with illustrated the romantic development between a wealthy prince and a poor girl over the course of the year. A fifth grader made numerous comic books about a stunt dragon who demonstrated his courage again and again by narrowly pulling off dangerous stunts.

Through storytelling, we make meaning from our experiences and shape identity, and we create a shared culture that is passed on through the generations. Storytelling is how we give order to the jumble of events, ideas, and emotions that we experience, so that we can find the meaning in them. Storytelling combines our real experiences with fantasy, and through fantasy we can grapple with difficult emotions and profound psychological themes, such as death, love, and power, in ways that make them easier to grasp.[10] Nearly all societies use stories to pass on cultural knowledge and themes to their children, but the way stories are constructed and shared is different around the world.[11] By encouraging children to tell their stories, we also give them a valuable tool for expressing empathy and having more meaningful relationships. Through storytelling, children learn how to connect events and experiences in their own lives to lives of others. They learn how to take on different perspectives, as a storyteller must show how each of their characters is unique and sees the world through different eyes and must create relationships among characters with different perspectives.

By telling their stories, whether with words or physical materials, children learn to contribute to social narratives and become adults who can use this ability to shape the invisible structures of society, such as policy and culture. The rules, mores, and laws that govern society are based on social meaning that comes from storytelling, not from physical laws. Drug criminalization laws are an example of how policy advocates persuade voters using the power of storytelling. In the past twenty years, marijuana laws have changed in thirty-four states, not because the physical properties of marijuana have changed, but because of shifting narratives about marijuana use and users, for example, as stories involving medicinal uses become more prevalent. The third grader who creates an elaborate story of romance between a wealthy prince and a poor girl might someday be an advocate for children living in poverty, using metaphor and emotional storytelling to persuade politicians to fund school nutrition initiatives.

Building Relationships, Family, and Community

Six-year-old Malcolm is working on a collage self-portrait in art class. He was assigned to look very carefully at himself in a small hand mirror, then cut and glue paper shapes to represent what he sees in the mirror. He cuts a "c" shape out of yellow construction paper and glues it to the ear in his self-portrait. "I'm making an earring," he explains to the other boys at his table, then glues a yellow "u" shape around the neck, "and that's the chain people wear." Although the assignment was to show himself exactly as he looked in the mirror, Malcolm understood that there are other ways to represent yourself. He was not wearing jewelry, but the earring and chain were things his father wore. His self-portrait was actually a portrait of the connection he felt between himself and his father. On the surface, his portrait is an act of self-expression, but usually there is something deeper going on when someone is expressing themselves. When children make things that we call self-expression, they are sharing something meaningful about themselves, often driven by a desire to understand others and be understood, and to connect with others.

Whether expressing themselves or more directly expressing ideas about people who are important to them, one of the most common intentions that drives children's making activities is the desire to build relationships with others, by finding points of connection and expressing meaningful ideas about people who matter. "Visiting the carnival with my sister," "swinging in the backyard with my grandpa," and "riding horses with my friend," are examples of the human connections that are so prevalent in children's drawing and writing. Children use making activities to explore what is meaningful about people they care about, and learn to use devices such as metaphor to express complex ideas about their loved ones. When third grader Evan made a painting of his karate class, he described how the painting showed the meaningful influence that his teacher had in his life. "I'm doing Bushido, which is like fighting with yourself. But it's not like punching yourself. It's like fighting with your soul. The person that teaches me is Miss Kelly, and she's very important to me." Evan paints to explore ideas about the people who matter most to him and express his bond with those important people.

When children make things, they know that their creations have an audience and will have an effect on others. In school, if assignments are strictly teacher-driven, allowing little or no room for student meaning, the audience will only be the teacher and the relationship will be limited to teacher-pleasing. When assignments and classroom activities are open to children's personal meaning making, they learn to use this space to explore ways that they can connect with, relate to, and influence others. There are three main ways that children relate to others through making activities. First, children build relationships by representing the important people in their lives. By representing these people through images and stories, they can develop and express ideas about them that reveal what makes them important. Second, they interact with others as they make things, using the activity as a space to share their ideas, listen to others, and build relationships. Children working side by side in the classroom build relationships simply by showing each other what they are working on and talking as they work. Third, children use meaning-making activities to create gifts to give to others, as a way to show care and strengthen the relationship.

Self-expression is expected of artists, but it may be on the decline in schools. Curriculum movements that encouraged students' free expression, such as whole language, process writing, and memoir, have since been criticized for failing to teach the skills needed for effective communication. Critics argue that self-expressive methods such as these encourage students to do whatever they want, without providing them instruction in the skills needed for high-level thinking and effective communication of ideas. Worse, they argue, these methods teach students that they can express their opinions and feelings without considering how others will (or will not) make sense of them.[12] But as the examples here show, children use self-expression to build relationships with others, developing the ability to understand what is meaningful about others and effectively communicate that meaning through words and materials. The third grader who uses a school assignment to express his affection for his martial arts teacher is becoming someone who will create a connected and caring society by focusing on and expressing what matters most in his relationships with others.

No one is purely an inventor, storyteller, or relationship builder, although some people may favor one mode over others. All three of these intentions—experimenting and inventing, storytelling, and building relationships—may be present in everyone who creates things. Teachers, for example, might combine all three: teachers are tuned-in to relationships and often get into teaching because they care for children; they are storytellers who grasp big ideas in the world and interpret them for young people to understand; and they are inventors who create curriculum and lessons that will inspire children. Again, these are not the only intentions that drive children's making and playing activity, but they are the most prevalent from my observations, and they are essential for developing the capacity to participate meaningfully in the world and have purpose in life. When teachers look for intentions that drive their students' participation in school activities, they open the door to engaging students in deeper learning. By understanding the intentions that students bring to their making activities, teachers can use those intentions to make the activity more meaningful for students and motivate them to fuller participation.

When children can act on their personal intentions at school, they not only bring in what is personally meaningful to them, but they also make shared meaning in the classroom by doing so. They make shared meaning by contributing, along with their classmates and teachers, to the classroom community's understanding of what ideas matter. That doesn't mean they decide what skills or content are taught, but if their intentions and meaning are given space in classroom activities, they learn in two ways. First, they learn in the traditional cognitive sense of gaining the skills and knowledge of the curriculum. Second, they learn in the social sense of participating in the production of shared ideas, values, and understanding, just as we expect teachers do in a learning community. In this second way of learning, students develop a learning community in the classroom, where each child's meanings are valid and valued, and can shape the activity of the classroom. This happens naturally when allowed to happen. Students sitting next to each other at a table share ideas or copy from each other, if they are not prohibited from doing so. They critique each other, offering suggestions or asserting their own ideas about a classmate's work in progress. They work together on each other's projects. They ask questions that challenge the boundaries of a lesson.

Given sufficient leeway, students gravitate to this second type of learning by engaging intentions like those described above. Some students will experiment with the boundaries of a lesson, to see if they can do something new or inventive with the activity. One creative fifth grader I met was assigned to make a drawing to show his understanding of "what pollutants get into our water through the sewer." He turned the drawing into an imaginative exploration of how animals could adapt to survive with those pollutants. Some students will make a story out of the activity, even if it is not a writing assignment. A third grader I observed in her art class used a still-life painting exercise to develop the next scene in a story she was working on at home, and a first grader used her linking cubes to create the scene of a story she was making up in her mind. Some will find opportunities in their classroom activities to build relationships with others. In a second-grade class I observed, students spontaneously read their stories aloud to their tablemates as they wrote to share the ideas they found important or to make their friends laugh.

Through this intentional engagement, children learn to be contributing participants in the classroom community and develop among themselves a learning community shaped by what they find meaningful. The classroom becomes a place where children's meanings are valid and important and shape the activity of the classroom community. This is not the same as a democratic model, where students are given control over deciding classroom activities. It is simply allowing for the natural inclination of children to bring meaning to their interaction with materials and media, which they started with preschool play, by setting the boundaries of classroom activities a little wider to allow space for their meaning and intentions to enter.

MEANING, MEANINGFUL, AND PURPOSE

If we want to look for and nurture the seeds of purpose in elementary school, we should start by making room for intention and meaning in the classroom. We have explored children's intentions, but what do we mean by *meaning*? We do not often hear about children's meaning in life or what is meaningful to students in relation to what they are doing at school, but children can and do think about what gives them a sense of meaning in life, and they try to connect their schoolwork with what they find meaningful.[13] Meaning is similar to purpose and is often confused with purpose, but they are not the same. Giving children the opportunity to connect their schoolwork with what they find meaningful can help lay the groundwork for later purpose, but it is not the same thing as having purpose. We will get a better understanding of how children develop purpose if we take a moment to explore what meaning is and how it differs from purpose.

Psychologists give two broad definitions of meaning. First, it can be what something signifies, as in what a word signifies or what a story signifies. A life can also have meaning in this sense, and this is the definition we are using when we "search for meaning in life."[14] When I ask, "What is the meaning of my life?," I am trying to understand what my life signifies, and what makes it significant. This is the definition of meaning used by Victor Frankl, a psychologist who examined the meaning of life while a prisoner in Auschwitz.[15] Frankl believed that our main concern as humans is to search for our meaning in life, or what is significant about our life. For Frankl, the significance, or meaning, in our lives is found in the things we do to reach beyond ourselves. Psychologist Roy Baumeister took up the study of Frankl's definition of meaning in life and found that meaning comes from making connections that give order and coherence to our lives.[16] We find life meaningful when we see the connections between our past, present, and future. We make our lives meaningful when we connect to others through relationships, or when we connect our inner life with the social and cultural life that surrounds us. Cognitive scientist Jerome Bruner describes this active connecting as "acts of meaning" or what we are "doing or trying to do" in the world.[17] Our acts of meaning are the actions we do to assert our inner, personal selves into the world beyond ourselves, to connect ourselves to the outside world, and make our lives matter by shaping the community, society, and culture we are a part of. Through these connections, we can come to understand what our life means, and what makes our life meaningful.[18]

Many psychologists who study meaning in life today look way back to ancient Greece and Aristotle for the philosophical foundation of their work. In his writing on ethics, Aristotle's main concern was with understanding how people should live, and he determined that the primary goal for humans is to be happy. Aristotle described two types of happiness: the happiness that comes from pursuing pleasure, status, and material gain, and the happiness that comes from living in accordance with our best and highest selves. This second type of happiness he called *eudaimonia*, or the good life, in the sense that it involves identifying and acting on what is good in ourselves. Eudaimonia is associated with meaning because it involves discovering our strongest values and strengths, recognizing what makes our lives significant, and achieving a sense of order and coherence by living in alignment with our most important values.[19] The research suggests that living according to eudaimonia is a more reliable path to well-being than pursuing happiness in the form of pleasure or material success.[20]

That is the definition of *meaning* that we might think of as "big M" *Meaning in Life*. "Little m" meaning refers to what is *meaningful to me*. Personally meaningful things are the things that align with our values, interests, and concerns. They are the things that make us unique and that shape our identity. When we talk about or act on these personally meaningful things, we are expressing ourselves, and sharing what matters most to us with others. We gain *Meaning in Life* by acting in accordance with the things that are *meaningful* to us. Of course, what we find meaningful is unique to each of us, but researchers have identified some things that come up again and again when people are asked what is meaningful. Relationships (especially family), health, religious beliefs, personal growth, service to others, and life work are the most often cited sources of meaning, and not only among adults.[21] When the same researchers asked thirteen-year-olds about what was meaningful in their lives, these young adolescents were able to talk about what they found meaningful and identified many of the same things as adults. However, compared to adults, they were also likely to find meaning in school, activities, and physical appearance, and less likely to find meaning in thinking about their future life work.[22]

Having meaning in life means living in alignment with our values, so that we have a sense of coherence in our life. This is not the same thing as purpose, but identifying the things that we find meaningful and shaping our most important values is a first step on the purpose path. To find purpose in life, we need to have a strong sense of what we value, but we also need to be driven by our values to do things that will contribute to the world beyond ourselves.

Young children might not be ready for purpose, but they are fully capable of exploring what they find meaningful, what matters to them, and what they value most. When they can do so in the classroom, they integrate what is meaningful with what they are learning at school, and what they are learning becomes connected to what they find meaningful. They also get to sense that their meaning and values are respected in their school community, and they develop the agency that comes with asserting their ideas to shape the activity of the classroom. Given the opportunity to explore what matters to them at school, their values grow stronger and more nuanced, shaped by interaction with their peers and input from their teachers. They see how their meaning and values relate to the meaning and values of others and learn to negotiate the different values within their community. With the materials and skills available to them in the classroom, children can learn to express and share what they find meaningful in ways that others can understand them and respond to them. Taking a cue from Aristotle, we adults do not have to sit back and let them focus only on the things they like that provide pleasure or the promise of material gain. A teacher's guidance in this area can help students identify and grow the values that will enable them to become their best selves.

As childhood gives way to adolescence, meaning making merges with the more specific task of identity formation. Increasingly, young people become more aware of their social identity and having a role to play in the world. They will hopefully, with the right opportunities, develop a strong sense of the values that are most central to their identity, and will be motivated to act in accordance with those values. They will begin to think about long-term goals and who they want to become, and how they might contribute to the world through their unique strengths and values. In the next chapter, we will examine this aspect of purpose development—the desire to be someone who makes a difference in the world.

CHAPTER THREE

Purpose and Social and Emotional Learning

To answer the timeless questions of "What is my place in the world? Why am I here?," purpose needs to go beyond personal meaning and self-focused goals. There must be a drive to do something positive or constructive for the *here* in that question—for the family, community, society, culture, or environment. It is a question of what good I am going to do in the world as evidence of my unique and meaningful existence. This is a vast question that takes students into deep and murky waters, without the security of prescribed answers. It is a spiritual question, sometimes religious, and requires talking about those values, virtues, and morality that some think should not be of concern in school. One of the arguments I want to propose is that purpose is a way to bring these important aspects of being human into school, where children spend about a thousand hours every year and do so much of their developmental work. This chapter examines the social and moral dimension of purpose—what it is, how it fits in the school setting, and why it should take an important place in our schools.

Recently, mindfulness training has made its way into classrooms, with the goal of helping students be in the present moment rather than getting caught up in passing distractions or worrying about things that might not happen. The idea of school-based mindfulness training programs is getting students to focus on the *now*. Purpose asks students to engage in mindfulness as well, but with a focus on the *here* instead of the now. By focusing on our surroundings, on the world we live in and the people who share this space with us, we can develop compassion, and take action to make *here* better for ourselves and others. We see this in the earliest cases of purpose. Young people develop early purpose when they see problems and challenges impacting the people closest to them—family, neighbors, and members of their community—and feel compelled to do something to help. So, as we consider how to develop student compassion, and compassion's more goal-directed and driven cousin, purpose, we need to keep in mind how we support them in attending to the *here*, that is, the community and environment that they participate in.

PURPOSE AND SOCIAL-EMOTIONAL LEARNING

Today, social-emotional learning programs across the country teach children vital non-academic skills such as conflict resolution, community building in the classroom, and effective communication. Essentially, the focus of social-emotional learning is on managing one's emotions, behaviors, and relationships, and creating a caring climate at school so children can learn. More recently, some social-emotional learning theorists and practitioners have argued for the integration of social and emotional learning with character education, which aims to develop students' core values.[1] This is a big shift that takes social-emotional learning beyond teaching students how to think, respond, and act in the moment, to shaping the type of people students will become. Our character is made up of the virtues, or personal strengths, that we develop because they align with our most central values. If we value adventure, we will put effort into developing courage and being a courageous person. If we value peace, we will put effort into developing compassion and becoming a compassionate person. Character education provides the opportunity to learn and develop those virtues that will enable us to be our best selves. Purpose education is a natural outcome when educators merge the action-oriented aspects of social-emotional learning with the fundamental identity-shaping aspects of character education and make values central to not only *how* students pursue goals, but *what* goals students set in the first place.

Responding to perhaps too much emphasis on the notion of "soft skills" prevalent in social-emotional learning, the most recent movement in character education pushed for tougher performance strengths, such as grit (perseverance in the face of obstacles), self-control (control over impulses that distract from daily tasks and goals), and growth mindset (belief that basic abilities can be developed through hard work), to develop the whole child in service of academic achievement. The unfortunate, and likely unintended, outcome is that this makes academic achievement the goal of character education, prioritizing self-enhancement for self-fulfilling reasons. Ironically, one of the biggest criticisms of the recent push to teach character strengths in schools is the neglect of moral character. As one critic put it, this "character-based education is untethered from any conception of morality."[2] Attention has wholly been on the strengths students need to pursue goals, without any attention to which goals students are pursuing, or why. Purpose, with its focus on the world beyond the self, is a moral character strength. Educating for purpose means asking students to think about which goals matter and why. It does not negate the need for grit and self-control, but raises the question of "grit for what?" If you have been helping students to be gritty, to look beyond failure and persist in their pursuits, how often have you, or your students, taken the opportunity to ask whether the goal is worthy of such persistence, or if there might be more worthy goals to be gritty for?

We teach grit and growth mindset so students can succeed, but do we ask what they want to succeed at? Do we help them formulate a vision of personally meaningful success? Do we offer diverse visions of success that allow them to explore future options that fit with their core values? Teaching for purpose requires us to think more deeply about what we want for our students; not just hoping that they can stick to their goals, but hoping that they will be good people with meaningful and satisfying lives. It asks us to think about students as people who know what their values are, and know their own value in the world. Conveniently, teaching for purpose can support the academic goals we have for students. If students are setting goals according to their values and what gives them a sense of purpose in the world, they will be intrinsically motivated, which may make it easier to persist and use adaptive work habits in the face of challenging goals.[3] Moreover, purpose helps us organize and prioritize short-term goal setting, which can support planning and strategizing to stick with bigger goals.[4]

Although purpose might make it easier for students to develop grit, it does not appear that grit is necessary for students to pursue purpose, at least in the early years.[5] Some purposeful teens seem to pursue the path of least resistance to fulfill their purpose. They find ways to solve problems in their community by using the little time they have available for activities unrelated to college pursuit, or by doing things that require little skill. One fourteen-year-old girl uses Twitter to support other teens who struggle with bullying and suicidal thoughts. A high school senior said that he found purpose by simply living according to a philosophy that he and his friends came up with:

> God can't live life, that's what we're doing here for Him; just live life, be good, and be nice to people. Go rock climbing. He just wants you to live and experience it because that's what life is all about. And basically try to be the best us that we can be so that we can affect so many people.[6]

This is not to say that purposeful youth are never gritty. Some show tremendous grit in pursuing purpose, and many find purpose by overcoming hardship. However, we hear in our interviews with adolescents that it is not necessary to work hard or be gritty to fulfill purpose. In fact, they might seek easy paths so that they can pursue purpose outside of, and in addition to, their schoolwork. This raises some important "what if" questions: What if we made it more possible for students to integrate schoolwork with their pursuit of purpose? What if, in addition to encouraging persistence, we prioritize the more difficult but meaningful task of examining personal values and finding something worth committing to for a duration? What if, in addition to telling students to work hard, we ask them to focus on the connection between their schoolwork and their most important goals, values, and concerns about the world? The research is still developing, but emerging findings suggest that purpose can inspire students to develop grit, growth mindset, and self-control, whereas these performance character strengths can support purpose commitment, but will not inspire or encourage selection of values-driven, other-oriented purpose goals.[7]

THE BENEFITS OF HAVING PURPOSE

Purpose is a valuable outcome in itself. According to psychologists who do research on positive youth development, young people with purpose are believed to be thriving, and it is considered an indicator of optimal development.[8] That alone is reason to support students' purpose development at school. However, teachers may find it advantageous to support their students' purpose development because the research shows there are other social, psychological, and academic benefits to having purpose.

People who have a sense of purpose to their lives tend to be energized, optimistic about the future, and hopeful, and they report feeling positive emotions, like happiness, joy, and satisfaction, more often than those without a sense of purpose.[9] Purposeful people are even physically healthier than non-purposeful people, for example showing more stable levels of cortisol (the "stress hormone"), less inflammation, and higher levels of HDL cholesterol (the "good cholesterol"), and appear to live longer.[10] Contrary to what we might expect, people who make an intense commitment to a purpose do not focus all of their energy on just that goal, but instead are likely be involved in a variety of activities and pursue numerous interests. It is not clear if having purpose fills people with energy and optimism and provides them with greater well-being, or if it is the reverse, and naturally positive and energetic people are more likely to have purpose. However, we are starting to see signs in the research that it is at least partly the former. In a collection of purpose intervention studies edited by Jenni Menon Mariano and Sonia Koshy, school-based purpose programs resulted in some other positive effects in addition to purpose.[11] For example, Matthew Bundick found that students who participated in a purpose interview reported greater life satisfaction nine months later, compared to students who did not participate in the purpose interview.[12] In another intervention study with patients suffering from social anxiety disorder, both the patients and the healthy control participants reported higher self-esteem and positive affect after participating in a program designed to increase commitment to a life purpose.[13]

Purpose not only provides students with psychological and health benefits, it also appears there are academic benefits associated with having a fully engaged, beyond-the-self purpose as well. The research on whether purpose is related to indicators of academic performance, such as grades and test scores, is inconsistent, and our most recent research with eighth and ninth graders shows only a slight relationship between purpose and grade point average. However, we did find that students this age who are fully engaged in pursuing a meaningful, beyond-the-self purpose are also more engaged at school, meaning that compared to students with higher GPAs, students who were actively pursuing at least one purpose goal reported that they were more excited about their schoolwork and enjoyed what they were learning. Purposeful students feel a greater sense of social belonging at school, reporting that they fit in at school and that their teachers take time to get to know them. They feel more personal responsibility for their school performance compared with students with higher GPAs, saying that it is up to them to do well in school, and their fault if they get bad grades.[14]

Although most of the psychological, social, and academic factors examined in relation to purpose are positive, such as hopefulness, social belonging, and school engagement, we did find one negative factor—stress—that appears to correlate with purpose. It is no secret that many students today bring stress to school with them or develop stress in response to their schoolwork. Some students are dealing with traumatic home lives and bringing that trauma to school, others are getting sick from the exhaustion of excessive homework and multiple extracurricular activities, and all are facing pressure to compete for college at younger and younger ages. Among the eighth and ninth graders we surveyed, those with higher purpose scores reported feeling stress more often than their non-purposeful peers.[15] There are two likely explanations for this finding. First, the spark for purpose is often found in negative life events, so it is possible that students who have been dealing with negative events are both more likely to be feeling stress from those events and more likely to be coping with those events by finding purpose in them. A second explanation is that adolescents who are pursuing a purpose outside of school feel overwhelmed from doing both that and their schoolwork and may feel the tension of not attending to what matters to them most when they are at school. In either case, we can reduce student stress levels by making room for them to explore purpose at school, through curriculum connections, advisory activities, extracurricular activities, and other ways that are discussed more in the second part of this book.

Given the benefits of having beyond-the-self purpose, we might be inclined to require students to engage in prosocial activities, such as community service or volunteering. Prosocial activity is associated with many of the same psychological benefits found in studies of purpose, including increased energy, well-being, self-regulation, self-esteem, and a sense of mattering.[16] However, people only see these benefits from their prosocial activities when they are intrinsically motivated, that is, when they make their own decisions about what to do because they are personally motivated to get involved. They do not get these benefits when they are required to do them or when they do them for instrumental reasons, such as for college applications or to boost their grade. The question, then, is how to create an environment where students are motivated to engage in prosocial activity without coercion or external incentives. Making room for purpose exploration at school offers a way to do this.

HOW PURPOSE DEVELOPS

Purpose, when understood as contributing to the world beyond the self, is a moral achievement that follows from earlier development of empathy and compassion and internalizing moral values as part of one's identity.[17] In our interviews with children as young as eleven years old, we usually saw the first signs of purpose among those who expressed feelings of distress and concern about the suffering they saw around them. Many of our youngest interviewees talked about wanting to help others, such as a bullied classmate, homeless people in their neighborhood, or animals abandoned to the local shelter. An eleven-year-old interviewee thought of her less popular classmates when asked what was most important to her:

> Helping people that don't really do good in school, and people make fun of them. I'll be friends with them, and I'll tell people that I'd like for them to stop making fun of them because they're just like us. I don't like that people get made fun of just because they're different than other people.[18]

Another preteen expressed empathy for homeless people he saw around his town, "When I see people on the streets, I get real sad because they have nowhere to live. I feel like I need to help."[19] The evidence from decades of research on empathy suggests that most people feel so distressed at the sight of another person suffering that they are motivated to do something to help that person.[20]

Those empathetic feelings develop into purpose when young people have opportunities to act on them and learn that they can have an impact. If we do not act on our desire to do something about a problem in the world, we are dreamers, living without fully realizing our purpose. Many young people get lost on the path to purpose because they feel others' pain and want to fix a problem they see but do not act on it because they think they are too young or do not have the skills needed. They get the message that they are too young to have real responsibilities or get involved in real-world problems, like Serena, who said, "A lot of people don't take me seriously because I'm only sixteen. If I say I want to do something, they're like OK, you can try that but good luck. They don't really put trust in me."[21] Although it makes sense for a child to have dreams that they are not yet acting on, we should also consider what would happen if they found or were guided to opportunities to act on those empathetic concerns. In our interviews, teens complained that they were too young to volunteer at the local animal shelter or that their voices were not heard because they were students. Yet, we also know that young people are not provided enough opportunity to demonstrate their responsibility, and that the expectations put on young adolescents often do not rise to what they are capable of. We expect students to push themselves academically, but we do not give them opportunities to push themselves in being engaged and responsible members of their community. Worse, the opportunities for engaging in the types of prosocial activities that can promote purpose are unevenly distributed, with young people living in urban, high-poverty neighborhoods having fewer opportunities than their suburban and rural peers.[22]

Children and adolescents not only gain valuable experience and empowerment when they act on their goals and concerns, they gain important cognitive growth as well. By acting on the things that stir their empathy, young people gain access to a fuller picture of what causes the problems they see, and they can start to grasp the underlying moral structures of the social world.[23] When opportunities to act are structured, extended over time rather than a one-off event, and include reflective discussion and writing, they can support the cognitive development that allows empathy to become purpose. A girl who feels for homeless people in her community might experience the spark that could become purpose, but if she does not act on it, and does not think about what causes homelessness and how it can be alleviated, the spark will fade. If she volunteers at a homeless shelter every Saturday morning for a semester, she will have many opportunities to talk to the people she is volunteering with, hear about their experiences and varied perspectives, and ask questions to expand her understanding of the situation. If an opportunity for reflection is included, she can process the ideas she is hearing from the people at the shelter, consider the paths that different people took to get there, and think about the social factors that might have contributed to their circumstances. From this activity and reflection, she can reason about how society contributes to homelessness in her community and develop nuanced ideas about moral principles such as equality and fairness. Through this experience and reflection, she is not just having an emotional response, but has gained a complex understanding of the problem, and developed values that further inspire prosocial activity, enduring commitment, and ultimately, purpose.[24]

As teens develop moral reasoning, they are also developing identity, or their sense of what matters to them and who they are as a person. This parallel development of moral reasoning and identity is believed to be the basis of moral identity formation.[25] People with a strong moral identity will, when asked what kind of person they are, describe themselves as a good or kind person, someone with integrity or principles, or use specific virtues to describe themselves, such as honest, fair, or compassionate. Adolescence is also a time for developing ideology, or attachment to certain philosophical, social, religious, or political ideas, beliefs or principles. With ideology, teens start to shape identity according to abstract beliefs and values. If the ideologies they attach to are based on a growing sense of morality, they are more likely to develop moral identity, and with moral identity, young people will be more likely to aspire to life goals that reflect prosocial moral values. Teens also develop a sense of control over their thoughts and actions that they did not have when they were children. With this increased ownership of their thoughts and actions comes a stronger desire to be a good person—and a stronger sense of moral identity—because they feel personally responsible for what they think and do.[26] Research suggests that moral identity formation follows prosocial activity, not the other way around, and therefore the social context—that is, the opportunities provided in the community and society for prosocial activity—can play a role in moral identity formation.[27]

I do not want to suggest that younger and younger children should be expected to take on real-world responsibilities in pursuit of purpose. We should be developmentally responsive when thinking about how to give younger students authentic opportunities to explore and act on their early potential for purpose. However, rather than assuming teenagers, or even preteens, are too young to get involved, educators can tune-in and listen intently to students' empathetic concerns, questions, and emerging values, and identify next steps that students can take to act on those values in and beyond the classroom. An English teacher might hear a political voice in her student's poetry and encourage that student to join the debate team. A school board member might hear a student give a passionate speech at a student council meeting and invite the student to attend a meeting on public education at the state capitol. The second part of this book will further discuss how experiential learning opportunities can be shaped to support purpose. Here, I want to emphasize that purpose goes beyond goal setting and pursuit of success. Purpose is an enduring moral commitment and a moral achievement that often starts with an emotional response to a problem or lack in the world, or a desire to make a positive impact, and it develops when that initial emotion or desire is both acted on and internalized as a personal values system. This is not the only way that purpose develops, but it is a common path for teens, and one that can be supported by adults at school.

WHAT ABOUT MY STUDENTS?

Whenever we present our research about youth purpose to educators, the question of privilege is raised. Many educators are keenly tuned-in to the needs and wants of high-poverty students compared to their affluent peers. To some of them, purpose feels lofty and extravagant, and out of reach for students who are lucky if they get a foothold on the academic path that will lead them out of their current circumstances. Students who are not as lucky, from this perspective, will leave high school and head straight to jobs that, at best, pay the rent but do not inspire purpose. Asking these students to think about purpose seems almost unfair. How can we expect kids to think about, much less act on, purpose if they have chaotic home lives or struggle with basic needs? Fortunately, we have found again and again that the privilege of purpose is a myth. Purpose is not extravagant, or a luxury only accessible to those with stable lives. So, how does this relate to *your* students, with their diverse challenges and needs? Should you care about your students' purpose development if they desperately need you to focus on the basic academic skills that might get them on a more secure path?

These are very important questions, and there are many ways to think about them, so I will start with the evidence. In our research with adolescents, we found no difference in purpose between low-income students and their more affluent peers. In fact, low-income students (indicated by whether or not they were eligible for free/reduced lunch) had slightly higher purpose scores than higher income students.[28] The slight difference we saw was likely explained by another small difference we see in purpose scores, which is between Caucasian adolescents and students of other ethnicities: Caucasian students tend to have slightly lower purpose scores than other ethnic groups, which might simply be due to the different ways that parents from different ethnic cultures express religiosity and family expectations. We surveyed students from inner-city public schools as well as affluent private schools and many in between, and we saw no meaningful quantitative difference in purpose at different income levels.

What explains this finding? How can students struggling with poverty be as purposeful as students with unlimited resources? One of the most likely explanations is that purpose develops in response to one's life circumstances, and adverse circumstances can provide the spark that ignites purpose. For example, a high school senior we interviewed aspired to be an immigration lawyer after watching her father struggle with the legal challenges of being an undocumented immigrant:

> I've always wanted to be a lawyer, maybe because, growing up, we saw a lot of lawyers with my dad trying to fix his citizenship documentation. My dad has been with the same lawyer for ten years, and he still hasn't fixed his citizenship. And I just feel it's so wrong. I feel that they fill up the system so that they can drain and drain and drain that person.[29]

We met several young teens who started antibullying programs after dealing with bullying themselves. We met a girl who became interested in cancer research after her aunt died of cancer, and a boy who wanted to develop new tools for diabetes treatment because his younger brother had diabetes. Unfortunately, many of the students we met lived in poverty, but those high-poverty students often aspired to make a better life for their parents, siblings, and future family. All of these young people were seeking purpose *in* the challenges they faced, not using those challenges as an excuse to not pursue purpose in life. Not surprisingly, given these stories that we heard again and again from our interviewees, we found that young adolescents with purpose were better able to cope with negative life events than their non-purposeful peers.[30]

Our findings are supported by extensive research that shows purpose is associated with resilience following adverse events. At the worst extreme, studies done with survivors of natural disasters, war, and other significant traumatic events have found that purpose is associated with positive psychological outcomes from those events. Higher levels of purpose in life is related to better recovery from these negative experiences.[31] For example, among earthquake survivors in Pakistan, those with greater sense of purpose showed fewer symptoms of post-traumatic stress disorder.[32] This might be related to a reframing process called *post-traumatic growth*, which is seen in many people who suffer traumatic experiences. Trauma survivors often lose the path to purpose that they were on before their traumatic event, but those who experience post-traumatic growth find a new path by making meaning from what happened. They reframe their sense of what their life is about, and then focus on the future with a new purpose.[33] Those who try to make meaning out of their experiences, for example through creative expression or reflective writing, and then set future-oriented goals based on the meaning they find in their experience, are less likely to ruminate, which is associated with poor outcomes from negative life events.[34] These findings, along with some of the experiences our interviewees described, suggest that many people living with adversity can find purpose in their struggles.

Not all young people facing adversity will turn their pain into purpose, but they are more likely to if the adults around them recognize the potential for purpose in their life circumstances. As adults, we can guide these students to reflect, make meaning, and grow from their negative experiences, and steer them toward opportunities to take future-directed action in response to their suffering. A teen struggling with questions about her aunt's death from cancer will benefit from compassion and a listening ear, and when she is ready she may also benefit from a teacher pointing, in response to her questions, to resources for understanding why and how people get cancer and where the science is going in terms of finding cures. A student expressing frustration about the injustices he sees in his immigrant neighborhood can benefit from an adult suggesting he apply to be a youth representative to the city council. The simplest way for a teacher to support student purpose is to recognize the potential spark, which might be found in the difficult circumstances that stir a profound emotional response or beyond-the-self concern, and point the student to opportunities to act on that spark.

These days, students at both ends of the socioeconomic spectrum are experiencing extreme stress at school. Many high-poverty children arrive at school with heavy loads of toxic stress, which has a negative impact on school engagement and learning.[35] At the other end of the spectrum, some children in affluent communities put tremendous pressure on themselves to achieve, and suffer alarming rates of anxiety.[36] The social and emotional needs of these children differ, but both would benefit from a school environment that focused on supporting them to find and pursue purpose. As we have already seen, purpose appears to promote resilience and the ability to turn negative life events into something personally meaningful and beneficial for the world. Providing a classroom environment that supports purpose can help students better cope with their challenges, whether those challenges are stressful home lives or self-induced academic anxiety. Moreover, both groups of students need the type of environment that a focus on purpose provides: a classroom environment that acknowledges them for who they are, that provides opportunities to be meaningful at school, to participate, belong, and matter. They need a school environment that invites exploration of possible selves and encourages diverse visions of a successful future. By setting up the classroom environment to support meaningful participation, intentional engagement, and purpose, students with all types of social and emotional needs benefit.

Different People, Different Purpose

Although we do not find practical differences in the *amount* of purpose people have based on their ethnic group, gender, or income level, we do see some differences in *how* people seek and create purpose. Some young people are more inclined to seek purpose in their relationships and families, while others find purpose in religion, and yet others in their civic and volunteer activities. There is some evidence that people differ in *how* they create purpose in their lives according to ethnic background.[37] However, it would be inaccurate to attach certain categories of purpose to different groups of people. Instead, I want to connect these findings with research that examined cultural differences in youth attitudes toward aspects of life that relate to purpose, such as prosocial engagement, family values, meaning in life, and religion. For example, Gustavo Carlo and his colleagues found that Mexican American youth and European American youth differed somewhat in their prosocial tendencies. With more nuanced study of these results, they found that prosocial attitudes and behaviors among Mexican American youth vary according to how attached young people feel to their ethnic group, their family attachment, and whether they were raised in a home with more traditional Mexican values or mainstream American values.[38] Lisa Kiang and Andrew Fuligni found that Asian American youth are more likely than their Latino and European American peers to be searching for meaning in life, rather than saying they have already found meaning in their life.[39] Margaret Beale Spencer and her colleagues found that for African American boys, but not African American girls, religion and cultural pride are important resources for developing a healthy sense of self.[40] These studies, and many others like them, point to the very different ways that students from different backgrounds might be thinking about the role of purpose in their life.

The findings of these studies also suggest that openly exploring student purpose in the classroom would offer teachers a valuable window into the lives of their students when they do not share an ethnic, cultural, community, or social class background with their students. By getting to know students in terms of what they value and what gives them a sense of purpose, teachers can also get to know their families and community in ways that will enable them to make a more supportive connection between students' home and school lives.

We hear again and again that some of the most important sources of purpose for young (and old) people are found in family and community, in the things that are nearest to them and that occupy their daily lives. Another likely explanation for the finding that purpose does not vary regardless of socioeconomic status is that people seek and find purpose in the very fabric of life, in relationships, in faith, as well as in careers and civic activities. By making space in the classroom for students to explore and share what matters to them, and opening the boundaries of classroom activities enough to engage students' intentions, teachers can learn to recognize the potential for purpose and tap into that potential to increase student engagement and motivation. We will go further into *how* teachers might support purpose in the classroom in the second half of the book, but here I want to emphasize that the goal is to see all students as having not only the potential for purpose but the desire to express and explore their potential purpose in the classroom and connected to what they are learning—be it in a future career, civic engagement, providing for their family, supporting their community, solving environmental problems, creative activity, or any other way they see themselves being of consequence in the world. The payoff for making time for purpose in the classroom, as we saw earlier, is students who are more engaged and motivated, have a stronger sense of belonging at school, and have a greater sense of personal responsibility for their learning.

In our research, we have met people of all ages finding purpose in myriad ways and in many different domains of life. Young people are especially likely to describe finding purpose in their relationships with family and friends, by helping people in their community, by creating or inventing things, or by working to solve a problem they see in society or the environment. The following examples describe how adolescents show purpose in some of these areas. These examples describe purpose in a single area of life, but it is possible, and even likely, to have purpose in more than one area, either at the same time, or as an evolving purpose over the course of life. Purposeful people tend to be engaged in a lot of activities, so they will often describe several things that are very important to them and several activities that they find fulfilling. The domains and purposes described here are not mutually exclusive.

Family

Despite the tradition of teen rebellion—when young people distance themselves from the security and boundaries set by their parents—many teenagers say family is one of the most, if not *the* most, important thing in their lives. Among the eighth graders we surveyed, 56 percent ranked "provide support for my family" among their top three life goals, which is consistent with previous findings among older teens, who rated relationship and family goals higher than most other types of life goals.[41] The words of fifteen-year-old James were echoed by many of the young people we interviewed:

> Family is important because they will have your back no matter what. Every time I struggle, like with schoolwork, they're always there to help me. They helped me to grow to the person I am now, and if it wasn't for them, I probably wouldn't be who I am. Because they provide for me, I want to help pay them back. I want to get a good job, like a doctor or engineer, so I can take care of my parents.[42]

At this age, the goal of providing for one's parents and future family is usually aspirational, rather than fully realized purpose, though for some teens it provides strong motivation to do well in school. They aspire to autonomy, to give back to the people who supported them, and give their future children the things they did not have. Some dream of being the first in their family to go to college or becoming a professional athlete to make their family proud. Students with family-oriented purpose benefit from exposure to a broad range of possible roles they can explore that will fit with their unique interests and values while also allowing them to become an autonomous adult who can provide for their family.

Community

Many young people are drawn to the idea of community as a source of purpose, though what is meant by community varies. Students we met in a neighborhood largely populated by first and second generation Latino immigrants talked about the importance of their immigrant community and working together to stand up for their rights and protect each other. At another, more ethnically diverse high school, students put a strong emphasis on the school as their community, and many worked to make the school a safe and welcoming space for all students, free of racism, homophobia, and bullying. Even if students do not identify problems in their community to fix, many with community-oriented purpose will focus their energy on creating communities to be part of. Several of the students we spoke with said that they participate in sports, arts, and even philosophical debate groups, to be part of a community. Some found purpose in building community with their theater group or football team. High school senior Vanessa explained:

> What's important to me is having a community of people that can really connect and be honest with each other. Like in the cast of a musical, you practice together for two or three months every day after school. You really learn to trust people and talk to people. Helping people is also important to me, thinking about other people and how your actions are affecting other people, which I think ties in with community a lot.[43]

Students who seek purpose in a community effort can be encouraged in the classroom. They can be leaders in collaborative projects or take on some responsibility for establishing the classroom as a supportive community of learners. For students who are deeply attached to their neighborhood, ethnic, or faith-based communities, those attachments can be a source of connection to purpose at school, but only if they are invited to think about the issues that affect their community in the classroom and given opportunities to use what they are learning to address those issues.[44]

Society and the Environment

Children and teens readily identify problems they see around them in their communities, such as homelessness, bullying, and pollution. Some, especially as they get older, identify problems that affect society or the environment beyond what they see in their immediate surroundings. Though less common than family or community-oriented purpose, some teens find purpose by looking for ways to solve these big problems. Recent high school graduate Annie was concerned about the alarming rate at which students drop out of school:

> I felt really strongly about education and how important it is to get an education, and what a privilege it is to have that opportunity, so when I saw people dropping out it really upset me to see them wasting that opportunity.[45]

She responded to her concern by volunteering for a drop-out prevention program run by her city. Another socially aware teen, fifteen-year-old Sophia, was striving to make a commitment to veganism, because she saw it as a way she could address human rights, animal rights, and environmental issues. Adolescents who aspire to fix problems they see in the world often have strong values and are well on their way to developing convictions related to their values. They benefit from role models and mentors who can point them to opportunities to act on their values, which can give them a fulfilling sense of purpose.[46]

Creating, Discovering, and Inventing Things

The experimenters and inventors of the previous chapter may well continue those activities and come to find purpose in creating, discovering, and inventing things that have a positive impact in the world. These are the artists, scientists, journalists, inventors, and entrepreneurs, who find purpose in changing how people think or feel, or in creating things, solving problems, and making discoveries that can improve lives. Sam, the musician we met at the beginning of chapter 2, finds purpose in creating music that has an emotional impact on people, while Cassie, an eighteen-year-old actress, performed in *The Vagina Monologues* because she wanted to use theater to raise awareness about social issues. Gabriel, the boy described previously whose brother had diabetes, was more scientifically oriented in his creativity and invention. He spent his afternoons tinkering with objects around the house to learn engineering. "I want to use my engineering skills to help people. I have already been developing things, like prosthetic limbs. I want to make them more lifelike, like prosthetic limbs on the Terminator, but not so expensive and hard to come by."[47] Young people generally find opportunities outside of school to explore and develop their interest in creating things. Few of the teens we interviewed talked about pursuing these interests in their classes. Many of these creative young people would benefit from better access to materials and technology and facilitated or mentored opportunities to explore their artistic and scientific interests at school.[48]

Religion

Purpose is often associated with the mysterious side of religion. For many people, purpose is a spiritual feeling of connection to something larger than the self. This feeling alone does not meet the criteria that purpose be an engaged aspiration to contribute to the world beyond the self, but we do see a strong relationship between religion and purpose as we define it in our research. Young people who find purpose in their religion talk about serving God, living by the positive social values taught by their religion, and serving their community as part of a religious youth group. Researchers who study religious and spiritual purpose in adolescence have found that teenagers might find purpose in the spiritual aspects of religion, which imbue experiences with profound meaning and shape attachment to values, or in the structured traditions and community activities of their religious group, or both.[49] A high school senior described the sense of spiritual attainment she felt in participating in Zen Buddhist tea ceremonies, and wanted to give others the same experience. Another described finding purpose in the service activities of his church youth group. Maryam, a Muslim teen, sought to live by the values taught by her religion, especially by respecting others' beliefs and contributing to her community:

> I usually focus on how I can help others. With the Muslim community, we have something called *zakat*, which is basically giving money to the poor. My way of doing that is helping the community through community service projects. I think a good person is someone who holds to his or her own beliefs and is respectful and helps the community.[50]

However, like many purposeful young people with strong faith, her ultimate purpose was not religious, but guided by the values taught by her religion: "My father had a stroke and he couldn't work. Because of that episode, I want to look into studying the brain, because I want to prevent such a thing from happening to other families." For many young people, purpose is found in the social aspects of their religion, such as being part of a youth group community, or in their growing desire to be of service to others. For others, like Maryam, purpose is found in the values taught by their faith that are not inherently religious, such as compassion and gratitude. We can acknowledge these important sources of students' purpose at school without delving into the contentious aspects of religion.

If we just look at the domains of life where adolescents are developing purpose, we might get the impression that purpose is extracurricular, and that students are largely finding purpose outside of school. I hope this chapter has demonstrated that we should be bringing student purpose into the classroom. Purpose is an achievement in its own right, indicating optimal moral and character development. However, it also supports student development in ways that can positively impact academic achievement. As we saw above, purpose is associated with psychological and social well-being, school engagement, and sense of belonging at school. It provides a way for teachers to understand and support students to achieve a personal vision of success. It promotes equitable achievement by enabling students from diverse circumstances and backgrounds to connect and engage with teachers and the curriculum. So much emphasis is put on supporting students' academic achievement, yet the research suggests that it may not be grades but other school indicators that are stronger predictors of future success, such as attendance and behavior, and those things may be more closely associated with having an engaged, beyond-the-self purpose more so than getting good grades.[51]

Having purpose—an engaged aspiration to be of consequence in the world—is more motivating than academic achievement as an end in itself and as a path to further academic achievement in college. Rather than using college as the motivational end, getting students to think in terms of purpose could inspire them not only to pursue college, but also provide a tangible and specific understanding of what they need from college that will motivate them to finish. Some students, after taking time to explore and pursue purpose, may decide that college is not the right path, but that decision will come from identifying an equally proactive and future-directed path that will take them further in pursuit of their purpose. This is not a diversion from college readiness, and the decisions about preparing students for the next steps after high school should be taken very seriously. If "college readiness" is a mantra used to avoid letting students slip through the cracks, purpose-readiness should let even fewer slip by, and it would get more students who do go to college prepared to succeed all the way through. We need to examine what it means to achieve at school and be successful in school and beyond. Do we give students the space, time, and opportunity to examine what success means to them? Do we give them different visions of success to consider? Or do we repeat "college and career," pushing and pulling them to a place where they can hopefully start to think about what they want from life after they have left our classroom?

CHAPTER FOUR

The Three Dimensions of Purpose

Purpose is abstract, spiritual, and mysterious; an inner sense of awe that is unique to each of us. It is a force in our lives that drives and gives direction to our goals and activities.[1] It can therefore be daunting to think about how to introduce it into our schools or consider helping students develop it. However, as previous chapters allude to, purpose is also composed of components, or dimensions, that can be developed and that are familiar to teachers. At the heart of it, the dimensions of purpose are: goals, motivation, and activity. That awe-inspiring, driving sense of purpose occurs when we have (1) a higher-order and meaningful goal, (2) motivation stemming from a desire to contribute to the world beyond the self, and (3) goal-directed activity. We can support student purpose at school by providing opportunities to work on each of these dimensions in a safe and open forum. With some understanding of these dimensions of purpose and how purpose is supported from the outside, we can make school a place for purpose to grow.

Although the dimensions of purpose—goals, motivation, and activity—are familiar aspects of education, most schools do not have the environment needed to support purpose. Over the decades and across the US, schools have been pushed toward a narrow vision of what it means to be educated and successful, a vision that sees students as future labor. Because of this, we provide students a standardized education and track their progress against their peers according to narrow indicators of learning, such as test scores and grade point average. Children are norm-referenced by the school system and measured according to where they fall on the bell curve of these narrow indicators: average, below average, or above average. We tell the students on the left side of the curve that they are failing. In this system, the job of teachers is to push students on the left of the curve so that they can be more average and hope to move some of the average kids to the above-average end of the curve, yet this simply results in the whole curve being shifted. Regardless, the outcome is that students are seen by the system as averages, not individuals.[2]

Goals, motivation, and activity are critical components of this system, but not of the sort that can be integrated to become purpose. In this system, students set goals related to raising their position on the academic curve, and are told to aspire to college with or without any sense of how college connects to who they want to become. They are motivated through discipline systems that reward good behavior and punish bad behavior, or by the promise of better grades if they work harder. They fill their time with activities that they hope will increase their chances of getting into college.

Educating for purpose looks beyond averages to draw out the unique strengths, values, and aspirations that are students' greatest assets. It means striving to support students' individual development, so they can work toward goals that align with their values and interests, participate in shaping their own learning experiences according to who they hope to be, and gain awareness of the unique strengths and gifts they can contribute to the world that is based in an understanding of what the world needs from them. Rather than seeing students as points sliding up and down a normal curve, the goal of educating for purpose is to support all students to identify and develop their unique strengths and address the challenges that will be obstacles to their pursuit of purpose. Because purpose is made up of multiple dimensions, there is no such thing as having "average" purpose. Each of us has different goals, motivated for different reasons, and we find different ways to act on our goals. Todd Rose, a psychologist who studies human development by looking at individual development, calls this multidimensional development "jagged." That is, there is no straight line or curve indicating average level of purpose. Instead, everyone has a unique—and jagged—profile with more or less developed goals, stronger or weaker commitment to acting on their goals, and greater or lesser inclination to contribute to the world beyond the self through their goals and activities. Moreover, everyone will have different content to each of these dimensions, so two people who are highly committed to their purpose goals will have different purpose because they are pursuing entirely different goals for different reasons.

Purpose is very different from what we are accustomed to supporting in school because it cannot be measured with a single score or indicator; it is different for every student. Yet, it is very familiar to what schools strive to do, because it is essentially about supporting student goals, motivation, and activity. In this chapter, we will look at these dimensions of purpose individually, to see how they differ from the goals, motivations, and activities we generally associate with student achievement, and how we can support student purpose by rethinking the role of each dimension in students' learning and development. We will also look at what the research tells us about the social and environmental factors that support purpose development. Up to now, we have been learning about how purpose develops within a person. We have seen how meaning making and intentional engagement with the world of play and making activities can build an early foundation for purpose development. We have seen how emotional and cognitive processes develop into purpose as a young person experiences the emotions of empathy and compassion and responds to those feelings by taking action. Later in this chapter, we will see how the social environment contributes to purpose development. It is up to individuals to seek out, identify, create, and act on possible purposes for their life, but the conditions and circumstances of their life will greatly influence whether and how they are able to do that. By understanding how the social context can support purpose development, we can start to see how adults in the school setting can support purpose, and how doing so can contribute to a healthy school climate.

PURPOSE IN THREE DIMENSIONS

It is daunting to think about helping a class full of students find their purpose. We are lucky if we can identify our own purpose and make the most of it. For that reason, it might be easier for educators to see purpose as its parts, and understand how those parts can be nurtured from the outside. By seeing purpose as made up of three different components, or dimensions, educators can identify which aspects of purpose their students need more help with. For example, rather than having an overall sense that students are lacking purpose, teachers will be able to see that one student should focus more on identifying meaningful, higher-order goals, while another needs opportunities to organize and act on goals.

The model of purpose described here and shown in figure 4.1 includes not only the three dimensions of purpose, but also the essential, underlying strengths that enable students to develop and integrate each dimension. Those underlying strengths are *self-regulation* (the set of skills that enable students to select appropriate goals and regulate their behavior to pursue their goals); *agency* (students' ability to take effective action and determine that their actions are having the desired impact in the world); and *values* (a strong sense of what matters to them and why, and awareness of what they believe is good and right for the world). Self-regulation provides the skills needed to commit to meaningful goals and act on those goals. Values reflection increases individuals' capacity to find beyond-the-self motivation and commit to meaningful goals. Agency, especially social agency, provides the attitude and efficacy needed to act on meaningful goals and increase beyond-the-self motivation. Throughout this chapter, I will refer to self-regulation, values reflection, and agency as the "core capacities" because they represent the skills and attitudes students can strengthen within themselves to support their developing purpose.

FIGURE 4.1 Purpose Development Model

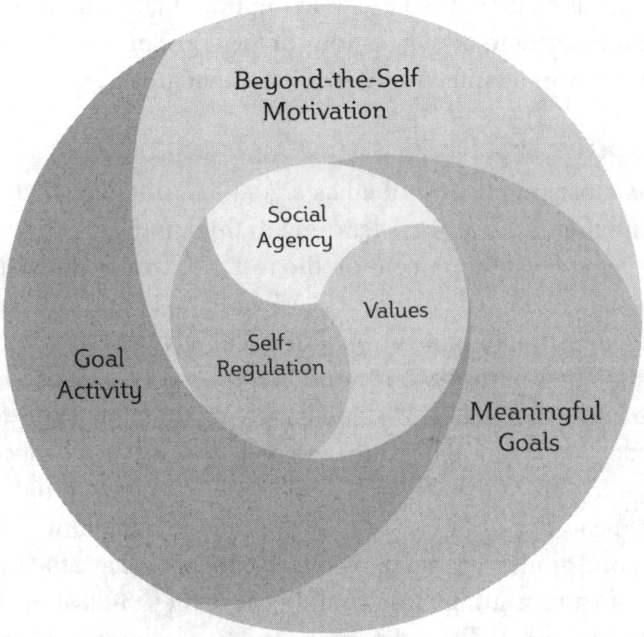

Thinking back to the image of purpose as a boat, charting a course through life, the core capacities might be thought of as the internal engine powering the development of the three dimensions of purpose, and those three dimensions provide the direction, drive, and sustained momentum of purpose. As values, social agency, and self-regulation develop, they increase the capacity for individuals to commit to meaningful goals, find motivation for meaningful goals in contributing to the world beyond the self, and take action to realize meaningful goals. We get a sense of purpose when these three dimensions are integrated, so we can imagine the core capacities as a propeller that drives the cyclical development and integration of these three dimensions. The emphasis in supporting students' purpose development should be on the key dimensions of purpose, as described below, but attending to the core capacities will make that job easier.

The following descriptions of each dimension of purpose includes questions to discuss with students to support that dimension. These questions are meant to be suggestions of the types of questions that can be used directly or adapted for use with content area curricula.

The First Dimension: A Meaningful Goal

Purpose is most simply described as a goal, but not just any goal. Students spend their school years learning to think in terms of goals: "My goal is to get at least 90 percent on the test," ". . . raise my math grade next semester," ". . . write a great essay," or ". . . get into college." Each of these is an example of a sub-goal that can give students a concrete path for pursuing purpose, but none is a source of purpose by itself. These are important goals for students, giving them the skills and attitudes needed to get through school and on to the next stage successfully. However, they are not intrinsic, meaningful, or future-minded. They give the appearance of future-thinking because a student who is working to get good grades and get into college appears to have their future in mind. But, are they setting those goals because they think about the kind of person they want to be in the future and have a strong vision of who they want to become? Or, are they setting those goals because it will get them from this phase of their education to the next phase according to the rules of the game? Future-thinking is important to developing purpose, even if the future-minded goals they aspire to evolve over time. Students can, and often do, find purpose in acting on goals that are not projected far into the future, however those goals are likely connected to a vision of the type of person they want to be, and it is a vision of self that is likely to direct higher-order goal setting well into the future. For example, the student working on an LGBT advocacy campaign at their school might have a short-term goal of raising students' awareness of fellow LGBT students' challenges and rights. That shorter-term goal is not projected very far into the future; however, it is purpose if the student sees it as connected to a broader, enduring intention such as being an advocate for underrepresented groups or working for social justice throughout their life.

In education, we tend to shy away from asking students to set broad, future-minded, or abstract goals, because they lack the specificity and time frame necessary for students to work toward them effectively and see them accomplished. If students have goals such as "improve my score on my government test," we can scaffold them to take the concrete steps toward accomplishing the goal and they can see the success of their efforts. Broad, future-minded, personally meaningful aspirations, on the other hand, are messy. They can rarely be achieved in a short period of time, and they may never be fully accomplished. They can be elusive and slippery, evolve over time, or branch off into other meaningful goals. They can feel impossible to pursue. However, by looking to the future with a sense of what really matters and envisioning the kind of person they want to be, and then setting intentions that align with that vision, students can create a life of meaning. And when that vision of who they want to be includes being someone who has a positive impact in the world, students are more likely to feel the force of purpose driving them to organize their short-term goals and activities toward being that person. The path they set out on will not be a straight line but will be more like the boat finding its way on open water, directed but not direct, taking in experiences and allowing their experiences along the way to influence the course. That is purpose. Purpose does not mean creating a narrow vision of future success and driving blindly toward it. It does not mean saying, "I want to be a lawyer" and rushing headlong toward that outcome without stopping to reflect on what makes life meaningful.

Young people can think about questions like the following to work toward identifying potential purpose goals:

- What kind of person am I now, and what kind of person do I want to become?
- What do I need to do during my lifetime to feel that my life has a purpose?
- What does a successful life mean to me?
- Which of my strengths or values do I want to define me in the future?

Their responses may take the form of a career aspiration, but not necessarily. They may take the form of several possible career options to explore, or they may not be that concrete. For many young people, the answers to these questions are abstract, or disconnected from traditional ideas of success. They might think, "I want to have good relationships," or "I want to be someone who learns about all the cultures of the world," or "I want to make my family proud." They may have more than one idea; in fact, it is a good idea to have a couple or a few broad ideas that can take the shape of purpose goals.

It seems that we are always expecting students to think about their future. After all, isn't school all about preparing students for their future? But future-thinking is not a content standard in any area of the curriculum. When students are asked to set goals, they are short-term goals set by teacher expectations, school requirements, or college admissions criteria. We need to find more opportunities to ask students to think about who they want to be in the long term. Doing so not only supports purpose development, but can also improve academic effort, so it can be advantageous to nurture students' future-minded goal setting, provided it is scaffolded with strategies to organize short-term goals that lead toward more far-reaching goals.[3]

To support young people in developing the first dimension of purpose, opportunities for future-thinking should be grounded in reflection on one's personal values. Higher-order, future-minded goals can give life a sense of purpose when they are an expression of what we find meaningful, our identity, and our values, so students should first take time to reflect on what matters to them and why. With values-driven goals in mind, students can then take steps to accomplish those goals by setting and working on intermediate goals that are more concrete, specific, and achievable in a short time frame. Some, though not all, of the interim goals toward a higher-order purpose goal are the same as the academic goals that support students' achievement at school. When academic goals are clearly seen as steps on the path to the future self, then they support purpose development. Self-regulation skills that support academic success, such as persistence, delayed gratification, and resource identification, will also support the pursuit of meaningful future-minded goals. Therefore, the first dimension of purpose—meaningful goal commitment—is supported by the core capacities of values reflection and self-regulation.

Kelly, a college student we interviewed for our study of youth purpose, showed how purpose goals are rooted in values and propelled by self-regulation. What she valued most was the sense of community and mutual support she shared with her family and friends, and because of these values she had a strong desire to do work that could give back to her community. She aspired to be a nurse practitioner so that she could use her career to give back. At the time of her interview with us, she was following the incremental steps toward this higher goal, completing coursework in biological sciences and working in the orthotics department of her local medical center, helping doctors make casts and fit leg braces. She also volunteered as a tutor in her spare time, so that she could be giving back to the community even before starting her work as a nurse. With self-regulation skills—recognizing which activities and goals to prioritize, managing her time to accommodate multiple activities, and identifying resources that would help her pursue her goals—she was able to manage all of these different activities to make progress toward her goal.

Much younger children are also capable of setting big goals rooted in values, especially when adults support them in doing so. A class of first and second graders in Northern California was primed by their teachers to think about environmentalism as a value. The teachers read picture books on environmentalism and asked their students to think and talk about the question "What places are special to you?" The students talked about a redwood grove adjacent to their school playground, where one of the giant redwoods was dying from the drought. As a class, they set the goal of saving the tree and determined the steps they would need to take, which included learning how drought affects trees and what was necessary to reverse the damage. Together, they dug up the soil and planted new plants around the tree so that more water could get to the roots, and they made signs telling their schoolmates to stay away from the tree so that the soil would not become compacted. Sadly, their effort did not save the tree, but it did teach them about aspiring to values-driven, beyond-the-self goals, and taking the steps to accomplish those goals.[4]

By following the stepping stones toward a higher-order, values-driven goal, students develop skills and gain experience that will be useful even if they change to different higher-order goals. They need not set a purpose goal that they will stick to for life. The point is to gain practice in identifying such a goal and taking the steps needed to work toward accomplishing it. Schools can support this type of goal setting by providing opportunities for meaningful project work that requires students to identify goals that align with their values, setting high expectations for students in terms of their future-thinking, and by creating an environment of encouragement and respect so students can feel that their goals are supported and matter.

Second Dimension: Beyond-the-Self Motivation

Purpose goals are personally meaningful, but what differentiates them from other important, higher-order goals is that they emanate from our desire to make a positive difference in the world. As educators, we too often ask students to think in terms of personal achievement, or assume that students are best motivated by self-oriented visions of success. Our goal as educators is to encourage students to develop into successful people, which means that they can clear life's hurdles, go to college, find employment, and be happy. Though well-intended, this emphasis on personal success may prevent students from finding purpose in life, and might not be as motivating as we think. In our interviews, adolescents who said the adults in their life encouraged them to pursue academic and financial success were less likely to be purposeful than those who heard messages of encouragement for their meaningful interests and beyond-the-self concerns. Young people who focus on self-oriented success are looking away from the points where they come into contact with the world. They are focused on winning at the competitions of life set up for them rather than attending to how they can contribute to the greater good. By focusing on personal success, we narrow our vision to only see the forward path and necessarily block out anything that might distract from our progress on that path, such as our emotional reactions to the things happening around us or abstract thoughts about making the world a better place.

The second dimension of purpose is the drive to contribute in a beneficial way to the world beyond the self. Although it is a strong drive and the heart of human purpose, it can be drowned out by more self-enhancing motivations in our success-oriented society. Young people need encouragement, role modeling, and support to listen to their other-oriented concerns and interests over the racket made by our self-absorbed, individualistic society. Moreover, they need the conditions to connect their beyond-the-self inclinations with their higher-order goal setting. Purpose does not come from having a generally kind or empathetic personality and also having meaningful, self-satisfying life goals. It is created when we *integrate* our compassion for others, sense of social responsibility, and moral virtue with our thinking about who we want to become and what we want to accomplish in life. Young people who are developing beyond-the-self motivation consider questions such as:

- What do I want my life to represent?
- What would I change about the world if I could change anything?
- What are some things I am grateful for? What do I do to express my gratitude?
- Which of my strengths can I develop to become my best self?

Adolescence is an important time for the integration of a moral sense of self with higher-order, future-oriented goals. This is the time when young people have a lot going on in terms of social development, identity formation, and moral development, so it is a critical time for supporting purpose development. In terms of social development, teens' sense of social agency is growing well beyond those early days of childhood play, when they explored their ability to have an impact on the world around them. They are increasingly able to participate in shaping their community and society. With healthy social development, adolescents make gains not only in developing social agency, but also in developing a strong sense of social responsibility. They may come to see that the success of society depends on everyone's contribution, including their own. At the same time, they are developing greater capacity for moral reasoning. They go from simply being aware of the social rules that they should follow, to having more nuanced ideas about justice, fairness, and equality.[5]

Adolescent social and moral development is concurrent with one of the most important phases of identity formation, when young people are figuring out what kind of person they want to be and what role they want to take in society. In early adolescence, their increasing social awareness causes young people to attend to who they want to be in the eyes of others. Later, adolescents come to see their identity in terms of the abstract principles or ideology they adhere to, such as a set of political ideas or their religious beliefs.[6] When social agency, social responsibility, and healthy moral development are able to flourish alongside identity formation, a young person develops moral identity, defined as seeing themselves as "acting on the basis of respect and/or concern for the rights and/or welfare of others."[7] In the early stages, moral identity is simply a child's desire to be a good or kind person. Moral identity gains complexity and nuance as a child grows into adolescence and wants to be an honest person, or a compassionate person, or someone who stands up for the rights of others. That growing moral identity comes from the values that the young person has developed through experiences in the world and their reflections on those experiences.

With a well-developed moral identity, young people have a strong foundation for the second dimension of purpose—beyond-the-self motivation—because they will be inclined to set life goals that accord with their identity. Of course, younger children can pursue beyond-the-self goals, before moral identity is fully formed, but we found in our interviews with pre-adolescents and young teens that they were motivated by beyond-the-self intentions related to the people closest to them, and in ways appropriate to their young age. For example, we met an eleven-year-old who wanted to make a better world by befriending people at her school who were bullied or shunned and a fourteen-year-old girl who joined boys' sports teams because she thought it was unfair and sexist that certain sports at her local Boys and Girls Club were considered for boys only.

The conditions that support beyond-the-self motivation include having adult role models of moral, prosocial behavior and opportunities for real-world experiences that develop social agency and responsibility. We saw these conditions supporting a fourteen-year-old we interviewed, Jenna, who found purpose in taking care of the environment. Jenna's role model was her aunt, who does species conservation work. Jenna found an opportunity to develop her curiosity about environmentalism through her school's capstone program, which had all eighth graders complete an independent, yearlong "passion project" with the guidance of a mentor. Jenna used this opportunity to volunteer and do research with her aunt's conservation project. In writing about the findings of her research, she learned that writing magazine articles to advocate for environmental issues was a perfect match for her personal strengths and interests.

Maryam, the Muslim teen we met in the previous chapter, found role models of moral living in her Muslim community. Although her long-term purpose was to work in medicine, she wanted to act now on the values she learned from her religious group by doing something to improve her community, so she looked for something that would match her deep interest in reading and literacy. She found an opportunity to connect her values and interests in her school's newspaper, where she wrote an article to advocate for her public library. "My latest concern involves the libraries. They're trying to charge each person annually to use the public libraries. I think it's an important place to have the accessibility of resources. So, I recently wrote an article about that for the school paper." Although advocating for libraries does not align with Maryam's future goals, it does give her practice in following through on her beyond-the-self motivations. It also reflects her underlying purpose, which is to improve the lives of others and her community.

It is easiest to think about beyond-the-self motivation in terms of the prosocial and issue-oriented activities that teens like Maryam and Jenna are involved in, such as volunteering in the community and environmentalism. However, having a desire to make a positive contribution can take forms that are not prosocial or rooted in a cause or issue.

Artists, for example, can contribute to the world by transforming visual culture through their creations. Athletes might seek to make innovative advances in how their sport is played. Scientists make discoveries that expand our knowledge of the physical world. Sam, the musician quoted at the beginning of chapter 2, finds purpose in connecting with others through music and having an impact on how people think and feel. Although morality is not immediately evident in the beyond-the-self motivations of these young people, a strong moral identity is vital to ensuring that their creations, discoveries, and innovations are aimed at making positive contributions to society. Therefore, the process of developing healthy social and moral identity described above applies to all different types of beyond-the-self purpose.

Above we saw that the first dimension of purpose—meaningful goal commitment—is supported by values reflection and self-regulation skills. The second dimension of purpose—beyond-the-self motivation—is supported by the core capacities of agency, especially social agency, and values reflection. As young people shape their identity by reflecting on their most central values, they can identify and commit to meaningful, values-driven future goals. When the central values relate to a strong moral identity, adolescents are more likely to be driven by beyond-the-self motives, so that their most meaningful goals align with that moral identity. The other core capacity that drives beyond-the-self motivation is social agency, or recognizing that one's actions have a desired effect in the world. We are more likely to be motivated to do things that contribute to the world beyond the self when we can see that our actions will have the desired impact. In the next section, we will see how agency integrates beyond-the-self motivation with the third dimension of purpose: action.

Third Dimension: Action

The first two dimensions of purpose capture what we tend to think purpose is—a goal for life and a reason to live—both of which are ideas. However, purpose is actually in what we *do*, not in what we think about doing. We have purpose when we commit to a goal or intention and take action on it. This is not simply a matter of how purpose is defined; the actions people take to realize their purpose affect the extent to which they feel purposeful. A recent study found that people who took action to pursue their important goals have a stronger sense of purpose than those who were taking time to evaluate their goals and decide how to pursue their goals.[8] Young people can plan for purposeful activities by reflecting on the following questions:

- What are some actions I can take to demonstrate to others what my most important values are?
- What steps can I take to become the kind of person I want to be?
- What small, specific goal can I work on right now to make progress toward realizing my dreams?
- What resources will I need to act on my goals and overcome challenges along the way?

Lofty purpose goals can be difficult to act on. Where do you start when it comes to your biggest and most abstract life goals? There are two main ways that action integrates with goals and beyond-the-self motivation to ignite purpose, and neither is as daunting as it sounds. First, having a purpose goal can organize and give direction to our actions. In other words, when we commit to a higher-order goal that is grounded in our values and desire to do something positive in the world, we have already taken the first big step toward acting on the goal because our commitment will serve to guide the steps that come next. Looking back to the purpose metaphors from chapter 1, these steps may not form a straight and direct path to purpose, but might instead appear to meander. What matters most is that steps are identified and taken. Sometimes, however, purpose begins with activities, even when there is no guiding aspiration, because our activities can provide purpose sparks and contribute to values formation. A purposeful musician might have started with piano lessons that were not meaningful at first but discovered purpose as he connected with his audience and saw the effect his music had on others. If we lack a purpose goal, we do not have to sit around doing nothing, waiting for one to arise. We can engage with the world intentionally, recognize what we value about our activities as we do, and reflect on how our activities can make us into the person we want to be. In that way, purpose can be created out of our actions.

One of the criticisms of our contemporary culture is that we do too much, and we ask students to take on too many activities. As the criticism goes, we never stop to reflect on or appreciate the moment. This suggests a point of tension between mindfulness and purpose. Mindfulness asks us to stop, be in the moment, and reflect more rather than going full speed all the time. Purpose asks us to be future-driven, engaged, and active to accomplish our goals. This tension uncovers an important point about the third dimension of purpose. It is not just activity for the sake of being driven or doing as much as possible. Purpose activity can be challenging, but should not be stressful in the sense of harried or overwhelming. By engaging in activities that reflect our values, or are based on future-minded goals and beyond-the-self motivation, the activities are focused, mindful, and intentional. Priorities are identified and activities that are not prioritized can fall away. A purposeful student might not get an A in all their classes but will feel that their time was allocated according to what mattered most, with personal values and meaningful long-term goals in mind. For our activities to attain this level of focus, they must go hand in hand with reflection. We need to reflect on our activities to check their alignment with our most meaningful goals, examine how our actions express our values, and cause the impact we hope to have in the world.

Acting in accord with values-driven—or personally meaningful—goals requires well-developed self-regulation skills. Self-regulation is the core capacity that integrates the third dimension of purpose with the first (meaningful goal setting). Ongoing commitment to purpose activities requires that we develop agency, in the sense of increasing autonomy, but also social agency, meaning we can see that our actions have the desired outcome or impact in the world. Social agency, again, also supports beyond-the-self motivation and integrates goal-directed activity with beyond-the-self motivation to result in purpose. Isabelle, one of our college student interviewees, demonstrated how acting on meaningful goals (aided by self-regulation), and developing agency in the process helped sustain her purpose activity. She aspired to be a teacher because her strongest values were education and relationships with others. In addition to majoring in child development, Isabelle volunteered with children whenever possible. She had developed the self-regulation skills needed to volunteer while attending college, for example, she considered the options she had for working with children while taking classes and decided the best opportunities would come from volunteering. She quit her retail job and persuaded her parents to provide her with an allowance for volunteering to cover her expenses. Isabelle knew she wanted to lead a Girl Scout troop, and applications were due in the summer, so she spent the school year researching what she would need to know and be able to do to lead a troop. Through her volunteer activities, she had the opportunity to work one-on-one with children, and because of that she could clearly see the effect she had on the children she worked with. "I was working with a girl who once said 'oh wow, you're in college?' I think it was a new experience for her, because she didn't know that college exists and people actually go there."[9] With a growing sense of agency, Isabelle's motivation to develop a career helping children strengthened.

Younger teens can also develop self-regulation skills to support their purpose activity, and in fact might rely on those skills as much as a busy college student. Many young people find purpose in goals and activities outside of what they are learning in school. If they do, they need to find opportunities to act on their interests without a support structure, set their own learning goals to make progress, shut out distractions, and find resources to engage in their activity. In the previous chapter we met Gabriel, a middle school student who liked to tinker on engineering projects at home. After school every day, he would come home and work on projects to develop his skills, such as re-engineering household objects and making simple prosthetic limbs. He enjoyed engineering, and as his skills increased, he saw the potential to use these skills to realize his goal of making life better for other people. Because he lived with a younger brother who was diabetic, he had daily opportunities to reflect on the role that medical technology can play in improving people's lives. Although still young and in an exploratory phase of thinking about his future, he aspired to be an engineer so that he could use his skills to help people. Gabriel's resourcefulness is inspiring, but he would be more likely to achieve his goal if he had structured opportunity to pursue his interest in engineering, which would give him access to mentors, material resources, a network of encouragement and support, and opportunities to see some social impact from his efforts.

SOCIAL SUPPORTS FOR PURPOSE

The model of purpose just described shows how purpose is created by integrating beyond-the-self motivation, meaningful goals, and intentional activity, propelled by an internal engine of values formation, self-regulation, and agency. What are the external conditions that support the development and integration of these dimensions of purpose? The research suggests that adults and institutions play an important role in providing the conditions that support youth purpose development.

The research on what supports young people to develop purpose is emerging, but again and again it points exactly where we might expect: purpose begins at home, and relationships with family matter. Recent studies have found that teens and college students who have positive relationships with their parents are more likely to have purpose. For example, one study found that college students who reported healthy parental attachment—with less anxiety and less avoidance in their relationships with their parents—were more likely to have a sense of purpose in life. In the same study, college students who had more difficulty separating from their parents and feeling secure as individuals were less likely to have a sense of purpose.[10] In another study with adolescent girls, those who reported good communication and trust with their parents were more likely to engage in prosocial behaviors, which in turn made it more likely that they would have beyond-the-self purpose.[11]

Family, friends, and other important people support purpose by noticing and encouraging a young person's interests, values, strengths, and goals. In our interviews with adolescents, those with purpose were more likely than their peers to say their family members encourage their personally meaningful goals and interests. They also got the message from their family that they could take risks in pursuing their goals because there would always be a safe landing for them at home if they failed.[12] When these important people in teens' lives notice and encourage their interests, they affirm the value of those interests, support their purpose by pointing to new opportunities to pursue their interests, and offer guidance in the form of advice and information that furthers their purpose.[13]

Purposeful teens in our study of youth civic purpose reported that their family was particularly supportive of their prosocial interests and activities. When asked what was important to them, the most purposeful of our interviewees typically started by talking about moral values and said that those values came from outside sources, such as their family, church group, and community.[14] They said that their family members promoted beyond-the-self values and behaviors by talking about issues like social injustice or religious faith. For example, one purposeful teen said, "my dad teaches me all the injustice that's going on right now, or has been going on in history."[15] Another said, "[my parents] influence me to be a better person, to make things better so I can influence people in a good way."[16] Family members of purposeful young people model prosocial behaviors, such as volunteering at a food bank or attending school board meetings. Parents sometimes provide material support for beyond-the-self activities, such as buying books to learn about an interest, providing transportation to meetings and events, or like Isabelle's parents, giving their children an allowance for volunteering so they do not have to choose between working for pay and volunteering. On the other hand, teens who said their parents emphasized and encouraged academic achievement and career success were less likely to show purpose.[17]

Another distinction of purposeful young people is that they describe being invited to participate in activities that led them to find purpose.[18] Some purposeful teens said that a caring adult noticed something they were interested in and found them opportunities to pursue that interest. Alex, the tenth-grade history teacher we met in chapter 1, is a real teacher who was described by one of our interviewees. The interviewee was Tony, a college student, who was working to become a movie director. He found purpose in making films about issues that people do not often think about, such as biracial dating. Tony started filmmaking in high school, when Alex invited him to help with a production company he worked with outside of school. Often, these purpose-nurturing adults are teachers and other people working in schools. We will meet more of them in the next chapter when we look at the ways that relationships at school can support student purpose.

The structure provided by organizations and institutions, such as religious programs, youth groups, and nonprofit organizations, is another important support for adolescent purpose development. Purposeful teens described their participation in these organizations as multifaceted, with opportunities to learn about new interests, develop moral values, create social networks, engage in community service, and find emotional encouragement, all in one place. For example, a church youth group that gets teens involved in building houses for homeless people integrates four forms of support for purpose development. It teaches the knowledge and skills needed to build houses, provides the social network of peers that encourage each other to engage in prosocial activity, connects house building with values found in religious teachings, and provides the opportunity to do something tangible for the community.[19]

The structure offered by these organizations provides a firm foundation, on which young people can layer multiple resources to initiate, build, and sustain their purpose. Non-purposeful students also participated in structured groups and organizations, but they did not describe the same opportunities to integrate multiple forms of purpose support. Instead, they described only the social aspect of the organization, or only the lessons the organization was trying to teach them. So, it is not simply that structured organizations inherently support purpose, but those that offer a range of purpose supports, when attended by young people who bring initiative and motivation, can be powerful foundations for those young people to build purpose. Schools, likewise, have the potential to provide this integrated purpose support because they have the structure to offer sustained exposure to skills and knowledge, social networks and adult mentors, and opportunities in the curriculum to reflect on how human actions impact society.

By thinking of purpose as the integration of components or dimensions, rather than as a mysterious, ephemeral state of being, and by looking at the ways that adults and organizations can support youth purpose in general, we start to see how educators can nurture student purpose and make schools places of purpose. The three dimensions of purpose—meaningful goal commitment, beyond-the-self motivation, and goal-directed activity—come from within, supported by outside sources such as positive and trusting relationships, caring adults who offer encouragement, role models of prosocial activity, help acquiring the resources needed to act on beyond-the-self goals, and opportunities to explore beyond-the-self interests. Behind and between each of these dimensions of purpose are the gears that keep it moving forward: self-regulation, values formation, and agency. We can further enable young people to develop purpose by helping them build these valuable life skills.

In the early years, educators can support purpose by allowing and encouraging children to bring their personal meaning making to classroom learning activities. One way to do this is to provide time for playful, open-ended making activities (such as drawing, tinkering, or writing) in response to lessons, which allow students' intentions to become part of classroom learning. Further, by having open dialogue in the classroom, teachers can generate inquiry questions based on students' intentions and go deeper into the curriculum content guided by what students find meaningful. When the curriculum reflects students' intentions and meaning, they feel that their voice matters, and that their participation has an impact on what happens in the classroom. The classroom becomes a place where students can develop self-regulation and agency in the context of personally meaningful activities. Moreover, classroom activities support values formation when they are responsive to students' intentions to connect with and contribute to the world beyond the self, such as when they seek to build relationships, invent new things, or create stories that make meaning from their experiences in the world (as described in chapter 2). Even early on, a school context that develops self-regulation, values, and agency through intrinsic, student-driven inquiry will provide a stronger foundation for purpose than a school context made up entirely of extrinsically motivated, teacher-driven learning activities.

As students get older, educators can build on this foundation by supporting students to develop more advanced values, social agency, and self-regulation skills, and do so in the context of pursuing meaningful, beyond-the-self goals. Teens can develop and integrate these dimensions of purpose when they have opportunities to act on their values and reflect on what causes the problems they see in society. With ample opportunity to act on their values and reflect on their values-driven activities, the purpose cycle is set into motion. Students increase their sense of social agency, and their stronger sense of agency becomes a catalyst for further beyond-the-self motivation and goal setting. When they see that they can make a difference, students come to see themselves as people who can and should have a positive impact in their world. At the same time, teens are thinking about what roles they will take in the world, and school can shape how they envision their future roles. If they have exposure at school to adults who model prosocial activity, values-driven activity, and purpose, they will see themselves taking on roles that have those qualities as well. Moreover, adolescents are supported in developing purpose when adults at school invite them to participate in real-world activities that reflect their values.[20] Ideally, as students get older, they will find increasing opportunities to reflect on their values and practice setting big, future-oriented goals based on their values, then working on smaller goals that take them step-by-step toward achieving those bigger goals. By doing so, the roles they envision for themselves will be shaped by purpose.

PART II

PURPOSE IN SCHOOL AND IN THE CLASSROOM

WHAT IF WE WANTED to create a school with the foremost goal of ensuring that all students have a sense of purpose to give them direction and drive when they graduate? What would the place be like? What would the curriculum consist of? What content would be prioritized? What instructional strategies would be used? While there is no widely accepted "purpose-based" approach to curriculum and instruction, and no scientifically proven strategies for teaching purpose, there are existing and emerging pedagogical ideas that align with what we already know supports purpose development. In our schools, we see increasing attention to students' social and emotional needs, which paves the way for more purposeful schools by changing school climate and nurturing more positive student-teacher relationships. There are widely practiced pedagogies, such as project-based learning and student-led inquiry, that can be shaped to provide the conditions for students to explore and develop purpose at school. There are also new programs and interventions emerging that directly aspire to develop student purpose and makes schools places of purpose.

The goal of part 2 is to inspire and encourage educators and anyone who works in schools or with young people to turn their schools into places of purpose. The ideas in the following chapters are more investigative and theoretical than scientifically based. That means that they come from theory about what purpose is and how it develops, combined with pedagogical approaches and teaching strategies that have been shown to have outcomes related to purpose or the dimensions of purpose. To prepare this section, I also investigated several purpose programs and interventions, and report about them in terms of what they consist of, how they are designed to support purpose, and how teachers and students respond to them. Evaluation of these programs is an ongoing process, but the anecdotal feedback about them is overwhelmingly positive, and they are increasingly in high demand, attesting to the positive impact they have had in schools. Profiles of six of these programs are woven into this section, between chapters on purposeful school relationships and climate; purpose curriculum topics; and purpose projects as an approach to instruction. If you work with students, or are a school or district leader, I hope you gain inspiration from the following chapters, and feel empowered to try new strategies for supporting student purpose in your schools.

CHAPTER FIVE

Purposeful Schools

Creating a socially and emotionally healthy climate at school has become a pressing challenge. Many children arrive at school unprepared for the physical, social, and cognitive demands of the classroom, bringing with them the adversities they face at home.[1] In this climate of greater demands coming into the school, teachers are under pressure to provide more academic content in younger grades and attain not only higher achievement for their students, but show growth in student achievement each year.[2] Teachers who are not provided the social and emotional training to handle these challenges can fall into a cycle of stress in which they feel helpless and exhausted, which can lead them to resort to punitive, controlling, and criticizing responses to challenging student behavior, which in turn causes student behavior to deteriorate. Positive student-teacher relationships are virtually impossible under these circumstances. Teachers are not only less able to manage their own social and emotional responses but also cannot support social and emotional learning and development among their students.[3] Teachers working under these conditions may leave teaching, or to regain control, they might resort to the rigid teaching methods that keep the cycle spinning and are antithetical to purpose.

The good news is that there has been a recent surge in efforts to improve the social and emotional climate in our schools and provide conditions that support more positive relationships between students and teachers. More and more, educators are prioritizing relationships in their schools, and striving to create an "optimal classroom climate" that is characterized by minimal conflict and disruption, smooth transitions, respectful communication, focus, and responsiveness to the needs of individual students.[4] The school climate research suggests that there are four dimensions of schools that shape the climate, which have the following qualities in schools that provide a positive and healthy environment: (1) people in the school feel socially, emotionally, and physically safe; (2) instruction is high quality, connected to real life, engaging, acknowledges student diversity, and is evaluated for continuous improvement; (3) relationships are positive, cooperative, and respectful of diversity; and (4) the structural environment is clean and inviting, and supplies are adequate to support curricular and extracurricular activities.[5]

When purpose is a prioritized outcome of education, these elements of a positive, healthy school climate are reinforced, because the elements of a school setting that support student purpose overlap with the elements that contribute to a positive school climate. This chapter links the research on positive school climate and student-teacher relationships with what we have learned about the role of relationships and social context in supporting youth purpose. The first consideration is what you thought about in chapter 1: If you work with students, what is your purpose? How can you engage your purpose in your work? How would your practice be different if you did? One of the tools that teachers have available to support them in creating a purposeful climate in their classroom is to reflect on their own purpose for being there. Another tool is found in focusing on student purpose as an important outcome of education. By focusing on purpose, teachers can employ strategies for classroom climate and student-teacher relationships that not only support purpose but also have the benefit of supporting students' social-emotional development, motivation, and engagement in the classroom and academic performance and achievement.[6]

Looking back to previous chapters provides some additional guidance for establishing a purpose-supportive environment at school. In a purpose-supportive environment, students feel safe to share their authentic selves, to expose what matters most to them, and to explore their deepest concerns and their biggest dreams, and they know they will be encouraged and supported for being who they are. A purpose-supportive environment is a space where students can reflect on their values, strengths, and goals, and make connections between the curriculum and what matters most to them. There is an assumption in this space that playing openly with ideas and materials is vital to learning, at any age and in any area of the curriculum, because that is how students can make meaningful connections to what they are learning. In this purpose-supportive environment, students can identify a purpose for what they are learning because learning activities are relevant and reflect an authentic, beyond-the-surface understanding of students' questions and interests. A purpose-supportive school environment is active, because students have opportunities to act on their values, concerns, questions, and goals. They have opportunities to take the lead in acting on their personal learning goals, and they are invited by adults in the school to get involved in activities that will enable them to develop their interests. Finally, in a purpose-supportive environment there is a strong sense of community. Students feel connected to and responsible for the well-being of the community. The classroom and school community provide learning relationships and collaborative experiences that are authentic to real-world purpose pursuit. With a sense of community, the school environment provides a space for students to practice identifying potential sources of purpose and working with others to act on their purpose.

The following conditions can contribute to creating a purpose-supportive environment in a classroom or school: student voices are heard, the teacher models compassion, students feel a sense of belonging, learning activities are relevant and promote student autonomy, students feel responsible for maintaining a positive environment, and they see themselves as members of an active learning community. If you are an experienced teacher, these conditions of a healthy and positive school environment will be familiar to you. The goal in sharing them here is to make the connection between specific aspects of a healthy school climate and purpose. Each of these conditions is selected because it can contribute to the purpose-supportive environment just described, and they are also among the conditions frequently described in the literature on positive school climate. This section is intended to point to the conditions that can lead to such an environment and suggest that interested educators will find additional resources for creating these conditions in the positive school climate literature.

Voice

Student voice is a widely used term in education in recent years, and can mean anything from empowering students to express their beliefs, ideas, and values in the classroom to giving students a say in what and how they learn in school. It first enters when teachers look beyond preconceptions about students and listen so they can know students authentically. In a classroom that nurtures purpose, students' voices are heard, and students are seen and acknowledged for their unique interests, experiences, values, strengths, and goals. They sense that they are valued stakeholders in the school community and can contribute to classroom decisions that have an impact on their learning experience. If there are never opportunities for students to share themselves in class discussions or participate in classroom decision making, school will be a place that shuts down purpose rather than supports it. When students have a strong voice in the classroom, it can be a place of purpose because young people can develop the potential for purpose as they learn to share their unique strengths and interests to have an impact in the world.

Purpose is supported when students are seen and heard in the classroom, but that does not mean every student must be seen in all of their individuality and uniqueness by the teacher for purpose to flourish. Rather, the climate is set for purpose when students have a voice in the classroom and learn to respond to each other in ways that show they see, hear, and respect their classmates' perspectives and contributions. In this environment, students feel that they can reveal themselves in the classroom, be meaningful, and share their emerging goals and values as they engage with the curriculum. They can also develop a connection between what they are learning and their goals, because they have opportunities to make this connection through class discussions and activities.

To create the conditions for purpose by encouraging student voice, consider these questions: Do classroom discussions and activities invite students to contribute their own ideas? Do class discussions invite students to respond to each other by acknowledging their classmates' ideas and expanding on or thoughtfully critiquing each other? Do students sufficiently understand the purpose of what they are learning to make meaningful contributions during class discussions? Are there opportunities for open-ended dialogue so that students can engage with curriculum content in ways that connect with what matters to them?

We will see later in this book that teachers can use dedicated purpose activities to directly encourage student voice, but how do you invite student voice into the classroom when you have a curriculum of content knowledge and skills that must be taught? Sara Stillman, the art teacher we met in chapter 2, demonstrates how a content lesson can provide numerous opportunities to invite student voice. Sara needed her students to learn what analogous colors are (those that are next to each other on the color wheel), however, she also wanted her students to develop their voice in her classroom. She asked them to practice using analogous colors by painting a picture of something meaningful to them: their favorite toy. She created a climate where students felt safe to speak up and make the activity even more meaningful. Her students challenged the boundaries of the assignment with questions such as: "Can it be something I play with that isn't a toy?," "Does it have to be a toy I play with now, or can it be one I used to play with?," and "What if the thing I like to play with is not a toy, but my friend?" The students then talked with each other as they worked, discussing what their favorite toys were and why they chose the toys that they did. They talked about why they chose a color scheme to paint the toy, such as a girl who said she chose shades of red and orange to make her toy dragon look fierce and fiery. After completing their paintings, Sara invited students to share about their painting experiences by describing what surprised them as they painted, and what they found challenging. Her students had voice in this project from the beginning, when they questioned the limits of the assignment to make it more personally meaningful, to the end, when they shared their experiences in completing the assignment. Though young, these elementary students gained a sense that school is a place for them to explore what is meaningful to them in connection with what they are learning, which provides a foundation for creating purpose at school.

Compassion

Compassionate people are aware of the suffering of others and are moved to relieve the suffering they see. Compassion is similar to purpose in that compassionate people, like those with purpose, want to have a positive impact in the lives of others. A study of eighth- and ninth-grade students found that compassion and purpose were significantly correlated among young adolescents, though the relationship was not strong.[7] In his book *A Fearless Heart,* Thupten Jinpa, co-author of the Compassion Cultivation Training program at Stanford's Center for Compassion and Altruism Research and Education, suggests that compassion leads to purpose because compassion inspires us to be kind and drives us to be useful and help others. Therefore, he suggests that increasing our compassion is also a way to have more purpose in our lives.[8] A compassionate classroom, then, might set the stage for purpose by providing a space where students are inclined to help each other and learn the value of caring for others. It also provides the sense of safety students need to share themselves and explore potential purpose at school.

The Compassion Cultivation course Jinpa helped to create uses mindfulness techniques such as meditation, mindfulness in daily activities, and reflection to cultivate compassion, and a study conducted with adult participants in the training showed it significantly increased compassion compared to a group who wanted to take the course but were on the waitlist.[9] Mindfulness programs for children and adolescents are on the rise in schools, aimed at improving attention, reducing stress, increasing compassion among students, and improving student behavior and academic performance, and there is some evidence that they work.[10] Although, according to a review of research on mindfulness practices with school children, the evidence is thin.[11] Therefore, mindfulness practices may contribute to compassion in the classroom, but other ways of creating a compassionate climate might be considered. The first condition for a compassionate classroom is a compassionate teacher, one who models compassion and can listen deeply to students and react with kindness and care. A compassionate teacher puts humanity before the demands of the system when responding to issues that arise with students. Being a compassionate teacher does not mean fixing the traumas, hurts, or problems that students bring to school with them. Instead, teachers should strive to be kind to themselves and not exhaust themselves worrying about their students. Compassion means opening your heart to the suffering of others; it does not imply that we can or should eliminate the suffering of others. In fact, students benefit from facing their personal challenges more so than they benefit from having their problems fixed for them by someone else.

Beyond this first condition, creating a compassionate classroom requires that students are seen and heard, as described in the first element of a purposeful school climate—student voice. Teachers can go further in creating a compassionate classroom by doing what at least one educator calls "checking in" with students.[12] Checking in is a daily activity that starts the class, either formally in a class meeting, or informally as the teacher assesses the emotional energy of students as they arrive, and asks check-in questions to make sure students are ready to learn. Teachers can also create compassion by checking in at specific times, such as when they see a student struggling, misbehaving, or failing to work at their usual level. Rather than defaulting to punitive reactions, teachers in a compassionate classroom respond by listening deeply and probing gently to find out what might be causing the student to act out or fall behind. Beyond checking in, teachers can create a compassionate classroom by reflecting on how they currently engage with students to consider whether they have preconceptions that color their interactions with students. Compassion means being aware that others are suffering, and for teachers that requires turning off preconceived ideas about students so they can tune-in to the emotional cues their students express and invite students to authentic dialogue by checking in.

Another way that teachers can create a compassionate classroom is by maintaining high expectations of students while being tuned-in to the challenges they might be facing that will impact their ability to engage fully with their schoolwork. Compassion does not mean being permissive or overindulgent with all the issues students are dealing with. It means listening with care and letting the student know that you understand what they are going through, and then working with students so they can be accountable for the work that is expected of them within terms that are reasonable for their situation. Aside from unnecessarily lowering expectations of the student, overly accommodating one student may be perceived by other students as unfair, which will prevent them from seeing the classroom as a compassionate space. In a compassionate classroom, students are given the opportunity to learn how to address their personal challenges and rise to expectations, which teachers can support by accommodating students in a way that acknowledges their challenges without releasing them from their obligations.

A compassionate classroom goes hand in hand with having a culture of purpose at school. When teachers show compassion, for example by responding with empathy rather than punishment to a student's misbehavior, they develop relationships of trust with their students. A trusting relationship with a teacher allows students to have deeper and more personally meaningful engagement in classroom discussions and activities, which in turn gives them greater potential for creating purpose at school. Moreover, a compassionate classroom environment supports students to develop compassion themselves, which can be a precursor to purpose. Although compassion is not the same thing as purpose, students are more likely to develop purpose if they are aware of the needs of others and inclined to respond to those needs. At the same time, when teachers prioritize student purpose, they can create a compassionate classroom in the process, because compassion results when students share what matters to them in the classroom, examine their values through dialogue with teachers and classmates, and participate fully as contributing members of the classroom community.

Belonging

Students have a sense of belonging at school when they feel that they fit in as members of the school community. Belonging starts with positive relationships but goes beyond that to include feeling accepted, valued, and supported by the community.[13] When students feel accepted, and like members of a community, school is an entirely different place than it is for those who feel rejected or do not feel connected, supported, or accepted at school. On the extreme end, students who have a greater sense of belonging at school are less likely to drop out.[14] More generally, students who have a sense of belonging at school are more engaged and have more positive feelings about school, class work, and teachers.[15] They also show more of the skills and resources that may support them in developing purpose, such as intrinsic motivation, self-regulation, internal locus of control, and higher expectations for their future success in attaining goals.[16]

Students who are members of groups that tend to be stigmatized at school are especially vulnerable when it comes to not feeling a sense of belonging at school. For example, African American students show a decline in their sense of belonging at school over the course of the academic year, and accumulatively over the course of their school lives.[17] As their sense of belonging at school declines, so does their academic performance, physical health, and happiness.[18] However, African American students are also more likely than their Caucasian peers to benefit from interventions that support sense of belonging at school. Even a simple activity to help new students see that feeling out of place is normal reversed African American college students' decline in sense of belonging as well as the negative impacts that accompanied that decline. The same effect was not seen in Caucasian students.[19] These findings suggest the important role that teachers play in supporting sense of belonging in students who are at greater risk of feeling out of place at school.

Students' sense of belonging at school is critical to their academic success, but it is also vital to unlocking their potential for developing purpose at school. When students feel that they are valued members of the school community, they are more likely to trust their teachers and classmates, and expect that what matters to them will matter to the community. With that trust and sense of mattering, students can be more vulnerable in taking risks with their ideas and values, and expose themselves in a way that makes it possible to explore their purpose at school. On the other hand, students who do not feel a sense of connection to the people at their school will be unlikely to speak up, ask questions, wrestle with ideas, or express controversial opinions in class.[20] Students who feel that they belong in the school community also feel that they can and should contribute to the success of the community. Students who feel that they are valued members of the school community are more likely to internalize the values of the community, providing a foundation for purpose.[21] Having a greater sense of belonging can increase our feeling that life is meaningful.[22] The connections and positive relationships that students experience when they feel a sense of belonging at school contribute to their sense that their lives have significance in a larger social context that extends beyond themselves. When students gain a sense that their lives are significant in in a larger social context, they are taking steps in building both the agency and the beyond-the-self mindset that can serve as a foundation for their developing purpose.

Autonomy and Relevance

Humans have a fundamental need for autonomy. Autonomous people are self-governing, are in control of their actions, and feel a sense of being the cause of events in their lives.[23] Students with a sense of autonomy feel that they are responsible for their actions and will learn to self-regulate their behaviors rather than relying on others to regulate their behaviors for them. They also feel that they can act and live according to their own intentions, drives, and values, and can pursue goals that are personally meaningful. Therefore, a classroom environment that supports student autonomy will also provide the conditions for students to develop purpose.

The environment of the classroom plays an important role in determining whether students will feel a sense of autonomy at school or will instead feel that they are controlled by others and not responsible for their behaviors. Some common features of classrooms are known to inhibit students' autonomy. When students are rewarded for good behavior, their autonomy is undermined because they learn to seek out external rewards for their behavior rather than being motivated because they find challenge, enjoyment, or meaning in their classroom activities. Likewise, punishments and threats, such as the threat of a deadline, can reduce students' personal motivations and inhibit autonomy by causing them to feel controlled by others. Students' autonomy is also inhibited when they feel they cannot express criticism or unpopular opinions in the classroom. Autonomy is further inhibited when students are interrupted excessively while working on learning tasks and expected to transition in the middle of an activity.[24] Finally, students are likely to feel less autonomous when they are being observed or evaluated. For example, in one study, students who were told they were learning something in order to teach it to other students reported higher intrinsic motivation (which is associated with both autonomy and purpose) than students who were told they were learning something in order to take a test on what they were learning.[25]

A classroom that supports autonomy does not rely on rewards, threats, or surveillance to manage student behavior and does not suppress student opinions. Instead, an autonomy-supporting classroom offers students choice in their learning activities and invites students to express their ideas and opinions. One important aspect of a classroom that supports autonomy, and purpose, is relevance. When students feel that classroom activities are responsive and relevant to their interests, goals, and values, they become more engaged in their learning and gain a greater sense of control over, and responsibility for, what they learn. In this environment, students develop a stronger sense of self-worth, show more desire to be challenged, and are more curious, compared to students in classroom environments that do not reflect their personally meaningful goals and interests.[26] Students need to see that what they are doing in school is relevant to their lives and feel increasing control over the environment and their learning in order to see the classroom as a place where their values are respected and where they are safe to share the things they find meaningful. When teachers allow for student control, trust students, encourage students' personal goals and values, and provide learning activities that are responsive to students' curiosities, they create the conditions for students to develop autonomy, self-regulation, meaning, and agency, all factors that contribute to student purpose development.

Social Responsibility

In the school climate literature, social responsibility is generally defined as students' willingness to follow classroom rules and social norms to make for a healthy, safe, and effective learning environment.[27] However, beyond the classroom, social responsibility is a broader concept about contribution to society, from which we can take ideas for creating a school climate that supports students' purpose development. People with social responsibility, from this broader perspective, are aware of interdependence in society, that is, they understand that their own lives suffer when others are suffering, and their own lives are improved when society is improved. They feel responsible for acting in ways that contribute to the greater good and show commitment to improving their communities.[28]

School can be a place where purpose grows when students recognize their own responsibility for creating a positive classroom environment, not just by following social norms, but by contributing to the greater good of the school community. Students can begin to develop social responsibility in the classroom by being made aware that their own ability to learn and thrive is improved when everyone else in the room is happy and learning, and little time and energy is spent on behavior problems. Beyond that, students can gain awareness that creating a positive classroom environment means more than simply good behavior. Socially responsible students recognize that their role in the school community includes being aware of others, caring for other members of the community when they are in need, and taking personal responsibility for addressing problems and making improvements when they can. This does not mean that students take on full responsibility for the state of the classroom, but that they are aware of the social environment and respond by doing their part in developmentally appropriate ways. A kindergartner might notice that his classmate needs a hug. A seventh grader might notice that a student is being excluded because she is different and sit with her at lunch. One socially responsible (and very purposeful) high school student we interviewed learned that state budget cuts were going to result in some teachers being laid off, so she formed a fundraising club to contribute to teacher salaries. She recognized that fixing the problem was not someone else's responsibility. It was her school; therefore, it was her responsibility.

Several factors contribute to students' developing social responsibility at school, but one of the most important is the school climate. Teachers can support students' social responsibility by nurturing supportive, respectful, and trusting relationships in the classroom.[29] Two seemingly contradictory aspects of school climate, already described above, merge to promote students' social responsibility. On the one hand, students report greater social responsibility when they feel a sense of belonging at school and feel that most members of the school community try to take care of each other. At the same time, a classroom environment that supports student autonomy, by enabling students to voice contrary opinions at school and even disagree with teachers, also contributes to students sense of social responsibility.[30] When the school climate encourages students to be autonomous and lets them know that they are valued and cared for members of the community, students come to feel responsible for the community and empowered to act when they see something that should be changed.

Community of Practice

The communities of practice concept is typically used to describe informal learning that happens in professional organizations or domains of practice, such as among teachers in a school, physicians in a medical practice, or musicians working in a particular style of music. In a community of practice, learning occurs through interaction among all members and is not just transmitted from a teacher to a student. All members of a community of practice contribute their ideas and expertise, changing the practice of the whole community through their participation.[31] Classrooms can also be communities of practice if we look past the formal structure of the curriculum to look at how students engage in classroom activity together and how they shape the learning that occurs through their engagement.[32] In a classroom community of practice, students have opportunities to share with each other their personal knowledge and insights about the subject as well as their personally discovered ways of engaging with the ideas, activities, and materials of the subject. For example, a teacher who uses math talk is taking steps to build a community of math practice in the classroom. Teachers can create the conditions for a community of practice in their classroom by opening the boundaries of their lessons so students can make connections to what they find meaningful, creating the conditions for students to collectively develop shared meaning, and encouraging students to share ideas, respond authentically to each other, copy from each other, and instruct each other.

Designing the classroom as a community of practice creates the conditions for purpose in two ways. First, it invites and privileges student meaning in the classroom, and second, it introduces the possibility of shared purpose. Students can make meaningful connections to what they are learning, and they can build shared meaning with others as they collaborate on classroom learning activities. In a classroom community where students work together to understand and solve problems, students learn that solving difficult problems is not an individual task but a collaborative effort. They can recognize that they have shared learning goals and can work toward greater understanding by sharing their ideas and learning from each other. We often think of purpose as an individual concern or interest, yet in practice, we rarely work independently to realize our purpose. Purpose is not about setting out into the world to solve enormous problems all alone. Rather, we identify ways that we want or need to contribute to the world, and then find ways to connect with others to be part of something that fulfills our purpose—working as a nurse with a neonatal intensive care team at a hospital, collaborating with other musicians to produce an album, or fighting climate change by working with a team of engineers to develop parts for a fuel-efficient car. Rarely can we fulfill our purpose aspirations alone, which means that we usually must adjust our individual purpose to collaborate with others toward a shared purpose. Therefore, classrooms that are set up as communities of practice prepare students for a more authentic approach to pursuing purpose in life.

ADULT ROLES AT SCHOOL THAT SUPPORT PURPOSE

Aside from generally striving for positive relationships with students, there are four roles that teachers, and other adults in the school community, can take on to create the conditions for purpose: Interested adult, mentor, purpose role model, and community facilitator.

Interested Adult

Teachers support student purpose by acknowledging what matters to the student, or what the student's unique strengths are. Young people are more likely to pursue purpose if they receive encouragement from important adults that validates their goals and interests, and they are less likely to pursue purpose if they instead hear adults encouraging academic achievement with no attention to what they find meaningful outside of their teacher-directed schoolwork. In addition to verbal acknowledgment and encouragement, interested adults can support purpose by pointing students to opportunities to act on their interests.

In our study of civic purpose among high school seniors and college students, we met several students who became meaningfully involved in political activity because teachers recognized their interests and pointed them to ways to act on their interests. Luis had been interested in politics since childhood, and learned everything he could about political science. When his US history teacher suggested students write to President Obama to express their concerns and anger about how education budget issues were impacting their school, Luis not only wrote the letter, but also helped organize students to participate in a teach-in that teachers staged to draw media attention to the issue. The principal noticed Luis's interest in politics and pointed him to opportunities to further his interest. He urged Luis to attend events with local politicians and go to the state capitol to advocate for the issues he cared about. With this support from his teacher and principal, Luis met numerous state politicians, became a regular speaker at political events, and after graduating from high school became the youngest person ever to run for city council in his city. In addition to his own political activities, he mentored younger students at his high school, such as Elena, another exemplar in our civic purpose study. Elena was also recognized by her teachers and principal for her passionate interest in policy and law. Luis brought Elena with him to the state capitol, and to political events, and by her senior year she was highly involved in civic and political activity that reflected her concern for immigrant issues and education policy.

Another young woman we met in the civic purpose study, Dominique, was deeply involved in closing the education gap for young people living in poverty. At the time of her interview, Dominique was a college student, and at the same time was leading an organization she started to help at-risk youth in the community get to college. She had also started a leadership program at the local continuation high school and had spent a semester working with the Children's Defense Fund in Washington, DC, among other activities aimed at developing opportunities for at-risk youth. Dominique had these interests and concerns starting early in high school. However, she had not considered her potential to have a real voice in policy until her sophomore English teacher read one of her poems and said, "Whoa, you have so much to say. You're really socially and politically aware of things that are happening. You have a powerful voice."[33] The teacher encouraged her to join the debate team, and from there, Dominique started using her powerful voice to advocate for the issues that she cared about. Because a teacher read beyond the needs of the assignment in Dominique's poem, and heard and encouraged her political voice, Dominique started taking effective action on her deepest concerns about poverty and youth before even graduating from college.

Mentor

Teachers support student purpose when they facilitate meaningful work or provide opportunities for students to learn skills to act on a potential purpose. They can become mentors for students in several ways that fit with classroom practices, for example by integrating project work into the curriculum, assigning capstone projects, providing instruction in skills that enable students to extend the curriculum, and connecting students with resources in the community to extend their learning beyond the classroom, like Alex did when he introduced Tony to professional film production. Mentors usually start off as interested adults who then go a step further by making opportunities to teach students the skills and knowledge needed to pursue an interest or by providing the emotional encouragement and wise guidance that enables students to pursue an interest on their own.

Adult mentors are often found outside of school, but these community-based mentors provide examples for school-based adults to follow. Manny, a young man we met when he was a high school senior, said that as a child he found trouble by getting into fights and had been using drugs and alcohol since he was nine. By the end of eighth grade, he was well on his way down the wrong path, when his aunt guided him to a youth organization that showed him other opportunities for his life. There he met adults who acted as mentors, who taught him job skills so he could imagine himself doing something other than selling drugs to make money and showed him that they cared for him like family. The organization's focus on drug prevention spoke to his worry for his younger brother and fed his interest in helping younger kids get on the right path in life. A friend also suggested he get involved with a local boxing organization to channel his interest in fighting into something positive. At the boxing ring, he met coaches who not only taught him how to channel his fighting skills and energy into boxing, but gave him opportunities to coach younger boxers. Through the guidance and opportunities provided by these mentors, Manny turned his life around and was planning to go into business or start a nonprofit when he got older. When we met with him again two years later, Manny was in college and still working with at-risk youth through community organizations. He was lucky to have caring adults paying attention to him and resources in his community that explicitly provided mentorship for troubled youth. Teachers and other school-based adults cannot give this level of attention to all the troubled students in their school, but Manny's example shows the life-changing difference adults can make for a young person by providing some targeted guidance that shows they care. The coaches and other adults who mentored Manny gave direction to his life by encouraging him and providing him access to activities that matched his interests. They made a difference because, as he said, "It seemed like they cared."[34]

Role Model

Adults can support students' purpose when they model the dimensions of purpose and live according to their purpose. At school, teachers who model their values and social-emotional skills are most effective at supporting their students to internalize the same values and develop those same skills.[35] The purpose research suggests that adults who model beyond-the-self thinking and activity are a source of purpose inspiration for young people because they establish norms of compassionate action and social responsibility.[36] Perhaps just as important, adults who live a life of purpose, and are explicit with students about what gives them purpose and how they act on it, can support students to develop and pursue their own purpose. This requires that teachers reflect on their own purpose or purposes in life, and then share their own understanding of purpose with students.

Among the young interviewees in our studies of youth purpose, those who most clearly demonstrated the important role that teachers play in modeling purpose were those who aspired to be teachers themselves. One of these was Andrew, a high school senior who aspired to be a music teacher, inspired by his own music teacher, Mr. Stevens:

> Mr. Stevens came in my ninth-grade year, and I've never met a teacher like him. He's been probably one of the most influential people in my life. He's the reason I decided to become a music teacher. He'd have me stay after school with him and help the clarinets, and I just love seeing the joy on their face when they couldn't get something, when they can finally get it and play it.[37]

When we interviewed Andrew again two years later, he was in the military and still hoping to be a music teacher after his deployment. He saw teaching as an important aspect of the life he imagined for himself, focused on family and community, raising children, making the world better by helping others, and having an impact on people's lives through music. He spoke again about his high school music teacher as a role model: "Mr. Stevens has a little quartet band that plays downtown. That's something I'd love to do, go out and do a little benefit concert with my students, just do charitable things, and work with the community whenever I get spare time."[38]

Community Facilitator

The idea of purpose in life often conjures images of people going it alone to pursue their unique passions and accomplish important goals. However, purpose is rarely an individual endeavor. On the contrary, purpose typically involves participating with others in a community, toward a shared goal. One of the ways that teachers can support student purpose is by being a community facilitator in their own classroom. As described above, schools can be places of purpose when students feel that they are participants in a community of learning, or practice, to which they can contribute meaningful ideas and shape the shared knowledge of the group. In a classroom where students learn this way, teachers can play the role of facilitator, empowering students to collectively take responsibility for their own learning. As community facilitators, teachers establish the potential for school-based relationships to nurture student purpose by creating a sense of community in the classroom and then encouraging students to support each other's interests, values, and goals.

In chapter 2 and above, we saw the inside of an elementary school art room where students had formed a community of art making. It was a particularly effective community, where the children's personal meaning came through in their art making, and they often collaborated and shared ideas with their classmates. The community of art making was so effective because the art teacher was a community facilitator. She wanted them to learn art skills and content, but she also prioritized their development as people and members of society, so she structured her lessons to create a somewhat student-driven art-making community in her classroom. Her assignments were open-ended to allow ample room for students to interpret each project in their own ways. She often gave them opportunities to collaborate with their classmates on art exercises and projects, and allowed them to interact, share ideas, and give each other feedback while working on individual projects as well. She supported them in having thoughtful discussions, as a class or in dyads, about their ideas for art projects and their critiques of each other's work. The ideas and experiences that students brought into the art room were shared through these discussions, collaborations, and artistic interactions and became part of their collective understanding about what it means to express yourself through art.

Outside the classroom, school activity directors have the opportunity to show how being a community facilitator supports student purpose. Eighth grader Alisa participated on a local diving team and particularly loved being a member of the team. She enjoyed diving, but what she found most meaningful about it was being part of a community with her teammates and coach. The coach cared for his team and taught them to not just excel at diving, but to be a community of divers, who supported and encouraged each other. Alisa described the influence of her diving coach:

> My coach and I, we're really close. It's almost like he's one of the people on the team, and not even a coach. I do really love the sport, but I've also developed a lot of connections with my friends there. The reason why diving is probably the most important thing to me is the people I met there, because we know each other so well, and we're there if someone is scared of a new dive, or needs encouragement.[39]

The coach acted as a community facilitator who made the team not only about diving, but about having a community of divers who were supportive of their teammates, learned from each other, and cared as much about each other as they did about diving.

In this chapter, I described the conditions and relationships that can help make a school into a purpose-supportive environment. The remaining chapters are also about the school environment, but with greater emphasis on instruction and learning activities. The next chapter is the first of three that introduce programs that educators are adopting to bring purpose into their schools. The two programs profiled in the next chapter follow this chapter because they emphasize the importance of having an encompassing impact on school culture, and therefore they resonate with the purpose-supportive conditions and relationships described previously.

CHAPTER SIX

Quaglia Institute and The Future Project

An approach to purpose education that is gaining traction is the creation of purpose development programs by external providers, which schools can adopt or adapt. The field of purpose interventions is growing, as educators, social entrepreneurs, and psychology researchers with a passion for meaningful education seek ways to apply what we have learned from purpose development research. They are people who think often and intensely about what it means to be human, and like Aristotle, think about how we can live a good and meaningful life. They work closely with students, teachers, and school leaders to shape programs that can fit into the rigor of a school day while creating space for meaning and purpose. Some of these programs aim to impact the school relationships, climate, and culture, whereas others aim to teach students the values and skills needed to pursue purpose in life. In practice, however, there is little distinction between activities designed to teach students how to pursue purpose and activities that create more positive and purpose-oriented culture in the school. This chapter profiles two organizations that have created programs for schools, partially or entirely aimed at supporting student purpose development. Throughout the remainder of this book there are four more program profiles. The six profiles are loosely arranged to echo the chapter that precedes them. In this case, the two profiles below strongly emphasize their role in transforming school relationships and culture.

The six programs profiled were developed either to directly support student purpose or aim for broader social-emotional outcomes that encompass purpose. The profiles investigate these programs in terms of how they are being created and implemented in schools; how they address youth purpose development; what other benefits they might have for students, teachers, and schools; and the challenges they have faced along the way. Each profile highlights the aspects of these programs that relate to the research on purpose development and points to methods that appear to be having positive impacts on student development and school environments. They offer insight into how public schools integrate these programs into an already overwhelming schedule of requirements and priorities. The six programs profiled here and in later chapters are:

- Quaglia Institute for Student Aspirations (based in Maine, with programs in school districts across the US)
- The Future Project (based in New York, with programs in cities throughout the US)
- Open Future Institute's QUESTion Project (based in New York, with programs in the Bronx and Los Angeles, California)
- MOSAIC (based at Rutgers University Social Emotional Character Development Lab in New Jersey, with programs in Jersey City Public Schools)
- Noble Impact (based in Little Rock, Arkansas, with programs in Little Rock and other locations in Arkansas)
- Project Wayfinder (based in Palo Alto, California, with programs in the US and around the world)

These six organizations represent just some of the purpose education programs that are burgeoning in public and private schools around the country. They generously shared their work with me and invited me into their classrooms to offer their programs as models of what is possible in purpose education and to inspire other educators to lead the charge in making their schools more purposeful. They all use the research on purpose development, which says that purpose begins with well-developed personal values and grows through opportunities to contribute to solving problems in the community or improve the lives of others. Relationships, role models, and mentors play a vital role for each of these organizations. In some cases, mentors and role models are included in the program by design, whereas in others, relationships with teachers are strengthened through the program, making it more likely that they can support students' emerging purpose. Most begin the year with values-exploration activities, either giving students an open forum to examine their personal values, or asking them to discuss specific values selected to support purpose development, or both. Some support students to envision a path to a meaningful life, others engage them in future-minded goal planning, and still others ask them to dream big. These programs ask students to think about real-world issues or problems in their communities that they want to work on, and some have students take action to solve those problems. Across these programs, there is an emphasis on voice—giving students and teachers voice in the school so they can create a learning experience that is meaningful and aligns with their sense of purpose.

There are also differences that give each program a unique character. The Future Project brings "dream directors" to schools to guide students in shaping and pursuing their purpose. Project Wayfinder uses the Polynesian Wayfinding tradition as a powerful metaphor for students' journey to purpose. Noble Impact uses a social entrepreneurship model to prepare students to live by their values and follow their purpose even after they graduate. Quaglia does not work with students, but instead develops teachers' voice and purpose so they can do the same with their students.

QUAGLIA INSTITUTE FOR STUDENT ASPIRATIONS

Addressing teachers at a conference, Quaglia Institute for Student Aspirations (QISA) leader Russell Quaglia challenged them, "Kids in our schools don't have a sense of purpose. What can you do tomorrow to increase your students' sense of purpose?"[1] School should be a place where students' aspirations and purpose are ignited and nurtured, but few are today. That is the belief driving over three decades of work by QISA. Quaglia founded QISA to create the conditions for student aspirations to flourish in schools, first and foremost by encouraging teachers to partner with students to ensure that students' voices influence all aspects of the teaching and learning environment. QISA offers a range of tools and programs that schools can use in adopting their Aspirations Framework, including student, teacher, and parent voice surveys, professional development, books explaining their frameworks and how to implement them, and online learning resources. They do not provide curricula per se, insisting that educators can adapt the frameworks to fit their schools and shape the framework according to what they learn by listening to their students.

The QISA Aspirations Framework defines aspiration as dreaming about the future and doing something currently to work toward the dream. To have high aspirations, according to the QISA framework, students must believe in themselves, be actively engaged in doing the work to accomplish their aspirations, and see a purposeful connection between their current efforts and their future goals.[2] Therefore, the three principles that that support the Aspirations Framework are Self-Worth, School Engagement, and Purpose. These three principles are supported by conditions that make up the foundation of the Aspirations Framework. Self-Worth comprises three conditions: Belonging, Heroes, and Sense of Accomplishment. School Engagement is also supported by three conditions: Fun & Excitement, Curiosity & Creativity, and Spirit of Adventure. Purpose is supported by two conditions: Leadership & Responsibility, and Confidence to Take Action to realize meaningful future goals.[3]

QISA uses a "train the trainer" model, working to cultivate these capacities in teachers so that teachers can then foster them in their students. For example, teachers participating in a QISA leadership academy think about school leaders (heroes) who helped them raise their voice in their school, collaborate with other participants to explore more fun and creative teaching methods, and reflect on their purpose as an educator and make concrete plans to enact their purpose when they return to their schools. The books and online support materials provide suggestions for how teachers can apply these principles in their schools and examples of teachers using strategies they developed through the training. For example, to create the conditions of Leadership & Responsibility and Confidence to Take Action, which students need to be purposeful at school, QISA suggests that teachers act as role models by setting and acting on their own meaningful goals and tell students stories about their own experiences working to accomplish meaningful goals.[4] Teachers can also support students to be purposeful in their learning by displaying purpose statements for the day's lessons and asking students to discuss the purpose of the lesson, and then reflect on their learning after the lesson.

Although they offer suggestions for educators to implement the Aspirations Framework, QISA fundamentally believes that schools should enact the framework with ideas generated using their school voice model. The school voice model has three steps. The first step is to *listen* to what members of the school community are saying by seeking input from students and teachers. The second step is to *learn* from what members of the community are saying by gaining new understanding of different perspectives. The third step in the school voice model is to *lead* by creating changes in the school based on understanding gained through listening and learning from members of the school community.[5] Kristine Fox, senior field specialist and research associate at QISA, emphasized the centrality of not only student voice, but *teacher* voice in promoting high aspirations in schools. Therefore, the QISA programs are specifically designed to support teachers' Self-Worth, Engagement, and Purpose in their teaching. Her experiences in schools have shown that teachers are often overwhelmed and defeated by top-down mandates, "with everything they're asked to do and measure and test, we want to give teachers a voice so they don't just feel helpless, so they can regain control of what they do. They need time to reflect on what they are doing, and they need opportunities to be creative."[6] By focusing their effort on teachers, QISA believes that teachers will in turn create an environment in their schools that prioritizes student voice, along with the three principles of Self-Worth, School Engagement, and Student Purpose.

Fox believes that the emphasis on voice must be a systemic shift, because it is ineffective to support teacher voice on a classroom by classroom basis if the overall school climate is repressive. The QISA Frameworks are therefore implemented on a schoolwide or district-wide basis. Schools begin their participation in QISA with students and teachers completing a survey to evaluate school climate and student voice, then adapt the QISA tools and frameworks as best fits their goals and their existing program. In Cobb County School District in Georgia, for example, the QISA Frameworks were adapted for their Teacher Leader Academy, which trains selected teachers to take on leadership roles in their schools and make changes that will have an impact on the school culture. The Teacher Leader Academy includes a four-day summer intensive, of which one full day is spent with the QISA team learning about the Aspirations Framework. Over the course of the year, Teacher Leaders participate in three more full-day professional development sessions in which they work with the QISA team in the morning to delve into the larger questions of teacher leadership using the Aspirations Framework, then meet in content area groups for the afternoon.

The Cobb County Teacher Leader Academy has evolved through their partnership with QISA and implementation of the Aspirations Framework. Melissa Morse, Cobb County director of Instruction and Innovative Practice said, "QISA's partnership took our program to the next level. It really gave it the focus on the Aspirations Framework in addition to the focus on content area leadership."[7] One example of this evolution is seen in the "legacy projects" that Teacher Leaders design and implement as part of their participation in the Academy, which are intended as a way for Teacher Leaders to have an enduring impact in their schools. The Aspirations Framework gave the legacy projects an emphasis on creating projects that reflect Teacher Leaders' purpose as teachers, and they are framed by the conditions that support purpose and engagement: Fun & Excitement, Curiosity & Creativity, Spirit of Adventure, Leadership and Responsibility, and Confidence to Take Action.

The legacy projects are key to bringing purpose into Cobb County Schools. In the Academy, Teacher Leaders are asked, "Why will it matter that you were a leader in Cobb County in your classroom?" They reflect on their own purpose in planning their legacy projects, and in turn they model purpose for students by acting on their own purpose at school. Students get to see their teachers doing something meaningful and that has a lasting positive impact in the school community. Morse said that the biggest impact on their schools from the Teacher Leader Academy has been from the legacy projects, because they make the ideas in the Aspirations Framework actionable and concrete. She described several of the legacy projects their teachers planned: A group of STEM teachers developed a coding program that all schools could use for teaching students to code; an art teacher started an art-making group among art teachers in the district, acknowledging that they would be stronger teachers if they were making their own art; and some middle and high school teachers came together to create a mentoring program for at-risk Hispanic students.

Kerri Waller, a middle school art teacher in Cobb County, wanted to expand her students' world by engaging them as artists in the community beyond the school. For her legacy project, she created several community-based art projects for her students that brought them out of the classroom and provided them opportunities to give back to the community through their art making. Some of her students created a mural for the school, others went to an adult living facility to lead a watercolor workshop for residents, and others created a digital coloring book that they shared through social media. Waller said, "I always wanted to do more with the community, but as an art teacher I felt isolated, I wasn't comfortable reaching out. The leadership academy helped me find my voice. I talk with the principal about things, I'm a vocal person now, which is different from before."[8] The legacy projects she started last year continue—the school mural is an ongoing project, and students she worked with last year are now emailing her to find out how they can come back to the school to help. Echoing her newfound voice, Waller finds that her students have become vocal about wanting to help the community. She supports their voice and their purpose through other changes in her teaching. For example, she said that she does a lot more choice-based projects in the classroom than before, encouraging students to question class projects and decide for themselves what materials they want to use.

Cobb County School District initiated the Teacher Leader Academy to develop the potential for leadership among their teachers and tap the resource of Teacher Leaders for their schools. In doing so, they partnered with QISA because they saw a fit with QISA's philosophy and believed the Voice and Aspirations Frameworks could be applied to their leadership training program. Morse said that the Teacher Leader Academy proved effective, initiating a grassroots effort that was more sustainable than if she had told the teachers what programs to implement. In the sessions led by QISA, Quaglia opens the training with an inspirational keynote speech. He shares data on student voice, arming teacher-leaders with research that they can use at their schools when their colleagues ask why they are making changes. Teachers spend the first part of their QISA training days learning the Aspirations Framework and tools, then in the afternoon they work with their content area teams and district-level subject-area supervisors to continue their leadership training and brainstorm ideas to bring back to their schools. Morse said that the Teacher Leaders return to their schools with newfound self-worth and sense of purpose for their teaching, which they model for the other teachers.

Waller returned to her school with renewed purpose for teaching. In the academy, she reflected on her purpose as an educator and defined the teacher she wanted to be in her school building. She developed as a leader with new awareness of the value of teacher and student voice and purpose. She said:

> It's easy to go in and teach what you want to teach, but harder to put what you need to teach in a way that students will find purpose in what they're doing. Students find purpose in it when their voice is heard. When they feel heard in the classroom and have a part in the classroom, and know their work is not just going to be graded and thrown away, it gives it more meaning. It helps them reach out and be willing to share more about what's impactful and meaningful to them.

By focusing their work on teacher voice, self-worth, and purpose, QISA energizes and inspires teachers, which they see as having a greater impact on schools than doing direct work with students. As Morse described, Quaglia's opening keynote address is pro-teacher, celebrating what teachers do, and seeing them as a solution to what is wrong with education rather than the cause. At the same time, he challenges teachers to do better, to pay attention to what students are telling us, set high aspirations for students, and help them reach those aspirations by providing the conditions in which self-worth, engagement, and purpose can flourish. "Teachers love it," she says, "It's non-threatening, data is communicated, and it's very effective for inspiring teachers. Teachers say it's life changing and changed the whole trajectory of their career. They see themselves as part of the solution."

THE FUTURE PROJECT

"The future is not fixed." That is the mantra driving dozens of Dream Directors who work with high school students across the US. It speaks to the *mindset of possibilities* that The Future Project aims to activate in students by placing inspirational mentors, or Dream Directors, in high schools as full-time members of the school community. Dream Directors begin the year with school culture work, conducting a Possibility Audit to understand the strengths and constraints and areas where they can contribute to improving the school culture. After an intensive phase of culture assessment, the Dream Director shifts to a coaching role, guiding students who want to take on Future Purpose Projects. Dream Directors encourage students to come to them with a project idea that is driven by passion or purpose. As a coach, the Dream Director then draws from an array of Future Project tools and curricula to support students to complete their projects. The tools are designed to help students develop three core beliefs that make up a mindset of possibilities: "I have purpose in life and know what my purpose is," "I can do anything," and "I belong." Dream Directors start by working side by side with students as they identify a Future Purpose Project to take on, coach them through challenges that arise, and encourage them to take the lead on the entire project. The ultimate goal is to develop students' agency to take the lead in conceiving, designing, and executing their project. In doing so, the students make personal gains in agency and potential for purpose, but they also change the culture at their school by influencing their peers to think in terms of possibility and purpose and to take on Future Projects of their own.

Fundamental to The Future Project's work with schools is the Dream Director's role in understanding and transforming school culture. Dream Directors spend the first month of each year conducting the Possibility Audit by interviewing the administration, teachers, staff, and students. They get to know the environment, the policies in place, the dynamics between students and teachers, the challenges the school is facing, the unique strengths of the community, and the needs and possibilities for culture improvement work in the school. The Chief Dream Director for California, Maria Tranquilli, noted that Dream Directors focus on bright spots and the extraordinary aspects of the school that they can amplify. However, they might also uncover challenges that The Future Project can help with, such as a staff exhausted by frequent leadership turnover or students frustrated by a lack of social justice programs in their school. With this rich insight, Dream Directors look for opportunities to transform the school culture, partnering with the principal, teachers, counselors, and students, to develop a vision and determine how The Future Project can be of greatest benefit to the school. The Dream Director then creates a plan of three to five initiatives to work on during the year. For example, in her three years as Dream Director at Academy San Francisco, Eve King has helped students install a music recording studio in the school, create murals of positive and encouraging role models who are representative of students at the school, and provide LGBT awareness and social justice programs for fellow students, among other initiatives.

The Possibility Audit phase is also a time for Dream Directors to develop relationships with students that will enable them to do purpose work. The Future Project recognizes that there must be a trusting relationship between an educator and students before the educator can successfully coach students in a Future Purpose Project. During this phase,

Dream Directors lay the groundwork for strong developmental relationships that will allow them to challenge students to grow, expand on their beliefs about what is possible, and go deeper in thinking about what purpose is. They do so by meeting with students and engaging them in introductory activities, conducting focus groups with students, having one-on-one meetings with teachers and counselors, and identifying other approaches useful for building relationships and gaining trust.

During that first month when they are conducting the Possibility Audit, Dream Directors also begin to recruit students to join the Dream Team—an extracurricular group of student leaders who develop and implement Future Purpose Projects. Through lunchtime pop-up activities and writing prompts such as "What's something you can do for hours a day?" they engage students in thinking about passion, purpose, and possibility, and introduce them to the work that The Future Project does in their school. Interested students can apply to join the Dream Team, and teachers can nominate students they think would benefit from the program. Students selected to be part of the Dream Team meet weekly to build a community, participate in Future Project curricula, collaborate on Future Purpose Projects, and share their projects with each other. The Dream Team commits to improving the culture of their school by sharing ideas and getting other students engaged in activities through assemblies and other schoolwide programs. In one school, the Dream Team implemented a wellness program to address the staggering rate of suicide attempts among students in their school. In another, the Dream Team waged a three-month empowerment campaign to get students to "show up for yourself, show up for your school, show up for your community." Dream Team members learn that purpose is collective, not individualistic, and that they are most effective when they collaborate. They learn to see themselves as part of a team that works for the good of their school or community.

Students in Future Project schools do not have to be on the Dream Team to work with the Dream Director. The principal introduces the Dream Director to the students as a coach and counselor, someone who is available to mentor them on projects, or even review college application purpose essays if that is what the student needs at the time. Students who are not on the Dream Team can go to the Dream Director with a project idea any time and ask for help. Students take the lead in identifying, developing, and acting on Future Purpose Project ideas, but the Dream Director acts as a coach throughout the process. As a coach, the Dream Director is intentional about developing students' skills and mindsets for creating purpose and engaging them in practices to develop their capacity for acting on possibility. They guide students to act on Future Purpose Project ideas by coaching them in five components of project development: Discover (self-discovery, identifying sparks, and developing passion; developing a practice of exploring to discover something that drives you, excites you, or fires you), Define (a problem or issue to work on based on the discovery phase), Design (the project), Do (act on the project), and Digest (reflect on what was learned from the project). Rather than unfolding a consecutive curriculum that leads students from interests to goals to project, the Dream Director starts with the student wherever they are. If students have a burning idea and are driven to act on it, the Dream Director will not start with a discovery phase but will dive into the design process with them.

The Future Project approach to coaching aims at making it possible for students to build the life and world they imagine. By building developmental relationships with students, creating Possibility Profiles, and coaching students to take action through five components of project development, Dream Directors combine the ideal conditions for achieving that aim. Students do not just complete projects, but reach a new level of thinking about purpose through their coaching relationship with the Dream Director. One student at Academy San Francisco shared how he transformed his love of video games into a meaningful and collaborative purpose. Through his participation with the Dream Team and coaching sessions with the Dream Director, the student worked with some friends to start a podcast on video games. Their goal was to restore passion in the gaming world by conducting a deeper analysis of their video game play and sharing their ideas with other video game lovers and game developers. In their podcasts, they talk about how they use competition and collaboration in their gaming, the influences different games have on them, and what they find most compelling about the games they enjoy. Through this project, these students were transformed from passive game consumers to vocal advocates seeking to improve an influential industry.

On a larger scale, Dream Directors might implement schoolwide initiatives with the goal of elevating student purpose. Eve King discovered in her Possibility Audit at Academy San Francisco that high school juniors were particularly disengaged. To get them more engaged, King held a daylong Future Project retreat just for juniors, focused on the themes of belief and purpose. In a workshop format, she engaged students in discussions about defining success, how they show up in the world, their biggest goals, how they could get more engaged at school, and not being treated like children at school. During the day, students vocalized what they wanted to change in their school. The retreat was so successful in getting the students engaged that the school asked King to repeat it with every grade level.

Dream Director training is critical to their success. They are experienced youth development professionals when they begin working with The Future Project, so their training is focused on the core ideas of the curriculum, specific coaching skills, and leadership. Every summer, they participate in an intensive two-week training, where they are immersed in the mindset of possibilities and social-emotional development. They learn coaching strategies centered on the "5 D's" curriculum (discover, define, design, do, digest) through their own collaborative project work. One summer, for example, Dream Directors were taught about the 5 D's, then like a student Dream Team, were tasked with developing a project. They planned an end-of-year celebration using the 5 D's process. Their training continues throughout the year, as they participate in Dream Director circles, meeting every week to talk about what they are doing in their schools and how they can improve their work. The circles are facilitated by Chief Dream Directors, who plan their training according to the needs of their group of Dream Directors each week. Tranquilli, the Chief Dream Director for California, said that being responsive to the needs of her team means something different every week. One week they might need to talk about the impact of changing leadership in their schools, while another week they might need support for managing the administrative aspects of their job. In the spirit of developing a possibility mindset, the Dream Directors spend about two hours every week discussing their limiting beliefs, such as their beliefs about how the year-end crunch limits what they can do, and talk about how to flip them to empowering beliefs. Doing so, they create more possibility in their programs while also practicing and reinforcing the human development work they do with students.

Every student who participates in Future Project programs takes a Possibility Profile survey at the start of their participation and again at the end of the year. The Possibility Profile assesses goals, values, and strengths to guide the Dream Director's coaching work with the student. It also allows The Future Project to measure growth in the mindsets that they hope to cultivate in students, such as optimism, collaborative leadership, and purpose. Their research with the Possibility Profile is in an early stage, but emerging findings suggest that more than 90 percent of students are experiencing growth in at least one of the mindsets they measure as a result of participation in the program. In a qualitative assessment, The Future Project found that the Dream Director model is effective for transforming school culture and impacting students' outlook on the future. Students say that the questions the Dream Directors are asking, about purpose, passion, and the future, are questions they have never been asked before. In case studies of program participants, The Future Project sees that students are thinking differently about their future, preparing not just for college, but for a meaningful life. They are thinking more about what they want their world to be like and planning for how they will contribute and make the changes they want to see in their communities. Looking forward, The Future Project plans to develop a scalable version of the program and is creating products and services that schools can adopt in modules. The goal is to make coaching more accessible at scale, for example by considering the potential of technology to extend the reach of their Dream Directors to more students.

CHAPTER SEVEN

Purposeful Instruction

One hundred years ago, education philosopher William Heard Kilpatrick published an essay urging a pedagogical method that would engage children in purposeful activity at school.[1] Called the *project method* in Kilpatrick's time, it had students learn by identifying and planning projects that fulfilled a strong interest or solved a compelling question or problem. Not merely arguing for the project method, Kilpatrick proposed that educators using the method might be thoughtful about how they define and implement it, suggesting that it was not "projects" but "purpose" that they were after: "It is indeed entirely possible that some other term, as 'purposeful act,' for example, would call attention to a more important element in the concept, and, if so, might prove superior as a term to the word 'project.'"[2] Kilpatrick deemed that a learning project was better described as "a hearty purposeful act . . . [with] . . . worthy social aims. . . . As the purposeful act is thus the typical unit of the worthy life in a democratic society, so also should it be made the typical unit of school procedure."[3] He is referring to students having a purpose for learning, which they do by planning and implementing projects that fulfill their life purpose. While he does not explicitly define purpose as a beyond-the-self goal, he does argue that the purpose he has in mind is the type that is socially embedded and relevant and that leads a student to becoming a good citizen in democratic society.

Today, the project method is seeing a resurgence as project-based learning, along with related pedagogies such as inquiry-based, problem-based, and service-learning. Researchers investigating how purpose develops largely look to this family of pedagogies for ways that teachers can support purpose, though the research on how effective they are for supporting purpose is still emerging.[4] In one sweeping example, Seana Moran at Clark University and Jenni Mariano at University of South Florida spearheaded an international research project to study the relationship between service-learning and purpose development, theorizing that service-learning is the most promising pedagogical approach for supporting purpose.[5] Among their partners in this study is a team from Brazil, led by Ulisses Araújo, who conduct action research with student teachers, training them to teach with projects using problem-based and design thinking methods, with the expectation that these methods will have an eventual impact on student purpose.[6] Araújo and his team see these methods supporting and integrating the three dimensions of purpose (beyond-the-self motivation, higher-order goal setting, and action):

> [A project] requires developing abilities to search for and select goals from a set of values and to anticipate actions that realize those goals. . . . These methodologies emphasize values and beyond-the-self impact because they focus not only on completing tasks but also on creating effects in the world . . . Students become immersed in real-world situations, so purpose is contextualized and not an abstract concept. Students listen to the needs, desires and necessities of others, so purpose becomes other oriented . . . These educational experiences support students to take an active role in constructing purposes based on moral values.[7]

In this chapter, we examine the project method as a potential framework for thinking about how purpose can be made central to instructional practice. As Kilpatrick's words remind us, project-based learning is not new. It has been long recognized as an instructional approach that can make learning more relevant and meaningful for students, and for engaging students in purposeful activity. However, even with the

Common Core Standards' emphasis on performance-based learning and assessment, which encourages teachers to have students demonstrate their learning through a performance or project, implementation of projects is uneven in schools across the US. One of the biggest obstacles is teacher buy-in and capacity to implement engaging, purpose-driven projects. As QISA and The Future Project acknowledged in the previous chapter, teachers need substantial and ongoing professional development to do immersive, purposeful learning activities with students, and it is even more so for sustained projects that also effectively teach required content. It requires significant commitment of resources, willingness among teachers to collaborate with each other and with mentors, and courage to prioritize content and learning experiences that do not directly result in test-score gains. This chapter includes examples that demonstrate not only the purposeful aspects of project-based learning, but some of the challenges schools face in implementing them and how they were overcome.

Before describing these approaches and their relationship to purpose, we should revisit the distinction between having a purpose for learning, understanding the purpose of a learning activity, and having purpose in life. All three are important to creating a purposeful curriculum, but the first two are primarily aimed at helping students learn the required curriculum content. The focus is on the lesson level, and engaging students in a lesson such that they know the purpose of what they are learning and find meaning in what they are learning. Getting students to understand the purpose of what they are learning is necessary to supporting students to create purpose in life because it shows them how having a purpose for our activities provides meaning, drive, and direction for completing them. However, understanding the purpose of our activities is only a foundational layer in building a life of purpose. Teaching for purpose means foregrounding students' efforts to create a life of purpose and fitting curriculum and instruction to that desired outcome. When we look at pedagogical approaches as they relate to purpose, all three of these ideas will be relevant, and all three should be considered in creating projects that are effective at both teaching core content and providing the conditions to support student purpose.

ELEMENTS OF PURPOSEFUL PROJECTS

The goal in this chapter is not to provide detailed strategies for project-based teaching, which are abundantly available from other sources and should be implemented with intensive and ongoing professional development. Instead, the goal is to focus attention on the elements of project-based pedagogy that are believed to support student purpose development. Most of these, referred to here as elements of *purposeful projects*, have also been identified as essential to high-quality project-based learning. They can be used as reflection on your own project work if you do project work, as a starting point if you are planning to start project work, or as elements that can be adapted to make other teaching methods more purposeful.

Purposeful Projects are Meaningful to Students

Students can explore and develop purpose in the classroom when the curriculum is responsive to their questions and interests. Purposeful projects are those that engage students in deeper learning about topics that are intrinsically motivating and personally meaningful. Making projects meaningful does not necessarily mean starting with content that is interesting to students but occurs in a dance between required content and students' emerging questions and interests. Projects are meaningful when the content and activities are responsive to students' questions and curiosities, not necessarily born directly from student interests. "What" is taught is less important than "how" the content is used to engage students.[8] The "how" is the dance that begins with the teacher planning for the content that needs to be taught, then setting the stage for student meaning and curiosity to enter. Projects become meaningful as students engage intentionally with the questions, ideas, or materials posed by the teacher, and the teacher shapes the project according to student emerging ideas and interests as they take shape. The goal is not to try to engage every student in a project that aligns with an existing passion or purpose, but to engage students in the process of pursuing an interest or concern at depth so they have those processes internalized when they do identify purposes they want to commit to.

Purposeful Projects are Inquiry-Driven

To have purpose, we need to discover what the world needs from us, so we must be inquisitive in our interactions with the world. Moreover, purpose gives a sense of being part of something larger than the self, which comes from reaching out to connect our inner selves with things in the world that fill us with wonder and curiosity, or that challenge us, or stir us to respond. The connection that the mind makes to these big mysteries and challenges in the world is inquiry. Projects that engage students' wonder or curiosity through inquiry can spark a sense of purpose. They engage students by starting with deep and expansive questions, or those that McTighe and Wiggins call essential questions.[9] These expansive questions are used to engage students in open-ended, critical thinking, as a starting point for shaping inquiry about more specific questions, topics, or problems that emerge from the interaction between the expansive question, students' interests, and the core content. Student-led inquiry is practice in seeking meaningful questions and problems in the world and engaging with them to discover solutions. Therefore, projects that start with meaningful inquiry can support students through one of the most challenging aspects of developing purpose, which is identifying worthy concerns or problems in the world to commit to.

Purposeful Projects are Sustained over Time

Purpose requires sustained commitment to a problem, interest, or question. Projects that support purpose development will engage students in exploring the topic over an extended period, with extensive planning and preparation, questions leading to more questions and a cycle of action and reflection. Sustained engagement in learning projects develops the capacity for commitment that purpose requires. With sustained commitment, students can develop attachment to ideas and topics, learn what it means to delve deeply into a topic or question, and make more meaningful connections between the topic of a project and other experiences and ideas. Developing a project over time also supports students to develop the skills and mindsets needed to successfully act on purpose, such as goal setting, self-regulation, persistence, and agency. Sustained projects send students the message that learning is about getting inside the things in the world that spark our curiosity or concern and staying with them until we understand them from all different perspectives.

Purposeful Projects Involve Reflection Throughout

Reflection asks students to pause their activity to take in what they have experienced, process it through writing or discussion, and make meaning from what they have been doing. Students then re-engage in the activity with a deeper sense of meaning about what they are doing and why. Reflection should not be saved until the end of a project, but should be used near the start of a project to examine the purpose of the activity early on and shape the project in a way that aligns with the purpose; then mid-project reflection can elicit new meaning and help students and teachers determine if they should change the project or redirect it in some way. When students stop to reflect on the meaning of what they are doing, they can also make connections between experiences, concepts, and content, both within the project and between the project and other experiences and curriculum content. Reflection in project learning tends to track progress in academic benchmarks, but that should not be the only or ultimate form of reflection if the goal is purpose development. For purpose, students need to reflect on what they are doing and why it matters, how it connects to their values, and what the impact is both for themselves and for the world beyond themselves.

Purposeful Projects are Collaborative and Community Building

Although purpose is unique to each individual and tied to identity, it is almost never pursued independently. Rarely do individuals make a positive contribution to the world by acting alone. Projects support purpose when they connect students with a community, engage them in collaborative activity with other students and mentors, and require them to look outside of themselves with empathy. Purposeful projects make learning authentic to the student through proximal connections (problems in the school, community, neighborhood, family, environment, or ecology).

Students look outward for ideas about purpose and what they want to work on. Purposeful projects blur the line between individual and collaborative purpose by supporting students to see themselves as part of the solution and not *the* solution.

Purposeful Projects Elevate Students' Social Awareness

By getting them to look outward, purposeful projects raise students' awareness of what is happening in their world. They become more aware of the experiences other people are having and the impact of human actions on the world. Purposeful projects are those that explicitly ask students to engage with the outside world in some way that raises their social awareness, for example by creating something new for their community, interacting with people they do not usually interact with, or seeking new knowledge that can have a positive impact on the world. Projects that stay in the classroom can also be made more purposeful, for example by asking students to examine social values, learn about people having different experiences from their own, or reflect on the social or environmental application of skills they are learning even if they are not applied at the time of the project.

Purposeful Projects Set High Expectations for Students

Project-based learning is not an opportunity to lower expectations for student achievement, and this is especially true of purposeful projects. Teachers' and students' expectations for student achievement should raise when learning occurs through authentic and meaningful projects that are sustained and inquiry-driven. Projects that are explicitly purposeful and steer students to think of their learning as preparation to play an important and contributing role in the world can lead to greater student engagement and performance in their schoolwork.[10] Purposeful projects allow for high expectations not only in academic learning, but also push students to pursue their personal interests and goals. In project-based learning, reflection and revision are critical to high-quality work and should be included in setting high expectations.[11]

TEACHING FOR PURPOSE WITH PROJECT-BASED PEDAGOGIES

Reggio Emilia

In a backlash against the overbearing push for standards-driven direct instruction, a growing number of schools are exploring diverse methods and philosophies for implementing student-centered and project-based pedagogies. Reggio Emilia, originally a child-development philosophy applied to early childhood education in the town of Reggio Emilia in Italy, is now being applied in a handful of elementary schools in the US. The Reggio-inspired approach emphasizes several of the elements described above; specifically, it is student-led, inquiry-based, and community-oriented, and it requires students to stay with a question or topic for an extended time. In Reggio terms, the program uses *investigations* (inquiry) to develop *emergent curriculum* (student-centered curriculum).[12] This section describes investigations and emergent curriculum as they are practiced by elementary level teachers at Ventana School in California. Ventana is a small private school affiliated with the local Episcopal church. It started as a preschool and used the Reggio Emilia approach, which aligns well with the educational values of Episcopal schools.[13] Responding to parent interest, Ventana expanded into the older grades and now offers a preschool through fifth-grade program. The school has adopted the Reggio approach to the upper grades through adherence to a unified school vision and set of values, applied to intensive teacher collaboration and ongoing professional development.

Emergent Curriculum

The content of Reggio-inspired programs is driven by student curiosity. Teachers can guide the direction of student curiosity in a number of ways, but follow students' questions to plan learning units and activities. "Emergent curriculum" refers to a curriculum that emerges from student curiosity, exploration, and questions. The teacher documents as much classroom activity as possible, noting student conversations and questions, photographing students in action and their finished products, and maintaining journals to reflect on daily student activities.[14] The extensive documentation serves as a record of student learning, but also provides the teacher with direction for shaping the curriculum. The role of the teacher is to capture emerging patterns of curiosity and engage students in meaningful conversation based on what stirs their interest, asking questions, sparking wonder, and making connections that extend student curiosity. The other role of the teacher is to provide an environment that enables students to explore what sparks their curiosity, with materials and resources that will push their engagement and learning.

Emergent curriculum demands a lot of the teacher, but often the greatest concern for K–12 educators is the incompatibility between an emergent approach and the demands of the core content standards. How can teachers both respond to the emerging interests of a classroom full of students and get through the required content their students need to advance through the standards? Elementary-level teachers at Ventana say that it is demanding, but integrating students' interests with the required content is not only possible, it is beneficial to student learning. Sometimes, the teacher can guide student interests toward the core curriculum, capitalizing on children's ready curiosity about so many things in the world. In other cases, the teacher finds opportunities in a project to follow students' interests as they emerge. In a first and second grade mix class, teacher Julie Kelsey started a life science project by engaging student interest in the ocean, reading books about the ocean, eliciting students existing knowledge about the ocean, and taking a field trip to the nearby Marine Science Institute. As they explored what they know about the ocean, students asked questions, which Julie then posed to the whole class to gauge student curiosity about the question. She discovered that many students were curious about lighthouses and wanted to investigate what they do and how they work. The class continued the life science aspect of the ocean project, exploring the climate and life forms at different levels below the surface, but they also took a field trip to a local lighthouse and a group of interested students worked with the science teacher to build a working model of a lighthouse. The ocean exploration project culminated with students creating a three-dimensional coastal scene in their classroom, with a coral reef mural, layered fabric "waves," clay sea animals, and the lighthouse with working light and foghorn.[15]

While first and second graders completed their ocean scene, third graders were out on the playground, immersed in imaginative play about dragons. They waged an epic battle, with some students choosing to be evil dragons while others chose to be good. Their teacher, Andrew Davis, observed their play and noticed that they described their dragon characters using qualities that they believed to be good or evil. Andrew fueled his students' interest in dragons and connected it to classroom learning by selecting *The Hobbit* as their read-aloud book. Then, building on their interest, he created a unit on "Dragonology" in which students created their own dragon characters. Through literature and art, they investigated the qualities of good and evil dragons, then wrote descriptions of their own dragons, examining morality in literature while expanding their descriptive vocabulary with adjectives that describe character, behavior, mental and emotional states, and physical qualities.[16] They connected with other subject areas, creating paintings of their dragons in art based on the character descriptions they had developed. Building on their curiosity about dragon eggs, they mapped out the life-cycle of dragons based on what they learned in science about the life-cycle of different species. A student who was not interested in the fantasy world of dragons but was inspired by the idea of fire proposed to investigate fire trucks and their technology instead. Andrew validated what his students' found meaningful by responding to their intense play activity. He allowed their interests to drive the curriculum, and as a result, they gained a sense that school is a place to explore the things that matter most to them. They are developing an early foundation for purpose by pursuing their interests at depth in the collaborative space of the classroom, and by discussing moral values in a way that is relevant to their interests and identity development. The teacher supported them in developing the skills for purpose by getting them to delve into the topic, and by asking questions that pushed their interest in dragons beyond superficial liking to a deeper understanding of what it means to have moral character.[17]

Investigations

Another key principle of the Reggio approach—*investigation*—provides strategies that teachers can use to be responsive to student interests while at the same time exposing students to new content and guiding their curiosity toward the content that they need to learn. At Ventana, a year of investigations is kicked off with a big, broad inquiry question, such as "How do we identify?" or "What is my place in the world?" Teachers then inspire students to explore topics related to the overarching question through *invitations* and *provocations*. Invitations expose students to an idea, object, or content area that might be unfamiliar to them. Provocations pose a challenging or open-ended question connected to an invitation, aiming to push students' thinking about the idea further. As students respond to the invitation and provocation, the teacher can get a sense for what most stirs students' curiosity or interest. In preschool, the Reggio teacher might put a small display of objects from nature on a table as an invitation for students to explore. In older grades, invitations are more complex to inspire intellectual curiosity appropriate to students' ages, such as tinkering materials to create with, photos from magazines, or a controversial story in the news. The invitations and provocations can be selected and posed to stir student interest in content areas that need to be addressed. The teacher facilitates students' investigations with open questions such as "What do you think is going on here?" and as they interact with materials, "What do you think will happen next?" The sequence of asking a big question, followed by invitations and provocations pursued through student investigation, which is pushed with open-ended questions from the teacher, results in an extended inquiry project that takes students deep into an interest or problem.

Teacher Amanda Stewart started a year with her third-grade class by asking students the overarching question, "Whose story is it anyway?" She read aloud books that shared the perspective of people with different life experiences, such as *Wonder,* about a boy with a genetic facial deformity. They also read Norse mythology, prompting a student to ask "Why is it called 'the creation of man' and not 'the creation of man and woman?'" Amanda followed up on the student's question of gender in storytelling by putting up pictures of superheroes in the classroom as an invitation, then as a provocation asked students to notice how the male and female superheroes were posed. The student's question, along with Amanda's invitation and provocation, led to several weeks' inquiry about gender representations in the media, including research on how toys are marketed differently for girls and boys, and the different messages on T-shirts designed for girls and boys. As they talked about their investigation, students reflected on their own responses to what they saw in the media images. Ultimately, some of her students were compelled to write letters to a T-shirt designer voicing their concerns about the negative messages their T-shirts were sending about girls. The superhero invitation deliberately raised students' awareness of a potential topic of interest (gender bias in children's toys and media), which they then probed both in and beyond the classroom. Early-grade student-led inquiry projects, such as the gendered media project and the Dragonology project, are scaffolded by the teacher so that students gain experience in sustained commitment to an idea, reflection, setting small goals in pursuit of big questions or problems, and engaging collaboratively toward a common goal or purpose. By fourth grade, students who have been so scaffolded are capable of greater autonomy in pursuing their own learning through inquiry projects, and the potential for purpose to take shape in these projects becomes increasingly evident.

In a fourth-grade class at Ventana, teacher Harfijah Oliver set up tinkering materials every week and invited her students to play freely with them. This invitation resulted in several different student-led projects that showed their growing ability to identify and act on meaningful problems in the world around them. One group of students explored the possibility of creating a marble run. After proposing and adding more large-scale materials like lumber and PVC pipes, they built a large prototype on wheels after several iterations, and introduced the rolling exhibit to several classrooms. With the teacher acting as a facilitator, they researched the physics and geometry of marble runs, experimented with designs, sketched iterations, tested different materials, and completed the project with presentations to younger students and parents. Another group explored with PVC pipe as a construction material and wondered what they could build with it. Bridging their curiosity about the material with a problem they experienced at school—the need for a place to occasionally escape the noise and chaos at recess—they wondered whether the pipe could be used to build a portable private space for the playground. They researched construction techniques, drew plans, and created a structure for the playground where students could have a quiet escape during recess. A third group in this class was unmoved by the tinkering materials, deciding instead that they wanted to understand "how does a smile affect us?" Harfijah supported their inquiry by providing them with articles to read, then the students created a research project to investigate their question by conducting experiments and interviewing younger students to collect data. In all of these group projects, students used core content math skills and knowledge (measurement, fractions, data, geometry), scientific inquiry methods, and communication skills, and also learned that the questions and problems they found relevant and interesting are valid topics to study at school.[18] In learning the math, science, and literacy skills needed for their projects, they deeply understood the purpose of learning those skills and saw that they could use them to pursue purposeful activity.

When teachers use invitations, provocations, and inquiry to guide the unfolding of the curriculum, they maintain control over the content while also creating a classroom culture where student intentions are valued. They expose students to new content and encourage curious exploration, then provide the space for students to probe the invitation to see what questions emerge. Then, students conduct research to investigate the questions they posed, with the teacher providing guidance and resources as needed. When the project is extended from inquiry to action, such as writing letters to T-shirt companies, or building new playground equipment, students vividly see a purpose for their learning. In elementary school, this inquisitive engagement with ideas and materials in the classroom prepares students to explore and act on purpose in school as they get older. They see school as a place where they should pursue their ideas and ask questions that require investigation, and they see teachers as the people they go to for resources and support. Describing her fifth graders as they prepared to leave for middle school, Amanda said she hopes they are reflective, believe in their own ideas but can also listen to others' ideas and build on them, and have learned to advocate for themselves and others. Feedback she received from parents about their middle school experiences suggested this was happening. "They're not afraid to advocate for themselves and usually ask to start some sort of club. They seem to leave with a sense that they can go to adults with their ideas and get support to act on their ideas."[19] By fifth grade, they are already developing the agency and autonomy to see themselves as someone who can take action to make a plan, organize others, and procure resources when there is an idea to pursue.

Projects in High School

The Reggio philosophy is rarely explored beyond elementary grades, but many of the principles are echoed in project-based learning that continues into middle and high school. Specifically, gold-standard project-based learning as defined by the Buck Institute for Education shares a number of elements with purpose projects as described in this chapter.[20] Gold-standard project-based learning is driven by a challenging question or problem; involves sustained inquiry; is led by student voice; is authentic in that it addresses a real-world problem, has a real impact on others, and is true to students' identities and concerns; involves reflection throughout the project; and sets high expectations for the quality of student work.[21] It has other requirements, but these are the elements that, when present, echo the elements of a purposeful project.

The New Tech Network, started at New Tech High School in Napa, California, and now including almost 200 schools, is a model that embraces the use of project-based learning in a culture that emphasizes empowerment, trust, and student responsibility for their own learning. New Tech serves as a design partner for schools seeking to implement comprehensive change, and provides network schools with resources such as learning tours of established New Tech schools, coaching, curriculum design guides, training institutes, and a pre-implementation visit to assess the readiness of the school community to implement the New Tech program.[22] James Lick High School, a public high school in San Jose, California, adopted New Tech in 2014, starting with the freshman class and adding a grade each year since. The following describes their experience with implementing project-based learning in a traditional public high school, including the challenges they overcame and mistakes they have learned from, to demonstrate that it is challenging but possible to transition to project-driven instruction.

David Porter, principal at James Lick High School (JLHS), came to see the advantages of project learning methods inadvertently. "I fell into project-based learning, not by choice, when I lost my hearing entirely in one ear. I was no longer able to do direct instruction well because I couldn't teach from the center of the room." As a science teacher, this made labs particularly challenging, because he could no longer manage student questions and simultaneously oversee distribution of materials effectively. He experimented with a new approach as a way to adapt to his new situation. "I started a lesson on blood pressure by giving students a purpose for what we were going to do. I asked the question 'why do we measure diastolic and systolic blood pressure?' I gave them resources for thinking about the purpose of the activity, which in this case was an opportunity for a student to tell his personal story about why his grandfather takes his blood pressure every day. I put the materials in the back of the room along with the procedures and, without further instruction, let them get to work investigating the procedures and the question. It worked. They were completely focused on testing the tools and investigating their use." It was a simple take on project-based learning, but it showed Porter that there were alternatives to direct instruction that could be more effective.

Years later, Porter's early experience with project-based learning echoes in the teaching found in all classrooms at JLHS. As they adopted the New Tech program, JLHS simultaneously developed a strong mission for the heart of their approach to project-based learning that is made up of four pillars: *Agency* (students learn to be autonomous in their learning, and can ask questions and seek out help to pursue their learning), *Communication* (students learn written and oral communication skills to defend their thinking, demonstrate their growth, and flourish beyond high school), *Collaboration* (students learn to work in teams, take on different roles in teams, and can accept and learn from feedback), and *Growth Mindset* (students learn that they can improve their knowledge and skills with practice).

Projects at JLHS are typically developed by teachers working in unlikely pairs, such as a math teacher working with a physical education teacher, or a biology teacher working with an English teacher. Teachers provoke student interest in the project with *driving questions* that stir intense and enduring curiosity, tap into problems or questions that are personally meaningful for students, or get students thinking about things they can do to make a difference in their world. Teachers can then control the direction the project takes by selecting the resources students will use to follow up on the driving question. Projects are sustained for several weeks and engage students through all phases of planning, development, and execution.

"Can art change our community?" That was the question used to provoke students' interest in a mural project. After a beloved elderly neighbor was killed in a home robbery, community leaders called for an effort to create a more livable and connected community, and asked JLHS students to clean up the litter around the school. Students were also offered the opportunity to contribute to a mural project planned for a wall at the main intersection of their neighborhood. The art teacher teamed up with a mural artist to plan a project in which students were involved through all phases, from planning through mural completion. They studied symbolism and representation as they planned the mural to represent important current and historical aspects of the neighborhood, such as its history as a farming community, the nearby Lick Astronomical Observatory that brought the roads and traffic that resulted in the small village that is now thriving there, the native Ohlone people who once lived on the land, and the Aztec ancestry of many of the current Mexican American residents. As students worked on the mural, members of the community came out to see their work and news crews came to film them, validating the purpose of their effort as making an important contribution to the neighborhood.

Another project developed by a math and PE teacher team posed the question, "If you could design a new weight room for the school, what equipment would you get and where would it go?" They challenged students to use systems of linear inequalities to conduct spatial cost-benefit analyses in planning their designs, because the space available was limited and had to accommodate up to sixty students at a time. Students worked in teams to create their designs and three were selected to present to the school board. The winning team developed a design that made calculations for the amount of space that would be needed around each piece of equipment, and to allow for exercises that required certain range of motion. The board approved their design and the new weight room is now being used by students. This project demonstrates well how a teacher-initiated project becomes a student-directed project. The teacher presented the need for a new weight room for the school, sparking students' interest, and then provided the resource of mathematical methods they should use to create their designs. At that point, students took the lead in creating their designs, with the teachers acting as mentors and facilitators. For their current project, the math and PE teachers asked students "How would you design a personal fitness program for yourself, based on your own fitness data?" The project requires students to use exponential, geometric, and arithmetic growth calculations. When finished, they will use their fitness plans to prepare for the state physical fitness exam.

In three years of implementing the New Tech program, JLHS has faced numerous challenges and made many mistakes. They planned carefully for teacher support and buy-in the first year, but did not consider that *students* would not come along willingly. After eight years of direct instruction, students were not ready to suddenly shift to a new way of learning. Another mistake they made was starting with the teachers who tend to be early adopters and separating them from those who tend to resist new programs, creating unnecessary tensions among the teaching staff and encouraging resistant teachers to dig their heels in. They also found that they were trying to do too much at once, changing the culture, partnering teachers, engaging students, and getting teachers to change not only their practice but their thinking about why the do what they do. These mistakes and challenges were in addition to typical structural barriers such as scheduling mandates, union requirements, and lack of funding for the resources and training that make project-based learning most successful.

Abiding their own mission as an organization, JLHS has used its four pillars to overcome challenges and continue building the program.

Porter strives to learn from their mistakes and to be transparent in communicating with the staff, students, parents, and union about their successes as well as their failures. They walked back their effort to engage students and started with teaching them about the new ideas, such as agency and self-directed learning. The administrative team aims to be in the classrooms and acting as instructional leaders as much as possible so that teachers see their involvement and effort at transparency, which also helps to prevent challenges from the union. As a school, they pulled back from doing too much at once, asking teachers to identify and focus on only three strategies they could use to move away from direct instruction. They also restructured their approach to teacher pairing to be more authentic and flexible. Rather than assigning teacher pairings for a full year, pairings were structured in weeks-long blocks, allowing teachers to try a partnership and then extend it or move on depending on how it worked. They also allowed for more flexible use of paired teaching time, so that teachers could use the pairing to splinter off students who might need extra time working on a certain concept, while the other students do supplemental activities in the partnered teacher's area. For example, a math-PE teaching team might split up a class for a few days to give a small group of students more time to work on a math concept they are struggling with, while students who have grasped the concept do PE. They identified teachers to act as coaches for their weekly training sessions to emphasize a teachers-training-teachers approach. They have learned to forego some traditional expenses to have money for needs associated with projects, such as field trips, teacher training, and planning release time.

Despite the challenges, Porter feels the program is worth pursuing, and the connection to student purpose development is evident. Students are more self-directed; they know what they are doing and why. There is more one-on-one contact between teachers and students, and teachers have more flexibility to meet the needs of individual students. Because they work in teaching pairs, they can bounce ideas off each other, and it shows in more creative teaching. Students are more invested in their work because they can see the purpose of their learning when they are designing a new weight room for the school or creating a mural for their community. They understand that there is an authentic purpose in the world for their activity. They gain social awareness and the agency to act on their social awareness by doing projects that respond to a need or concern in the world around them. They connect with a community in multiple ways, by collaborating on project teams, evaluating the needs and interests of the audience or user of their product, and sharing their results with a wider community. The projects are meaningful and inquiry-provoking and can sustain students' interest because their teachers identify driving questions to engage them with the topic.

For many high school principals and teachers, the biggest concern about project-based learning is that it cannot prepare students for high-stakes standardized tests. However, recent findings from a study of "deeper learning" schools, including New Tech Network schools, suggest that this concern is unfounded. The study examined the impact of schools that use deeper learning methods, including project-based learning (in addition to internships, group work, portfolio assessments, and student participation in decision making). It found that students in these schools on average scored higher than matched comparison students on the OECD Test for Schools, which is an internationally recognized assessment of core content knowledge and problem-solving skills, and also scored higher than comparison students on state exams in California and New York.[23] An impact report prepared by the New Tech Network suggests that New Tech students consistently outscore non-New Tech students on measures of critical thinking.[24]

Purpose Projects in the "Real World"

The examples above show that integrating student meaning and striving to develop students' capacity for purpose through purposeful projects does not preclude core content, and in fact purposeful projects can and should be based on a foundation of the core-content learning goals for the unit or project. With that foundation, the teacher can use some of the principles described above to inspire or connect with students' authentic interests or concerns.[25] One of the most powerful ways for teachers to support student purpose development is using curriculum to make connections between school and the world beyond school. Purpose is about being driven by a sense of what you can and should do to make a positive contribution to the world, so any time teachers can provide opportunities for students to make that connection will result in a stronger foundation for developing purpose. Problem-based service-learning is a specific type of project that gets students actively engaged in solving authentic problems with the goal of teaching students to be critical problem solvers while having a genuine positive impact in the world. When service-learning is effective, it not only activates purpose in a way that is beneficial for the individual student but benefits society as well, which more completely fulfills the concept of purpose. When there is a social benefit derived from a student's purpose activity, the student receives motivating feedback about the impact they have had on the world.[26] Teachers can ignite students' sense of mattering in the world by engaging them in authentic problem-based projects. Too many students, especially those in low-income communities, are not made aware of the gifts they have that they can share with the world. They have few opportunities to develop and express their gifts, which limits their awareness of their own value. By making contributions to their community through authentic service projects, students become aware of their personal strengths and abilities, and the value that they have.[27]

Service-learning can be applied in different ways at different ages to provide students with developmentally appropriate purpose-supporting experiences. In middle school, students are empathetic, capable, and ready to contribute to their communities, but they are not often provided opportunities to take action on the concerns and interests that stir their sense of purpose. Somewhat older students, around fifteen to sixteen years old, start exploring their interests and concerns to identify roles they might take in society. At this age, they might think more often in broader and more abstract terms about their purpose in life, for example by thinking of their purpose as "helping others," which they can act on by "starting an antibullying campaign at my school." Though they will likely want to explore different ways that they can be a helpful person. For these students, working on real-world problems gives them opportunities to explore different outlets for their potential purpose. By late high school, students are increasingly able to think of purpose as a general, higher-order goal that organizes and directs their goal setting and activities. They can be more independent in identifying a broader purpose for their life and creating a project that fulfills that purpose.[28]

As with more general project-based learning, there are specific elements of applied methods such as service-learning that can be emphasized to make it particularly suited to developing student purpose. These elements are among those identified in a framework for high-quality service-learning, which shares qualities with gold-standard project-based learning as defined by the Buck Institute.[29] To support purpose and be high-quality learning experiences, service activities should: (1) begin with significant planning and preparation that engages students to identify problems that are personally meaningful to them and of genuine concern to others, (2) include reflection alternating with action throughout the project, so that students make meaning from their activities, (3) be sustained over time and involve frequent or intense engagement, and (4) collect feedback to monitor progress. Here we look at these strategies through the lens of service-learning. However, in terms of supporting purpose, the same principles apply to other forms, such as civic engagement, capstone projects, and social entrepreneurship. The following section uses the example of Kevin, one of our youth purpose research interviewees who did community service by volunteering at a local homeless shelter. The example of volunteering in a homeless shelter is a simple and traditional one, and while there are more innovative examples of service-learning available, this one provides a familiar background to highlight Kevin's learning experiences.

High-quality service-learning starts with an investigation phase that establishes the learning goals of the core curriculum that will be addressed and investigates potential needs or problems in the community. Building on the investigation phase, students plan and prepare a service activity that meets the need identified. If one of the goals is to support student purpose, there should be an emphasis in the planning stage on identifying, eliciting, or connecting with what is personally meaningful to students while striving to understand the needs of the community to be served. Using an empathy approach to design the project can accomplish this. An empathy approach gets students to conduct research on social issues by interviewing or otherwise gaining the perspective of people who are impacted by the issue, and it gives them the opportunity to explore problems and issues they might not be aware of.[30] A service project is neither empathetic nor personally meaningful if students do not first deeply understand what the real needs and challenges of the community are. Doing something that feels good but that does not actually address an existing problem cannot give students a sense of purpose because the project does not meet a real need in the world. Student voice is essential during the planning and preparation phase to ensure that projects are personally meaningful.[31] Therefore, providing opportunity for students to plan their empathy research and discuss and reflect on what they are learning from this research is critical.

Planning and preparation are vital to service-learning that supports purpose, but it might be necessary or useful to begin with activity. One potent way to raise students' awareness of the issues impacting people around them is to engage them directly in activity in the community. Activity can be a purpose spark by putting students into physical and emotional contact with issues that might be unfamiliar to them. However, such spark activity should not be the end of a service-learning unit. Rather, it should precede the planning phase for a student-led service-learning unit. Starting with service activity should be followed with exploring that activity to identify real needs that can be addressed in a more sustained project and that will inspire students to make meaning from the experience. Kevin, a high school senior when we interviewed him, described his experience fulfilling a service project by volunteering at a homeless shelter. He started working at the shelter with little planning or preparation, but the activity sparked an intense interest for him so he stayed with it for several years. During that time, he developed ideas based on his interactions with homeless people at the shelter that led him to ongoing and purposeful political service in the community. Finding purpose sparks in activity is a useful skill for creating a purposeful life because there are many situations that require us to find meaning or purpose within required activities, such as work that is primarily a source of income. It is a reminder that purpose is not found only in an idea about how we want to live, but is created by our actions in the world and how we make meaning from them.

A second important aspect of service-learning that aims to support student purpose is reflection, and in particular reflection integrated with action.[32] Reflection is an important aspect of a purpose-directed education, regardless of the learning activity. To develop a sense of purpose, students need to reflect on what they are doing, why they are doing it, and the outcome of their activity for themselves and others. In service-learning, students should reflect throughout the project to make sense of what they are doing, strengthen their values related to what they are doing, and shape ongoing plans and future goals based on what they are learning through the experience. Through written reflection in response to critical thinking prompts and class discussion about challenging or controversial aspects of a service project, students can extend their service experience beyond the surface to see connections with other experiences and can draw larger and more abstract principles from their service experiences. Kevin did not just go to the homeless shelter and fulfill his assignment. He reflected on his experience between visits, challenged his own assumptions, and followed up on his reflection by asking shelter clients questions to make sense of their experience and what he was seeing. With reflection, Kevin gained deeper understanding of homelessness in his community and shaped his social values based on his experience, which in turn gave him purpose in pursuing political activity. "I saw the conditions and how a lot of people, even if they had the opportunity, they weren't looking for jobs. I talked to them, and they were actually happy living on welfare. Based on my experience, with talking to a lot of people, I just wanted them to have an incentive to work, to get a job, to support themselves. That was a pretty big turning point in my life."[33] With critical and challenging reflection, service-learning is not simply checking the "helping others" box, but it supports students to learn that they are the ones who should do what needs to be done in society and use values to drive and shape their activities in society.

Kevin's service experience at the homeless shelter points to a third feature of service-learning that supports purpose development. He did not spend an afternoon or a week volunteering at the shelter; he ultimately worked there for three years. Service-learning that supports purpose is sustained over time and usually requires frequent or intense engagement. Sustained involvement supports students to develop the self-regulation skills required for commitment and responsibility. Enduring and frequent service engagement also contributes to students' changing attitude about the issues they are addressing and their role in society. With sustained commitment to a service activity, students can deepen their reflection on the activity and develop a sense that serving the community is not something they do for a grade, but an aspect of who they are, and their social responsibility.[34] Service activities do not have to be several years, as Kevin's experience was, but should be measured in weeks or months instead of days. One study, for example, found that a two-day service project had no impact on students' attitudes, but a semester-long project did.[35] Service project duration and frequency should be developmentally appropriate, but within that guideline, it should be an opportunity to push students to greater commitment, deeper reflection about their activity, and internalization of the skills needed for higher-order goal pursuit, autonomy, and agency.

An essential element of high-quality service-learning is progress monitoring, or feedback that informs students how they are progressing in the goals of the project.[36] Students collect evidence of their progress over the course of the project, from sources such as the target beneficiaries, community leaders, and mentors. With this feedback, students can see the impact of their activity and change course if needed. In terms of their developing purpose, feedback completes a loop between intention to do something in the world and action, with positive feedback leading to stronger and more purposeful intentions.[37] The ideal form of feedback from a service activity for supporting purpose is seeing a change for the good in society, or a positive impact on the individuals or community that they acted on. However, this is an unlikely source of feedback because it is slow to come about and can be hazy with complexity, nuance, and the noise of less relevant feedback that accompanies the positive impacts. Therefore, the teacher is a valuable source of feedback in service projects for supporting student purpose, informing students about their progress both in the academic content and in taking steps toward addressing a need or problem that will impact others.[38]

Vocational Education

The principles that make service-learning likely to support purpose also hold for other applied problem-based approaches, such as social entrepreneurship projects and other vocational programs. Contemporary vocational education programs are not confined to the campus woodshop and mechanic garage. Today, students participate in vocational education programs that teach general professional skills, explore potential career interests, and provide internships and apprenticeships in medical careers, graphic design, engineering, or any field with willing mentors. The role of vocational education programs in supporting purpose is less explored than other project- and problem-based pedagogies, but there is some evidence suggesting that this is a promising avenue to investigate. Research from Finland shows that Finnish high school students report greater sense of purpose than students in the United States, which may be related to their access to high-quality vocational education.[39] In Finland, vocational and academic tracks are equal in status and equally likely to lead to career success. Therefore, sense of purpose might be higher among Finnish adolescents because more young people have the opportunity to plan for a meaningful career rather than aiming for the abstract goal of college whether it aligns with their interests and goals or not.

In the United States, a number of promising programs offer high-quality vocational education options for high school students that elevate vocational learning and increase the potential for supporting students to find purpose at school.[40] Big Picture Learning, for example, offers internship-based vocational learning but is grounded in student-led project-based learning principles that are the same as those believed to support purpose development: student voices are heard, projects are based on big and challenging questions or problems, projects are sustained over time, and a relationship with a mentor is key.[41] Purpose-directed vocational programs should not track students into a lifetime career decision, but should transparently provide skills and in-depth experience that can then be applied to other vocations throughout life. Students should be made aware of the process they are learning for engaging with a vocation, along with developing the skills and knowledge specific to the vocation they are exploring in school. Also, we know from purpose research that early adolescence is a time for open role exploration and values clarification, and therefore not a good time for committing to a vocational learning program. In terms of supporting purpose, these programs will likely be more effective with older adolescents in the second half of their high school years.[42]

CHAPTER EIGHT

Noble Impact and Project Wayfinder

The two programs profiled in this chapter—Noble Impact and Project Wayfinder—differ from the programs described in chapter 6 in that they provide curricula for teachers to implement during class time. The curriculum might be taught during a content area class, as an elective, or in a separate required course. Both programs also offer an action component, getting students engaged in projects that can be implemented in school or out in the community. Although they differ from the programs in chapter 6 in terms of delivery format, they are equally concerned with impacting school climate, relationships, and culture. All six of the programs profiled aim to support student purpose, but in every case this goal was not distinguished from the larger goal of making schools more positive, healthy, authentic, and humane environments for all members of the school community.

NOBLE IMPACT

Every one of us has a story to tell about who we are, about what has made us who we are, and about the dreams we have that guide us to our future selves. The stories we choose to tell about ourselves, and how we choose to tell them, have an impact on who we are becoming and the purpose we create for our lives. Chad Williamson, a cofounder of Noble Impact in Little Rock, Arkansas, noticed that young people could not effectively tell their own stories that connected to their aspirations and purpose. "They had a very difficult time expressing their stories, and we want them to ultimately control their own narrative through meaningful storytelling." Williamson and his cofounders started Noble Impact to help kids tell stories of their lives that would create and express their purpose and give them the skills to not just dream, but take action and live a purpose-driven life. After launching as a summer program in July 2013, Noble Impact piloted a full-time course at eStem, a K–12 charter school in Little Rock. It has since been expanded and adopted by several public middle and high schools in Arkansas. The founding vision of Noble Impact was a social entrepreneurship education program, with the purpose of providing students with entrepreneurial skills and a public service mindset. The team sought to achieve this goal by infusing the entrepreneurship training with social-emotional learning, taking students through intensive exploration of identity and then building from identity to innovation.

The Noble Impact program is offered as an elective course at the high school level, and students can, if they choose, complete a three-year sequence of courses. The Noble 101 class starts with a quarter-long unit on identity that engages students in values-exploration activities and encourages them to "pitch" their personal stories to the class. Through journal writing, class discussion, videos, and creative activities, students reflect on who their most significant influencers are and what they value, and they fold those ideas into their personal story. An eighth grader who named LeBron James as his biggest influence was challenged to describe the qualities that James has that he wanted to emulate. "What does LeBron stand for? How does he influence your values?" The student was then invited to stand in front of the class and give a sixty-second pitch, telling the story of what has made him who he is today. In the second unit, students learn entrepreneurship skills through the Civic Innovation Challenge. Working in teams, students identify a problem in their classroom, school, or community, and collaborate to come up with a plan to address it. The third unit of the course asks students to identify a company or organization that reflects their purpose and study how the organization develops branding and messaging to align with its goals. In addition to teaching students how organizations use storytelling to connect with customers and clients, the branding project provides students with networking experience by requiring them to contact the company or organization they select and meet with local professionals. Finally, in the fourth unit, students pull together what they've learned throughout the year to create a purpose action plan. Building on their values and the meaningful personal story they developed earlier in the year, students use their new entrepreneurship skills to come up with a plan for creating and marketing a product or service that will make a positive contribution in the world.

Each year of the high school program has a similar structure but increases in depth and expands the group of people students work with from classroom to school to community. In the third course, *Noble 301*, students take on an apprenticeship with a local business or organization. These apprenticeships are specifically designed for students to pursue something they are passionate about in a professional setting. One student pursued his passion for design by working with a local design firm, and another with an interest in photography worked with a local photographer. From beginning to end, students who complete all three courses in the Noble Impact series learn to create and pursue their purpose, starting with an exploration of their values and identity, and culminating with real-world engagement in public service, social entrepreneurship, and professional experience. Along the way, each course offers students an opportunity to develop a digital portfolio that they can use to communicate their story to their peers as well as colleges and prospective employers. As the year progresses, students design their online portfolio and populate it with the content they develop in the course, such as describing their most significant influences, their strongest values, their purpose in life, and their future plans. The digital portfolio process teaches students how to create a thoughtful social media presence and gives them control over the narrative and identity they present to the world.

The Noble Impact team learned some important lessons from the first years of doing the program with students. One lesson they learned is that high school is too late to be starting purpose work with students. They found that instilling the skills and mindsets that are the foundation of purpose would be more effective if students started younger. In a blog post on the Noble Impact website on December 23, 2015, CEO Eric Wilson noted that "Early exposure to problem-solving and project-based learning environments sets our students up best for success." Williamson agreed, students need to be finding their own meaning and developing their personal narratives earlier and learning the social and emotional skills needed to create their purpose before arriving at high school. To that end, Noble Impact started a course for eStem middle school students, making it a required daily class for seventh and eighth graders by aligning the curriculum with the communication skills standards that fulfill students' technology requirement. In fifth and sixth grade, students also take the course as part of the school's core curriculum. More recently, Noble Impact began implementing its program in fourth grade and introducing younger students to the concepts of the curriculum through morning meetings. The elementary curriculum introduces the content and skills of the program by teaching students to reflect on their personal narratives and introducing them to teamwork activities for making changes in their community.

A second lesson the Noble Impact team learned is that entrepreneurship skills are a useful byproduct, but what students gained most from the program were the social and emotional resources it offered. As described by eStem Junior High School director Jarrod DuPriest, they redefined entrepreneurship as it is used in their Noble Impact class to mean empowering yourself to get the skills and knowledge you need to create and live by your purpose. This realization did not change the curriculum significantly—they continue to teach students how to pitch their story and solve problems in teams—but it did shift how they think about their own purpose in working with students. More than just skills training, the Noble Impact courses provide students an opportunity to articulate and deepen their values and identify their purpose by setting future-minded goals according to their values.

Purpose is the driver for everything that Noble Impact does. The personal stories that students pitch early in the year are honed through values reflection, followed by in-class exploration of questions about purpose, dreams, and goals that arise from their core values. Students do not settle on surface-level goals and interests, but are challenged to make substantial connections between what really matters to them and their dreams for their future. The digital portfolios give students a platform to develop and express their integrated values and goals, articulating their purpose for themselves and to others. They write a purpose statement, which then serves as their "north star," and follow by identifying the "near stars" or small goals that will take them step-by-step toward fulfilling their purpose. With a clear, values-driven purpose in mind, students then work with a team to develop and implement a service project that reflects their values, and more advanced students act on their purpose by taking on an apprenticeship in the community. At each grade level of engagement, the digital portfolio is archived for students to continuously reflect as they progress through the program.

At Yerger Middle School in Hope, Arkansas, one of the public schools that adopted Noble Impact after seeing the impact at eStem, purpose is a critical aspect of the program not only for students, but for their teachers as well. Principal Josclyn Wiley introduced Noble Impact to her teachers through a summer professional development, during which teachers participated in the same activities that they would later share with their students. Wiley noticed that the teachers, most of whom had been in the school for twenty years or more, had lost sight of why they were there, and as a result the school was losing students because they felt disconnected. She saw Noble Impact as an opportunity to reconnect teachers, to tell their back stories about how and why they first got into teaching, examine their core values, and rediscover their purpose as teachers. The experience was effective. Teachers realized they get caught up in the pressure of getting content to their students and lose sight of the emotional side of working with children. The Noble Impact professional development tapped into the emotional aspects of their work and reconnected them to their purpose for being there.

Students at Yerger also see benefits from the Noble Impact emphasis on purpose. Wiley said the students, most of whom come from high-poverty backgrounds and are labeled as such by the public education system, are used to being recipients of support. The generosity of others has put their students in a victim role and taught them that they have nothing to give. By developing a values-driven purpose and using it to identify and work on an issue in their community, Yerger students are learning that they have something to give and can give without expecting something in return. Wiley said, "Students can come to me to pitch what the school needs that they can provide, like a movie night, or a community clean-up event. When they do, they learn that you get so much more from giving than getting, because being able to serve others improves who you are." Using the Noble Impact framework, students design these acts of service as civic-innovation projects. They work in teams to develop the problem they want to solve and figure out who the stakeholders are, then talk with stakeholders to understand their perspective and create a narrative to fully describe the problem and determine what they can do to act on it. They develop leadership skills and moreover, come to see themselves as having leadership responsibilities that go beyond the school walls. As Wiley explained, "Our Noble Impact students check their own behavior in the community because they feel responsible to the class. They say, 'I can't do that because I'm a Noble kid.'"

When I met Wiley, the Hope School District superintendent, Bobby Hart, met with us as well, so I took the opportunity to ask him the ever-present question: How is it possible for Yerger to implement this program when there are so many other pressing requirements and mandates competing for time in the school day? "Our priority," he responded, "is that our students learn to know their value." But he added, "You need to show schools and districts that there's a reason to have you in." The Noble Impact program, which teaches students not only to identify their core values, but through emphasis on purpose, teaches students to recognize their value, showed Hart that it was what Hope schools needed.

The impacts of implementing a purpose curriculum like Noble Impact go beyond the benefits to individual students and teachers.

When there is buy-in, the effects are seen in the school climate and culture. Williamson picked up on the potential for Noble Impact to make positive changes to the climate of classrooms and culture of the school, and partners with teachers and school leaders to capitalize on this potential. For example, in the Noble Impact classes, he works with teachers to emphasize the role of storytelling to establish a climate of compassion and trust. As I observed a class of eighth graders preparing to pitch their stories in front of their classmates, Williamson set the tone by reminding students to be respectful of the storyteller. "When people tell their personal stories, they are opening compassion in the group, because we can see points of connection between that person's story and ours and feel empathy with them." He reminded them that telling our personal stories to a group makes us feel vulnerable, so it is important that the speaker can feel trust before they tell their story. "If we laugh inappropriately at the speaker or don't pay attention to the story, we break that trust."

At a deeper level, eStem leaders and teachers work with the Noble Impact team to establish a culture that reflects their values and purpose as a school community. eStem High School principal, Johnecia Howard, said that the core values they developed as a district through their work with Williamson and Noble Impact—the HEART values (humility, enthusiasm, authenticity, reflection, and trust)—now shape the culture of their school. The HEART values are used at all levels of the school, with elementary students discussing them in morning meetings, high school students sharing how they have lived or experienced the core values in their lives, and teachers setting the direction of each day based on which HEART value the district is focusing on that day. In district-wide professional development, teachers and school leaders hold these shared values while reflecting together on questions that will shape their district identity, purpose statement, and culture; the story that they want to tell about eStem: Who are we? Why do we do what we do? How did we get here? Where are we going? With a set of shared core values on which to build their purpose, eStem students, teachers, and leaders can connect their personal purpose statements with grade-level and school-level purpose statements, resulting in a culture of shared purpose.

PROJECT WAYFINDER

High school is an optimal time for young people to embark on a journey of purpose exploration, but the current school system is antithetical to such open exploration. That realization led to the creation of Project Wayfinder, a program that envisions a new direction for our schools, as a setting for students to embark on a wayfinding journey. Project Wayfinder was created by Patrick Cook-Deegan and Kelly Schmutte at the Stanford d.school, who used the design-thinking process to address the problems they saw in schools today.[1] The design-thinking process begins with empathy, and through empathic research with end-users, seeks to understand what they need from you. In schools, students are the end-users, so Cook-Deegan and Schmutte started by interviewing teens about their experiences at school. Cook-Deegan said, "Over the past decade, I have had the chance to ask thousands of teenagers what they think about school. I've found that the vast majority of them generally feel one of two ways: disengaged or incredibly pressured."[2] The current school day, he argued, is not designed for human students, it is designed to meet the needs of the system. Students arrive at school too early in the morning for their brains to learn effectively and are expected to sit through one class after another for seven hours straight every day. On another level, he said, adolescence is a time for figuring out your identity and what you want to do with your life, which humans do best through exploration and working with a coach, guide, or mentor. The current school structure, in many places, does not provide this opportunity for students because schools must meet the needs of an elaborate system, shaped by the demands of bus schedules, standardized testing, and college entrance requirements.

Based on their empathic research with students and teachers and backgrounds as adolescent educators, Cook-Deegan and Schmutte started to develop a plan for a public laboratory school in Silicon Valley that would provide high school students with an innovative, purpose-driven learning experience, one that would make academic work more meaningful through project-based learning and prioritize a purposeful life as the most important outcome of students' education. Students at the Wayfinder School would have opportunities to explore who they want to be and work with guides and mentors to figure out how to get there. The proposed lab school was rejected by the school board, causing Cook-Deegan and Schmutte to regroup and find a new outlet for their purpose curriculum. They expanded on the wayfinding theme that had served as a metaphor for the envisioned school by immersing themselves in the study of Polynesian wayfinding—a traditional method of ocean navigation. Polynesian wayfinders are skilled navigators who create a vision of their destination, then use physical markers in the world around them, such as stars, waves, and the wind, to steer a course that eventually leads them there. Wayfinders do not plow over the ocean in a direct path, nor do they wander lost at sea, but navigate from landmark to landmark, making adjustments along the way, honing their instincts, and using the navigation experience to connect their inner selves with the natural world. As Cook-Deegan learned by interviewing students, too many in the United States are either charging straight toward their destination, with no time to reflect or go off course, or they are adrift, lacking the vision, skills, and tools they need to navigate a future course. The program he and Schmutte developed, Project Wayfinder, aims to create a wayfinding experience for students, supporting them to create a vision of their destination and giving them tools to help them on their journey.

Project Wayfinder offers a vision of a more human-centered education, with students having opportunities to explore their values, goals, and purpose, and provides schools with a menu of programs and tools they can select from to work toward that vision. The tools are meticulously designed paper objects that invite interaction, with instructions to fold, cut, tear, and glue. The paper objects are also worksheets that guide students on a purpose journey. They ask students to respond to reflection questions, such as, "What values do you aspire to?" and "Where am I ultimately trying to go, and why is that important to me?" Unlike traditional worksheets, however, the Wayfinder tools are crafted into origami-like objects that support an adventurous journey—a boat made up of paper "planks" that name the student's values, a "gratitude island" where students reflect on who and what they are grateful for and how to build more gratitude in their lives, and a "purpose compass" that guides students in planning a project that aligns their strengths and interests with a need in the world.

The tools lead students through three phases of a purpose journey, starting with activities that build self-awareness, continuing through activities that stir awareness of the world beyond the self, and finishing with planning and acting on something they want to do in the world. The three phases of the Wayfinder journey unfold over consecutive tracks, which students travel step-by-step as they work through the navigation tool activities. The first track, self-awareness, is about examining a student's core values, character traits, and emotions so that these personal assets can be used as resources and developed intentionally and with awareness of the impact they have on the life journey. The second track, building awareness of others and the world, is about identifying social resources in students' lives that can help them on their journey, developing empathy, and tuning in to the issues and needs in the world that they care about. The final track, planning and acting on a need in the world, guides students in developing a project to address a need they identified and taking steps to act on it. The journey can take a semester or a year, depending on the time the school allots for the program.

The guide on this journey is the teacher, who is typically a subject matter or advisory teacher already in the school. Wayfinder guides participate in an intensive summer training program or direct on-site training, where they learn how to use the navigation tools, practice using the tools with students, and experiment with adapting the tools. In the training, teachers are encouraged to be open and vulnerable with students when teaching the Wayfinder curriculum, to put themselves in the role of mentor or guide rather than teacher, and to tell their own stories and do the activities along with students. Reem Bilbeisi, teacher of the Wayfinder class at Averroes High School in California, made personal connections throughout the activities. Averroes is an Islamic school, so Bilbeisi made simple connections that would be meaningful to the traditions she and her students share, for example, evoking the pilgrimage to Mecca to describe how people can use the stars and sun to guide them on a long journey. She also got more personal, sharing her own response to a prompt that asked students to think about what they do when they encounter stormy emotions. "When I'm angry," she shared, "I need to let the person know." In the training, teachers are also encouraged to think about the setting where they teach the curriculum, and to rearrange or design the space to provide a setting that aligns with the goals of the lesson. Bilbeisi's students, for example, sat in a circle on the floor, so they could spread out their tools in front of them, easily rearrange themselves for small-group sharing, and feel connected as they shared out their personal responses to the Wayfinder questions.

The teacher training is essential for gaining familiarity and comfort with the Wayfinder curriculum. Erin Hayes, a Blue Valley Center for Advanced Professional Studies (CAPS) program teacher in the Blue Valley School District in Kansas, said that the summer training helped her wrap her mind around the innovative tools and prepared her to integrate the tools into her courses. Hayes teaches the Foundations of Medicine course for the Blue Valley CAPS program, which is available to all high school juniors and seniors in the district. CAPS is a semester or yearlong immersive career-development program that engages students in one of six professional strands (engineering, human services, medicine and health care, business, technology and media, bioscience, and innovate). Students spend three periods of a seven-period school day in CAPS activities, including working to solve real problems in one of the fields.

In the foundations class, students identify a problem in the medical community that they want to work on and develop a project to offer a solution to the problem. Students might develop a project to address insurance policy challenges, for example, or create an app to facilitate patient care. Hayes introduced some of the Wayfinder tools throughout the course to give her students opportunities to reflect on what they most value and problems they care about. By using the Wayfinder tools, they go into their projects with a strong and meaningful connection to a problem in the medical world and feel a sense of purpose as they work to solve it.

Because it is the first year implementing Project Wayfinder, Hayes selected five of the fifteen navigation tools, choosing to integrate a few of them well and taking time to discover how they work with students, rather than rushing through all of them. Hayes innovative adaptation of the tools aligns with the goals of Project Wayfinder. Cook-Deegan encourages teachers to adapt the tools to fit their program and students' needs and is happy to see teachers finding unique ways to bring the tools to their students. Another Project Wayfinder teacher incorporated the activities into a senior poetry elective, while another created a peer mentor program and guided the mentors in doing the Wayfinder activities with students.

Although in their first year implementing Project Wayfinder, teachers and program staff are encouraged by student engagement and responses. Hayes said that her students enjoy the activities. "So much schoolwork is content-based, it's always geared toward one specific thing—college. These tools let them step out of that to reflect on what they want to do and what they're good at. They tell me, 'Wow, that was great! We never have time to sit and think about this stuff.'" Bilbeisi's students at Averroes also had a positive response to the Wayfinder activities. Working on a navigation tool that asked them to draw themselves on an epic journey, Averroes students drew steep waves, or a meandering path, or a sky full of guiding stars. After finishing the activity, students shared the journeys they drew, describing career, family, and spiritual goals that shaped their path. They said that they enjoyed the activity. As one student said, it was hard, but she appreciated the challenge of doing something on her own and without direction from a teacher. At Blue Valley CAPS, Hayes found the design of the tools to be especially effective with students because they did not see it as just another worksheet to fill out. The navigation tools, she said, are different and special, more experiential than traditional worksheets because they engage students in cutting, folding, and gluing as they think about their values, strengths, and goals. She talked to some of her students, a group whose project was to create a "Break the Silence" mental wellness fair for their community, to see if the Project Wayfinder activities were having an impact on their project work. Their immediate response was, "yes!" In particular, they said, the "Powers of 10 Perspectives" tool, which engages students in deep thinking about the problems in the world that matter most to them, got them to brainstorm ideas about mental illness that resulted in their plan for the wellness fair.

Hayes said her students appreciate the discussions that are inspired by the tools and continue those discussions outside the class, with friends or in one-on-one conversations with her. She hears students encouraging each other using the ideas they learn from engaging with the tools, providing feedback to each other such as, "maybe that isn't what you want to do with your life," or "you'll be a great doctor, it's your passion." Since starting Project Wayfinder, Hayes said her students approach her more often for counseling-type conversations and do so using the framework provided by the navigation tools. She recognized that teachers must create an environment of trust and camaraderie to get students to open up, but the more they engage in discussions framed by the Wayfinder tools, the more trust there is in the room. At Averroes, Bilbeisi similarly sees the Wayfinder program as a way for students to go beyond the traditional work with counselors that they were already doing. "We are trying to be true to who we are as human beings, as a school." Continuing, she said, "We also want our students to be leaders in their communities and in society. For that, you need to know where you're going, you need to know your purpose. Wayfinder helps them find that purpose."

CHAPTER NINE

Purposeful Curricula

Student-led pedagogies like project-based learning suggest approaches to instruction that can support purpose at school; however, without attention to curriculum content, they can leave the impression that developing student purpose is the same thing as engaging students in a cause. Having a cause to work for can give students a sense of purpose, but it is not the same thing as having purpose. Projects, problems, and service provide students with the skills and tools to create or pursue purpose in their lives, but it is possible to engage in projects and service and causes and never gain a sense of purpose. Therefore, it is important to pay attention to supporting purpose outside of working toward a cause. The feeling of having purpose is transcendent. Learning to set meaningful, higher-order goals and act on them, as students do in project-based approaches, is critical to purpose development, because purpose is just a dream if we do not know how to act on it. However, that feeling of purpose is found in powerful self-awareness and connectedness, or integration with something larger than the self. It is a sustained, driving, and directional feeling, not a stagnant or centered feeling, which is more like meaning.

Achieving that transcendent sense of purpose comes from developing a moral identity, as described in chapter 3. Moral identity can be addressed through character education and social- emotional learning if we attend to specific aspects of these curriculum areas. Both character education and social-emotional learning have become popular in recent years, but only rarely do they aim explicitly at developing moral identity and purpose. Often, character development programs focus on performance character, teaching students grit and growth mindset, neglecting moral character traits, such as empathy. Social-emotional learning, on the other hand, too often focuses on teaching students skills for managing the immediate social context, such as conflict resolution and classroom communication. To support purpose, the curriculum in these areas needs to engage students in thinking about and internalizing moral character traits, social values, and social agency. Within these areas, there are three key ideas that teachers can focus on to support students to develop moral identity and purpose: empathy, values, the future, and power.

Empathy

Empathy is a complex aspect of character that begins with being aware that other people have feelings, thoughts, and perspectives that are different from ours. Empathy is both emotional, in that it involves having feelings in response to the feelings and experiences of others, and cognitive, in that empathic people can take the perspective of others and respect others' perspectives and feelings.[1] Empathy may be central to developing moral identity because the emotional impact of empathy can cause people to want to be a moral person (who helps others or does things that make the world better for others).[2] Empathy is a strong motivation for moral action.[3] When young people develop empathy, they have the start of a strong foundation for purpose, because they can understand and value the needs and concerns of others, and the needs of others come to affect their own well-being. The research with children suggests that empathy is not a fixed trait but is a character strength that can be nurtured through secure attachments in the early years, warm relationships, and empathy-building activities.[4] This section describes some of the research on teaching for empathy and methods some schools and teachers use to make empathy central to their curriculum.

Some pedagogical strategies that develop empathy include sustained involvement in community activities, such as service or performing arts, and using inquiry and reflection in learning activities.[5] Community activities require students to pay attention to others in order to have effective interactions and be successful in their collaborative activity. In general, providing an environment in which students find a sense of community appears to support students in developing empathy and engaging in more prosocial behavior.[6] Inquiry and reflection in learning activities require students to think about and question what they are learning through different lenses, including considering perspectives other than those that are automatic to them. For example, a unit on electricity that includes inquiry and reflection can get students thinking about what happens when there is no electricity, and how that affects people. Role-taking activities are another way to develop empathy. In several studies, empathy scores increased among participants who engaged in role-playing or perspective-taking activities, such as reading literary fiction, reflective writing about the feelings of others, and prosocial video games.[7]

The research on teaching for empathy has informed several recent programs aimed at making empathy a central and essential aspect of K–12 education. The Ashoka Changemaker Schools program, for example, is a global network of schools recognized for exemplary empathy teaching. Ashoka selects schools to join the network, structures collaborative learning opportunities for network schools, and provides resources to further support the schools in teaching empathy.[8] The key quality Ashoka looks for in selecting Changemaker Schools is an emphasis on empathy; however, they also look for emphasis on creativity, responsibility, and leadership, so that students are learning to be effective in applying their empathy in the world. Ashoka's other programs support social entrepreneurs, and their overall goal as an organization is to develop and support Changemakers all over the world. With their Changemaker Schools program, they assert that becoming a Changemaker starts with empathy, and by recognizing schools that prioritize empathy, they can spread the idea that schools must start with empathy to develop students who can create a better world. The Ashoka

Changemaker Schools program provides examples of how empathy is being taught and supported in schools today. As the following models demonstrate, much of teaching for empathy has to do with providing the conditions for a purpose-supportive environment as described in chapter 5. Teaching for empathy is handled as a comprehensive approach of providing a compassionate environment, where adults model empathy and students practice the skills of empathy.

One Changemaker school is San Miguel Elementary School in California. San Miguel was selected by Ashoka based on their success with the community-school model, as well as their commitment to social-emotional learning that prioritizes empathy in all aspects of the school. As a community school, San Miguel provides wraparound services for their families and the community, including counseling, dental care, and health and wellness programs. They partner with numerous local organizations to provide student support for social and emotional development and teacher professional development in social-emotional learning. Class meetings are a regular feature in San Miguel classrooms, both in daily morning meetings, but also whenever there is a need to address social challenges or bond as a community. These elements of the school make for a culture and climate of compassion, but student development of empathy is also directly addressed through the curriculum.

The core curriculum areas provide opportunity to engage students in thinking and talking about empathy and learning about the world from different perspectives. For example, second graders at San Miguel learned the parts of a letter by reading a model in which the writer described people who are "upstanders" to the recipient, explaining that upstanders help others and are brave. Later in the year, they completed a unit on exploring the qualities of heroes to learn about character development. First graders in a bilingual class learned how words can have different cultural significance in different languages and may not be culturally appropriate when directly translated. They learned this cultural linguistics lesson by sharing and reflecting on the caring words their families use when talking with each other, such as "sweetheart," "dear," and "corazon." Fourth graders watched a video of poet Kwame Alexander reading and discussing his poem "Take a Knee," based on the movement started by football player Colin Kaeperneck. Social-emotional skills are also taught directly in daily activities, such as in a third-grade class where students did an activity using cardboard frames to obscure all their faces except for their eyes, revealing how our eyes communicate what we feel. Through their community partnerships, San Miguel teachers receive training and resources to teach social and emotional skills, such as self-regulation, coping, positive self-talk, and empathy. Principal Christina Ballantyne considers these activities a priority for their school and essential to students' academic success. "We need to address students' social and emotional well-being in order to have academic gains. Kids can't learn if you don't address these things."[9]

Ashoka provides resources for current and prospective Changemaker Schools on their website, such as curriculum ideas and templates developed by the Center for Inspired Teaching.[10] The resources provided by the Center for Inspired Teaching show how empathy can be taught in all different subject areas. A sample science lesson on the website engages students in an extended and intensive investigation of water chemistry that is framed by the concept of water scarcity in some parts of the world. The investigation begins not with the science of water, but with a discussion about global water scarcity and how it affects people, including discussion of pollution as the primary cause of water scarcity and the costs associated with creating potable water. The inquiry unit guides students from the social study of water scarcity through a scientific investigation of water chemistry and water pollution and culminates in creating a water filtration device that can address the problem of water scarcity.[11] The unit is teacher-led, but it raises students' awareness of issues in the world that they might not have been aware of, engages them in taking the perspective of people living in different circumstances from their own, and gives them practice in taking action to address a problem that they see so that they can have a positive impact in the world. It shows how starting with empathy can lead students to developing the skills and values needed for pursuing purpose.

Values

Our values are the core of our identity. They are the principles or beliefs that guide our goals, actions, and behaviors. In the context of teaching values, it is important to distinguish values from virtues and manners, which are sometimes confused with values.[12] When we talk about engaging students in activities to develop values, we are not asking them to behave according to classroom norms, or internalize a specific set of virtues, though social norms and virtues might be some things that students value. We are asking them to reflect deeply about who they are in terms of what matters most to them, and to be aware of their most important values and act in accord with them. In reflecting on their values, students should be aware of different types of values that we all have. Some values reflect our interests, such as the arts, sports, or academic achievement, while others describe the kind of person we want to be, such as honesty, adventure, and creativity, or indicate the importance of relationships in our lives, such as family and friendship.

Values that support purpose are prosocial and moral, in the sense that they are oriented to being a good person and having a positive impact in the world. Beyond that specification, purpose-directed values are unique to the individual. One purposeful person might value family and tradition, while another values innovation, and yet another values social justice. These beyond-the-self values are the guiding light for purpose, and they are what gives purpose a sense of inspiration and awe. We have a sense of purpose in life when we know what we value most and are driven to act on those values to make a positive impact in the world.

Though essential to identity formation and purpose, values education is a controversial topic. In one sense, there is the controversy of indoctrination, and the belief that values should be taught at home or in religious institutions. In another sense, there is ongoing controversy about how values should be taught. Some believe that schools should preference specific values that prepare young people for life in society and inculcate these values in students, while others believe that students should openly explore and clarify their personal values, without a teacher telling them what they should value.[13]

With purpose as the goal, schools can resolve these tensions in teaching values. Purpose education requires values exploration, so that students feel connection, meaning, and identity related to the values that shape their purpose. They need to clarify what their most important values are, gain awareness of where their values come from, develop a strong attachment to their values, and be deliberate in living in accord with their values. However, they also need to reflect on moral values and need to know what it means to be a good person. Purpose requires that values are strong and personally meaningful *and also* outward looking and oriented to doing good in the world. In their study of moral exemplars, Anne Colby and William Damon describe this as a unity of our sense of morality and personal goals.[14] There is a long history of efforts to create this unity with strategies that engage students in values clarification, while also guiding them to internalize certain moral values. Three of these strategies are described here that can be especially useful for supporting student purpose.

Values Sort and Reflection

In a values-sorting activity, students see a list of words that represent different values (such as creativity, success, family, fitness, gratitude, and so on), which they sort into boxes ranking them in order of importance (most important to least important). To make a values-sorting activity relevant to purpose, teachers can extend the activity with writing prompts, discussion, and hands-on activities for students to further explore their values. Students can reflect on why they selected their most important values: Why do they matter? Who do I know that has those values? What does it mean to act in accord with those values? If students select family, for example, they will have to go a step further to reflect on what it is about family that matters to them. Do they value quality time spent with extended family? Do they most value the opportunities their parents provide for them? What do they do to act on what they value about family? Do they have any future goals that reflect their value of family?

In a powerful example of values reflection, the John Templeton Foundation created a contest to engage students in writing about their values. The Laws of Life Essay Contest inspired students around the world to reflect on the values that mattered most to them, and resulting essays have been published in at least two edited volumes.[15] In their essays, students eloquently describe values such as responsibility, helping others, love, integrity, and living life to the fullest. Their essays artfully narrate how they gained their values and how they experience them in their own lives, describe what they mean, and share their plans for living by their values into the future.

Through extension activities, students can externalize their values, such as by creating school displays that share student values and related goals, producing radio broadcasts or podcasts that express values related to a current event, creating mind maps or life maps that show how values connect to other aspects of life, or creating art or writing poetry that reflects key personal values. To guide purpose, our internally meaningful values cannot exist in a social and moral vacuum. By externalizing their values through reflection and extension activities, students can find connections between their innermost selves and the world and receive guidance to shape positive and socially beneficial values.

Role Models

The use of role models has long been advocated as an approach to teaching students moral values and good character. Typically, role models and their values are presented to students through literature, documentary videos, and biographical accounts of exemplars such as Gandhi and Martin Luther King, Jr., or through teachers' own expression of their values and action in accord with their values. A role models approach to developing students' values assumes that desirable values are "caught not taught," and students will best learn by internalizing the positive beliefs and behaviors they see in admirable others. The research on youth purpose development finds that adult role models are an influence in the lives of purposeful adolescents.[16] In another study of middle school students participating in an environmental education program, those who described having parent and teacher role models of environmentalism were more likely to develop environmental values and social responsibility.[17]

Another recent study suggests that the most effective role models for shaping values that lead to prosocial activity may not be adults, but peers. Middle school students studied either attainable (peers) or unattainable (historic figures) role models of exemplary moral activity and completed pre- and post-surveys to assess their participation in volunteer service activities. Students in the group that studied peer exemplars increased their volunteer activity significantly more than students in the group that studied unattainable historic exemplars.[18] This study suggests that role models can have an impact on different aspects of student values and character development, but exemplars they see as attainable or more like them, such as people their age, may have a greater impact on whether students will act on their positive values.

Deliberation

Usually grounded in a community or political event, issue, or controversy, deliberation engages students in discussion to address the issue. Because deliberation has roots in civil discourse, it generally involves democratic values, such as equality, justice, individual rights, diversity, liberty, and interdependence. Therefore, there is a body of socially normed values at the core of this approach, but it also involves discussion in which students use rational thinking, evidence, and personal meaning to support a position related to democratic values, which are fundamentally controversial when applied to real-world situations. Therefore, the reflection involved in deliberation is intensive and multifaceted. It requires students to apply thinking that is rational, philosophical, and evidence-based, but that also taps into personal relevance and meaning. Deliberation includes getting beyond differences to solve problems, so it is especially relevant to developing values for purpose because it supports students in going from values to action. Deliberation of democratic values requires students to reflect on personal values while also considering the societal consequences of their values. In practice, the act of deliberation requires social virtues such as humility, moral courage, and tolerance, so transparency about the role these values play in civil discourse can lead students to develop attachment to these values as well.

In civic deliberation, teachers do not tell students what values to prioritize or internalize but can expose students to examination of different civic values, and through critical engagement and discussion support students to develop their own civic values. Teachers cannot tell a student to value liberty or diversity or equity, but they can engage students in thoughtful debate about these values so students can form their own attachment to the values that matter to them. The practice and skills of deliberation can be used in different areas of the curriculum and do not have to be related to civic values. The goal of deliberation is to clarify values and recognize commonly held values for socially positive outcomes, and not to inculcate specific values.[19]

The Future

The future is largely framed as college and career readiness in schools today, with less attention paid to what students plan to do in college, how they will use their college education, and who they want to be in life after and around college. There is also little attention given to student futures that do not involve college. There is much more to students' futures than college, of course, and thinking more broadly about their future goals in school will give students a purpose for learning that can motivate and engage them, and it can support them to create purpose for their lives at school.

Future goals can be proximal (close in time, concrete, specific) or distal (distant future, abstract, broad). When distal goals are personally meaningful and impart a sense of purpose, they help to organize and direct the setting and pursuit of more proximal goals. Proximal goals provide scaffolding that make it possible to realize purposeful distal (referred to in this book as higher-order) goals.[20] College and career readiness scaffolds students to set a distant abstract goal that may not bear much meaning for many students. It also attaches to only one specific value—education. Education is an important value for many (though not all) students, but it is a narrow and shortsighted value for shaping a purposeful future. Students need opportunities to think about the future in terms of more meaningful and aspirational goals, which education is part of but not an endpoint.

Aspiration, optimism, and a hopeful future-outlook are associated with academic achievement, healthy psychological outcomes, and positive youth development.[21] In a study of adolescent life goals, high school students were asked to write in response to this open-ended question: "If you could do anything you wanted with your life, what would you most want to do and be?" About 37 percent described professional or skilled career goals (doctor, lawyer, engineer, police officer, chef), 26 percent described non-career lifestyle goals (marriage, helping others, religious goals, wealth, being important), 20 percent described creative or athletic career goals, and 13 percent described education goals.[22] These findings suggest that we should connect learning to students' ideas about the future beyond education goals, because that is where their minds are, that is what they are concerned about, and it is the vision of their future that will be most motivating and engaging. Education, including college, is a tool for achieving that future vision.

It is important that the future students envision is aspirational and holds high expectations for themselves. Most teenagers think of future goals in terms of lofty career goals, such as doctor, lawyer, and engineer, but these aspirations do not align with reality considering the percentage of adults who work in these roles. Unfortunately, the gap between aspiration, expectations, and reality is bigger for some groups than others. For example, adolescents from some ethnic groups set higher professional goals for themselves than others, and some, namely low-income and African American students, describe a greater gap than other students between what they aspire to, in terms of prestige, and what they expect to achieve.[23] Even if their aspirations are unrealistic, the level at which students set their expectations and aspirations predict their academic achievement and future outcomes.[24] Therefore, it is important that teachers provide opportunities for expanded and aspirational future-thinking in school, that they are aware of the level of students' aspirations and expectations, and that they ensure that all students are setting high expectations for themselves.

The *content* of students' future aspirations is also critical for their general well-being outcomes, but especially for their potential to develop purpose in life. There is clear evidence that some future goals are better than others when it comes to student well-being, life satisfaction, and purpose. In a study of college students' aspirations and psychological health, researchers found that attainment of some goals correlated with greater well-being, whereas another type of goals, when achieved, correlated with poor outcomes for psychological health. Specifically, students who set and attained *intrinsic* goals, that is, those associated with personal growth, having close relationships, and community involvement, also reported greater well-being after attaining their goals. On the other hand, students who set and attained *extrinsic* goals, such as those associated with fame, wealth, and image, reported more signs of ill-being, such as shame, anger, and anxiety.[25]

It might be that the motivation behind the goal content is more important for psychological outcomes of attaining a goal than the content of the goal itself. A study of volunteers who described wanting to volunteer for different reasons showed that the type of motivation had and impact on well-being outcomes for the volunteers. Those who reported other-oriented goal motivations, such as wanting to connect with others, wanting to understand the perspective of others, or wanting to do something good for others, attained a greater sense of well-being, higher self-efficacy, and higher self-esteem from their volunteer activity, while those who volunteered for self-oriented reasons, such as to enhance their career, showed lower well-being, self-efficacy, and self-esteem outcomes.[26] Purpose is a future-minded goal that is driven by intrinsic and beyond-the-self motivations. These findings about positive psychological outcomes for intrinsic and other-oriented goals and motivations reinforce the idea that purpose is associated with positive developmental outcomes for young people.

Activities that engage students in talking and writing about their aspirations and future selves can motivate student engagement and improve their academic performance. Yet, students often report that they have few opportunities at school to think about their future goals in terms of their interests, values, or purpose. Following are examples of programs that were designed to engage students in talking and thinking about the future that can be adapted for high school classrooms.

Possible Selves Intervention

One approach to future orientation that has proven to be effective in improving academic achievement while also supporting far-reaching, higher-order, and positive future-thinking is demonstrated in a *possible selves* intervention developed for students in an after-school program. Participants spent nine weeks thinking about their desired future selves and planning a path to attain the future self they imagined. They started to envision possible future selves by looking at images of adults in different life roles, careers, and activities. They selected from these images to create an image of their own desired future self, then wrote about the image they created. To make a bridge from their current schoolwork to their envisioned future self, participants then created a timeline from the present to their future self that includes possible roadblocks. They also mapped out the strategies they could use to accomplish their goals and collaborated with each other to solve problems that might arise as they worked toward their future selves.[27] Following the possible selves program, students who participated had better school attendance, felt more bonded at school, and were more concerned about doing well in school compared to students who did not participate in the program. They also were able to come up with more plausible strategies for achieving their school-related goals than students who did not participate in the program.

Postsecondary Future-Thinking Courses

Recently, college programs have developed courses for undergraduates to explore their future possibilities in ways that resemble purpose exploration. These popular courses offer ideas for activities that can be adapted for use with high school students to engage them in thinking about their future.

Life Worth Living is a course offered at Yale University in which students reflect on questions such as, "What is a life well lived?" and, "What do we need to do to lead a life well lived?" In the course, students reflect on these questions in the context of different religious faiths, including Buddhism, Judaism, Christianity, and Islam, by reading texts from these different faiths and hearing from invited speakers that represent different faiths. However, without the context of religious faith, these questions and others like them can shape a reflection activity for high school students, especially if they follow or accompany values clarification activities.[28]

Designing Your Life is a Stanford University course started by the design school to engage students in reflecting on their life path through a series of activities, readings, and discussions. The course gets students to integrate their ideas about future work with their values and worldview, encouraging them to think of their future in terms of an evolving vocation. The capstone activity asks students to develop an Odyssey Plan in which they imagine three different possible futures for their lives. Before writing their Odyssey Plan, students reflect on their "workview" and "lifeview," writing in response to questions such as "what is work for?" and "what gives life meaning and purpose?" Students create mind maps of the interests and activities in which they are most engaged and energized. Then, referring to their mind maps, students are asked to think like designers and brainstorm many different possible lives for themselves.[29]

The Odyssey Plan method was recently tested with high school students in a pilot conducted by Summit Public Schools.[30] Fourteen students who opted into the pilot program were asked to create a portfolio with three possible life plans. As described by Amy Sandoz, director of diploma at Summit, students benefited from extra prompting in several areas: thinking about areas of life other than future career plans, thinking about their future in terms of setting goals that they can work toward, and thinking through more specificity and detail about the steps they will need to take to pursue their goals. Sandoz recognized that the gaps in students' future-thinking are consistent with their developmental stage; however, the additional prompting they provided demonstrate how adolescents might be scaffolded to reach the next stage of development in their future-thinking.[31]

Engaging students in any open-ended discussions about the future is valuable, but the questions discussed in Designing Your Life and Life

Worth Living are notable for shaping discussions about life and the future in terms of meaning, values, and purpose. With opportunities to think about their future in terms of creating a meaningful life, students can tend to their purpose, nurturing its growth instead of relying on the chance of time and circumstances to present a purposeful path. Their growing purpose will then give them a sense of direction as they plan for their future.

Aspirational future-thinking can, and should, be tied to more proximal goals and activities, including the learning goals and activities needed to fulfill core requirements. Students' current vision of the future may not be the same as the aspirations they will have next year, but the point is not to foreclose on a future plan in high school. Instead, the goal is to motivate and engage students with a vision of the future that is meaningful and gives them a sense of purpose—something to work toward that matters. Shorter-term learning goals can then be directed toward that aspirational and purposeful vision of the future. We know that specific and concrete goals lead to better student performance, but that does not mean we should not make space in school for students' more far-reaching goals or their aspirational thoughts about the future. With these developmentally powerful future aspirations and purpose goals in mind, students can be scaffolded through classroom activities to learn the processes of setting concrete goals as steps on their path to a meaningful future. Strategies such as backwards mapping and SMART (specific, measurable, achievable, relevant, and time-bound) goal setting are effective ways to help students turn dreams into purpose.

Power

Agency, which has been identified here as an essential mindset for fully realizing purpose in life, can also be thought of as power. Power is defined as "the capacity or ability to direct or influence the behavior of others or the course of events."[32] There are many thoughts in the education research about how to develop student agency, which largely center on strategies to make instruction relevant, coherent, and challenging so that students are motivated to take the lead in their learning.[33] However, power is rarely considered as a topic of study, especially in the context of supporting students to develop agency. Eric Liu, civic entrepreneur and founder of Citizen University, argues that students need to understand power in order to be effective and see themselves as people who can play a role in shaping society.[34] In other words, he believes we must know what power is, who has it, and why in order to have social agency. He created a curriculum for people of all ages to learn about power that was adapted for high school students by the organization Facing History and Ourselves.[35] The curriculum is designed to help students recognize power in their community and understand how they can channel their concern for issues into effective action. Although the curriculum is based on civic action, Liu proposes that the concepts can be applied in any domain of life where people want to make an impact, such as in their family, at school, or at work.

The first principle that Liu emphasizes in teaching about power is that power is concentrated and tends to form into monopolies, but it is possible for a "catalytic minority" to cause change even within a concentrated power structure. Someone without power can gain the power to cause change by first "reading power" and then "writing power." Reading power means observing the power structure in the community or system that you want to change: Why are things in your community the way they are? Why do some people have resources and others do not? Who makes decisions that become policy, and how? Which people in the community are effective at making things the way they are? Writing power means deciding to be one of the people who is effective at causing change and then taking action to get involved by showing up at meetings, participating in campaigns, developing a plan of action based on what you learned by reading power, and practicing by continuing to show up and participate.

Liu then proposes several strategies to build from reading and writing power. For example, he suggests pushing against the boundaries when someone says, "that's not possible" by asking "what if?" "What if we eliminate homework on weekends?" "What if I use Twitter to support suicidal teens?" "What if we create a self-sustaining community farm at our school?" By asking "what if . . . ?" in response to "that's not possible" and coming up with concrete ideas in response to the what if question, students learn that they can change the frame of what is possible and take effective action. Another strategy Liu proposes is to create momentum with an early win. Success is persuasive, so one way to gain power is to act on possibilities generated by the "what if?" challenge and achieve some success. A little success sets in motion a positive feedback loop, inspires optimism, and draws support and resources.[36] These strategies have a natural fit with social studies, especially civic curricula, but they can be applied to project development in any content area where students aspire to have an impact but are starting without power.

Purpose

Purpose itself can be a topic of study in K–12 schools. The field of research-tested purpose interventions is growing, providing inspiration for teachers looking to use purpose activities in their curriculum.

The research team at Stanford Center on Adolescence developed an interview for conducting qualitative studies of youth purpose (which was the basis of the purpose exploration activity in chapter 1). The interviewer asked participants to talk about the things that are most important to them, their current activities and interests, and their future goals. Matthew Bundick, now a professor at Duquesne University, worked on the interview when he was a doctoral student at Stanford and wanted to see if the interview itself increased student purpose. In an intervention study, Bundick tested the impact of participating in the interview on purpose identification, a sense of having goals that give direction to life, and life satisfaction. The interview did not appear to have an impact on purpose identification, meaning that participants were not more likely than a control group to say that they had found a purpose for their life after participating in the interview. However, they were more likely than the control group (who had not participated in an interview) to report increased life satisfaction and goal directedness, both of which are related to life purpose.[37] These findings suggest that giving students opportunities to reflect openly on their values, concerns, and goals for the future can increase their goal directedness and sense of satisfaction with life.

Based on promising results from the purpose interview intervention, Kendall Cotton Bronk and her team at Claremont Graduate University developed a purpose intervention that unfolds the interview over a series of online reflection activities for high school students.[38] The activities are self-paced, but intended to be completed over about four days, for fifteen to twenty minutes at each sitting. Participating students watch videos that show celebrities talking about their purpose and read inspirational quotes about purpose, then respond to reflection questions such as, "What does the quote make you think of in regards to the things that matter most to you?" The reflection questions touch on different aspects of purpose, such as asking students to envision their best possible future, how they would change the world, and what matters most to them. It borrows certain principles from the purpose interview, such as providing students opportunity for reflection and scaffolding them through a guided reflection on purpose in life (rather than directly asking them to name their purpose). By spreading out the intervention over a week, students have more time to process their reflection on the questions and deepen their thinking about purpose in their life. This intervention is currently being tested, but initial evaluation results suggest that it has a positive short-term impact on student purpose.[39]

Another research-based purpose intervention turned the tables by testing whether giving students a beyond-the-self purpose for learning would improve their academic performance. Ninth graders were primed for beyond-the-self purpose with a writing prompt that asked them to reflect on what they think would make the world a better place. Next, students read an invented report, suggesting that surveys and interviews with older students showed that they are sometimes motivated to do well in school because it will enable them to make a positive difference in the world.

Students who participated in the intervention had a higher post-test GPA than a control group that did not participate in the intervention. This effect was strongest among low performing students—those who had pre-intervention GPAs lower than 3.00. Students who participated in the intervention were also more likely to persist on tedious learning tasks, compared to the control group, as measured by their willingness to complete long blocks of boring math problems. Another group of students was primed to think of self-serving reasons for learning, such as getting a high-paying job in the future. This group of students performed the same as the control group on the boring math challenge, showing a precipitous decline in the number of problems they were willing to solve.[40] This promising intervention study suggests that integrating beyond-the-self purpose with school learning activities can support academic performance, especially among less-motivated students. It also suggests that this can be done with simple writing reflection activities and by showing students that school learning can prepare them to make a difference in the world.

CHAPTER TEN

Open Future Institute and MOSAIC

Each of the programs profiled throughout this book aims to develop purpose by engaging students with topics such as those described in the previous chapter. We saw, for example, that The Future Project engages students in active learning about future possibility, QISA trains teachers on the topic of self-worth, and Noble Impact and Project Wayfinder ask students to examine their personal values at depth. The two programs profiled in this chapter—Open Future Institute's QUESTion Project and the Rutgers University Social Emotional and Character Development Lab's MOSAIC program—exemplify the approach of engaging students with selected topics that can provide a foundation for a life of purpose. Though very different in their approach, both programs see the need to make purpose and related topics integral to the school environment and students' every day experience.

OPEN FUTURE INSTITUTE QUESTION PROJECT

"What is purpose?" It is an expansive, deep, Big Question, the kind that is endlessly open and has no right answers, and the type that students have so few opportunities to address in their middle and high school classes. However, Gerard Senehi and Francesca Rusciani, founders of Open Future Institute, believe that these big, open questions are exactly the ones teachers should be asking students. Questions such as this are the foundation of the Open Future Institute's QUESTion Project, which engages students in semester or yearlong exploration of their future and the path they will take to get there. The QUESTion Project provides schools with a set of programs for engaging students in asking big questions and thinking about meaning in life. The two key components of the QUESTion Project are the QUESTion Class, which offers a semester or yearlong curriculum, and a student ambassador program, which provides selected students with intensive training in leadership and communication skills in connection with the concepts taught through the QUESTion class.

For students at five high schools in the South Bronx, discussing big questions is a weekly, and in some cases, daily experience. Their schools offer the QUESTion class, either as an elective, as a health class, or through their advisory program. The class is taught by teachers already in the schools who were carefully selected for having the qualities needed to engage students in open, expansive questions. QUESTion class teachers need to be willing to explore big questions with students without leading them to "the right answers." They must be willing to implicate themselves and share their experience when appropriate. They need to have an awareness of where students are coming from and respect students' capacity to shape their own ideas and insights. Selected teachers participate in a ten-session training program to prepare to teach the QUESTion class. After the initial training, their professional development is ongoing, with both one-on-one and group PD sessions throughout the year. Although they receive a fully designed curriculum, the teachers can adapt it to meet the needs of their school and students.

School leaders who have embraced the Open Future Institute saw the need in their schools that the QUESTion Project could fill. Senehi heard from some principals that they felt they were good at preparing students for college and career, but were not preparing them for life. The QUESTion class offered these schools a full curriculum to guide students through challenging questions about what they want from life and what they would need to do to accomplish their goals. More than just goal pursuit training, though, Senehi and Rusciani wanted their program to create a space in schools where students could bring their humanity, explore some of the most important questions about life, and think about their future in terms of meaning, purpose, and making the world a better place. As Senehi described it, "We don't help students 'find their purpose' but we help build the foundations for a life of purpose. In the curriculum, we approach purpose from many different angles as students can experience or have access to purpose in different ways."[1] They support students to build a foundation for purpose by providing the tools and sensibilities that enable them to connect with their authentic selves and empower them to reveal themselves in the classroom and beyond.

The QUESTion class supports students to build a foundation with five pillars that empower them to examine fundamental questions about who they are and to create a life that is meaningful to them and matters in the larger world. The five pillars are: Choice, Purpose, Fearlessness, Interconnectedness, and A Bigger Picture. Purpose is the primary outcome, but it is first empowered by the capacity to see possibilities and make choices that will lead to fulfilling purpose, then the other pillars of fearlessness, interconnectedness, and seeing a bigger picture provide the skills and attitudes that form a strong foundation for purpose.[2]

- *Choice*: To build the first pillar, students reflect on their own decision-making processes to understand how they make choices, the outcomes of their choices, and how the outcomes of their decisions impact their future goals. They are invited to think of their lives as open fields of possibility, consider how the choices they make define their lives, and take responsibility for their decisions.
- *Purpose*: To build the second pillar, students engage in open discussion about the meaning of purpose as well as the purpose of their own lives. They identify the things that are most important to them and are challenged to connect what inspires them to contributions they can make to the world.

- *Fearlessness*: The third pillar comes from students realizing their life is in their own hands and depends on the courage they show in pursuing a life that is true to their personal interests and values. They build this pillar as they find the strength within themselves to stay true to their convictions as they define and pursue their purpose.
- *Interconnectedness*: The fourth pillar is awareness of being part of a larger whole. Purpose is individual and personal, and at the same time it connects us to others and is most powerful when we work with others toward a common purpose. Students build this pillar by developing empathy and compassion, and a sense of responsibility for the common good.
- *A Bigger Picture*: To build the fifth pillar, students learn to step back and gain perspective on their lives as fitting into a larger context. They develop a big picture view of the world and reflect on the significance of their lives from this big picture perspective. They learn to think beyond their immediate context as they develop their purpose and envision a role for themselves that is part of a larger whole.

Each of these five pillars is a unit in the QUESTion curriculum. Students are invited to participate in discussions and activities during each class session that strengthen these pillars and create a foundation for purpose. Prior to discussing the question, "What is purpose?" students might have had several sessions in which they explored questions such as, "How do your decisions impact your future goals?" They might follow their reflections on purpose by discussing questions such as, "How do you maintain individuality as part of a group?" to address the tension between holding on to personal values and convictions while also developing connections with others. Senehi calls these kind of questions "paradoxes" because they do not have right or wrong answers. In addition to class discussions, these questions are addressed through various creative activities, including debates, role-playing, and writing assignments. In one QUESTion class I observed, students held a debate to discuss the paradox of whether life is meant to be lived for oneself or for others. In another, students watched a short inspirational video in which people were invited to share stories with a stranger about what makes them feel successful, then students did a pair-share to tell stories of their own most successful moments.[3]

The class discussions, activities, and writing tasks are designed to provide students with skills needed to think about their lives in terms of possibility, purpose, and being a significant part of a larger whole. Those skills include considering the positive and negative consequences of their decisions, and the impact of their decisions on their potential for realizing their purpose. In a class at Theatre Arts Production Company School (TAPCo) in the Bronx, for example, students engaged in a lengthy discussion about how a serious romantic relationship at this stage of their life could impact their future goals. The teacher sparked this discussion by playing the song "7 Years" (by Lukas Graham), which describes goals and relationships through different phases of life. As with all QUESTion class discussions, there were no right answers. Some students felt a meaningful relationship that endures from high school years into adulthood is beneficial, while others saw the potential for a relationship at this stage to derail their life goals.

The outcomes of the QUESTion class run deeper than the explicit goal of providing students with skills and attitudes for pursuing future goals. Teachers of the class described some unexpected changes in their school after they started teaching the class. As students engaged in meaningful, open discussions with teachers and with each other, they began to reveal themselves, and the teachers started to see them differently—as people with values, concerns, fears, and hopes that did not fit their expectations about students. Lola Osoria, English teacher at Bronx High School for Law & Community Service said, "these kids have layers I didn't know they have."[4] Another teacher said that she had always seen her students as self-centered, concerned mostly about how they could get to the NBA or how they could get rich in the future. In the QUESTion class, she learned to see her students authentically and found that many of them are deeply concerned about helping other people and thinking about what they can do for others. As I listened to a class at TAPCo talk about their purpose, this concern for others dominated the discussion.

One student said his purpose is to be the best big brother he can be, and another said that he finds purpose in helping others feel the positive things he feels. They also expressed concerns about their own future in terms of meaning, purpose, and happiness. Some students worried that they might not find purpose and would end up graduating from high school only to get stuck in a meaningless job and purposeless life.

The student ambassador program is a six-month program for selected students who want to have an intensive experience with QUESTion Projects. Ambassadors develop their leadership capacities by facilitating QUESTion activities in their schools and communities, producing podcasts, and writing blog posts to express their perspectives and experiences related to big questions about life. As ambassadors for the QUESTion Project, they take on responsibility for raising awareness about the importance of having opportunities to explore big questions about life at school through these different community and online forums. The ambassador curriculum was created with in-depth input from about 100 students who participate in the QUESTion classes at their school. Students are also involved in reviewing and revising the curriculum and developing new lesson plans.

Senehi hopes that the QUESTion Project can even more broadly impact the culture of the schools by prioritizing and elevating the humanity of students, and making schools places of connectedness. The QUESTion class teachers suggest that is exactly the impact the program is having in their schools. Jamila Blades, a teacher at Bronx Center for Science and Mathematics, noticed that since their school started offering the QUESTion Project, students and teachers increasingly connect with one another on a human level and through their shared human experience. Importantly, the connections go both ways between teachers and students. Novelette Foote, a QUESTion class teacher at Belmont Preparatory Academy, said that her students like to turn the tables and ask her questions about herself in relation to the topics they're discussing. "They want to hear my stories, and hear that, 'wow, you're a person, like me.'"[5] Through these genuine, human connections, the presumptions that students and teachers hold about each other fall away, and trust grows between them. This trusting, connected climate makes their schools places where students feel motivated to contribute to creating a positive community and feel safe to take the risk of sharing their personal values and exploring their purpose with classmates and teachers.

Teachers are sometimes resistant when they are first asked by their principal to teach the QUESTion class. Their resistance fades as they see students engage authentically with each other. The curriculum offers a new challenge for teachers accustomed to asking questions to which they know the answers, and some say they find it inspiring to talk with students about what matters to them and the possibilities for their lives. By the end of their first year, some teachers are not only embracing the curriculum, but also sharing it with their colleagues. Osoria loved the class so much she chose to create follow-up sessions in her English classes so students could continue building on what they experienced the first year. She found ways to align the content from the five pillars with her English curriculum so she can infuse her English lessons with QUESTion concepts. For example, she adapts content from the QUESTion class as critical thinking prompts in lessons about a text or literary theme the class is studying. Blades said that teaching the QUESTion class has affected her teaching in her social studies classes as well, by affirming that the right approach is to avoid teaching to the test, and instead focus on making meaningful connections in the classroom and connecting classroom learning with real-life experiences.

Senehi shared some of the insights he has gained over several years of developing and implementing the QUESTion Project. One is that a program that engages students in exploring questions about purpose in life is best started with students who are at an age at which they can articulate themselves but are still young enough to more easily shift their perspectives and open themselves to change. The Open Future Institute first worked with college students, but at the suggestion of a mentor, shifted their focus to high school students. The teachers they worked with found that older students, juniors and seniors, were better prepared to talk about purpose in life than their ninth-grade peers; however, ninth graders were more receptive to the open-ended questions than twelfth graders, who likely had already formed strong social bonds and expectations of classroom learning that could make them a little more guarded. In response to this feedback from teachers and educators, Open Future Institute hopes to adapt the program for students as young as fifth grade.

Another key takeaway is the importance of getting buy-in from both principals and teachers by conveying the value and potential impact on students. Senehi found that principals may have prior experience with social-emotional programs that lack substance, or have learned through experience that the social, emotional, and character-development concepts that fill their email inbox are little more than trendy buzzwords. He suggests that principals need to see that teaching for purpose can be done in a way that is educationally substantial and profoundly impactful for students. When principals see the substance of the program, they can support the teacher-leaders who implement the class and promote buy-in at all levels in the school.

MOSAIC

The research team at Rutgers University's Social-Emotional and Character Development (SECD) Lab has long known that students reap tremendous benefits from both social-emotional learning and character education. Both support students to have healthy relationships, develop a strong sense of self, and take on a positive and constructive role in society. Despite the clear relationship between these two aspects of a young person's positive development, they are usually treated as distinct paths, with character education focused on instilling students with moral virtues and social-emotional learning referring to teaching students the skills and attitudes that will enable them to function effectively in social situations. The SECD Lab noticed that school programs more often reflected the differences between these two paths, rather than capitalizing on their overlap, and found that many schools divided their resources between separate, and sometimes contradictory, social-emotional learning and character programs.[6] To address this problem, they created a program that integrates social and emotional skills learning with development of character virtues. This program, Mastering Our Skills and Inspiring Character (MOSAIC), uses purpose as an organizing principle. Specifically, they designed MOSAIC to support positive purpose development among students in high-poverty middle schools, though the model is applicable to all schools.

MOSAIC seeks to develop student purpose by instilling a constellation of virtues that support purpose, at the same time teaching the social and emotional skills that support students to act on their purpose goals. Therefore, MOSAIC offers schools a single program that teaches social and emotional skills and develops character virtues, all toward the ultimate aim of supporting students to create positive purpose for their lives. In developing the program, the SECD team implemented a participatory feedback process, soliciting reactions to the curriculum and lessons from students and teachers throughout the year and reporting back how they altered the curriculum in response to the feedback. The participatory feedback process was instrumental in creating a culture of respect for participants' opinions that the MOSAIC team believed could positively influence student and teacher engagement in the program.

The SECD Lab partnered with the Jersey City Public School District, where it brought MOSAIC to several middle schools.[7] The basis of the work was a pilot project carried out in New Brunswick Middle School, for which that school received National School of Character recognition. Students at MOSAIC schools participate in the program all three years that they are in middle school, attending a MOSAIC class in their homeroom, advisory, or another time set aside by the principal, for fifteen to thirty minutes every school day. Each month covers a theme, starting in September with the theme *Why are we here: Finding our positive purpose*. The following months cover different aspects of purpose, such as *Making our selves/school/world better*, *Planning for the future,* and *Connecting with others and being a leader.* Each one-month unit focuses on a supporting virtue, such as generosity, gratitude, and diligence. The school year begins and ends with monthly units that emphasize the virtue of positive purpose. Every unit also provides instruction in social-emotional skills that support purpose, including communication, social problem solving, empathy, and emotional regulation.

The overall experience for students is a yearlong, daily program that integrates character virtues with social and emotional skills while reflecting on who they want to be and what their purpose is or will be. Teachers use diverse methods to engage students, including small-group discussion, writing reflections, drawing and creative activities, and role-play. The class is often taught by subject-matter teachers, so they can bring the MOSAIC concepts into all their courses and display MOSAIC materials in their classrooms, connecting students to the themes, virtues, and social skills they are learning in MOSAIC throughout the day. However, the ideal implementation of the program has all staff members in the school guiding a small group of students through the curriculum in an advisory period so that every student has a small MOSAIC cohort and a strong relationship with at least one caring adult at school.

The curriculum moves in wider circles of influence over the students' three years of participation. In sixth grade, students begin the program by discussing personal identity, then move on to talk about building a classroom community with a climate of trust so everyone can feel safe to participate. Next, the class shifts to a broader perspective, with students discussing how they can contribute to the community beyond the classroom through a positive purpose. Finally, in eighth grade, students discuss how they can have a positive impact in society by addressing significant social causes and committing to act on higher-order values such as justice, equality, and love. Over the course of three years, students learn essential life skills and develop character, motivated by purpose. As described by Maurice Elias, SECD Lab director, the social and emotional skills are the propeller that make it possible to keep moving forward in pursuit of goals, the character virtues are the rudder that steer you in the right direction and keep you on course, and purpose is the driver, deciding where to go in life.[8] Students can see the relevance of the MOSAIC class, because they see that the skills they are learning will help them in life, with their future in college and beyond, in specific ways that the students find salient.

The year begins with an exploration of positive purpose as a virtue. The class defines positive purpose as a group and discusses why it is important to have purpose. In a seventh-grade class at PS 17, students' responses showed that they were thinking about why it is important to have purpose for themselves as well as for contributing beyond themselves. One seventh grader said, "It keeps me motivated and on the right path." Another said, "You have a reason for doing what you're doing, a right and positive reason." A third student noticed the impact of having a purpose on others, "When you do something good that's your purpose, you can get your friends to help too." Next, they studied a young person who exemplifies the virtue of positive purpose. The class watched a short video about Malala Yousafzai, the Pakistani girl who was shot in the head by the Taliban in 2012 because of her advocacy for girls' education and became the youngest person ever to win the Nobel Peace Prize in 2014. The students talked about her purpose, going beyond a surface description to consider the virtues and values that led her to go to school despite the risk, and then channel that experience to influential work as a global advocate. They discussed the impact of her purpose, as one student said: "Because of her positive purpose, other people can hear her now. She took a stand and that got her noticed, and now her message goes further." In a MOSAIC class at PS 24, students worked on the social and emotional skills that support purpose, first describing each of the essential skills—communication, empathy, problem solving, and emotional regulation—with their ideas for how to do them. For example, a student described emotional regulation as "calming down by breathing in and out." Students then did a role-play activity in small groups to demonstrate each of the essential skills by acting them out in scenes in which someone does not have the skill but learns how to use it. Later in the month, students work on applying what they have learned about purpose-related skills and virtues by thinking about their own purpose and setting SMART goals to pursue their purpose.[9]

In addition to the daily classes, MOSAIC provides an ambassador program in which one or two students are selected from each class to lead regular social action discussions within the MOSAIC curriculum and participate in a school improvement project. Ambassadors meet monthly and collaborate on a "positive purpose project" that addresses an issue for improvement in the school based on what students want to see changed. For example, one group of ambassadors wanted to address the problem of their school being dirty. They developed a program to encourage students to think of the school as their home and as their responsibility to keep clean, and they organized a school beautification competition to engage students in cleaning up the school. At another school, the MOSAIC ambassadors recalled their own difficult transition to middle school and remembered seeing their classmates stressed and crying in sixth grade. For their purpose project, they developed a peer mentoring program to support incoming sixth graders with the transition to middle school. The ambassadors at another school were concerned about tension and bullying among students caused by lack of understanding between different ethnic groups. They generated a set of board games for the school that consisted of games from different countries, so that students could have fun together while learning to understand and appreciate different cultures.[10]

Together, the ambassadors use the goal-planning skills they learned in MOSAIC class and take the extra step to complete the project. The ambassadors then participate in a year-end demonstration and ceremony, in which student ambassadors from all MOSAIC schools meet, share their positive purpose projects, and receive awards. The ambassador program emphasizes leadership development and community service as an extension of the social-emotional learning and character development of the MOSAIC class. It supports students to think beyond individual purpose to understand that purpose is also collective. The program is targeted at students who would most benefit from a structured opportunity to develop leadership skills, such as students who show potential but may not thrive in the classroom setting, or students who struggle with behavior at school because of the challenges they face at home. Rosalyn Barnes, principal at PS 24, said that the ambassador program is especially helpful for students who are required to take on adult responsibilities at home, such as taking care of siblings and preparing meals, because it allows them to shift their leadership skills to age-appropriate activities and pursue a purpose that aligns with their adolescent interests.

The principals of MOSAIC schools do not necessarily think of it as a purpose program, but emphasize its value as a social-emotional development program. They describe dramatic shifts in the climate and culture of their schools, and student behavior, since adopting MOSAIC.

Francine Luce, principal at MS 40, noted that the school dropped from a 12 percent suspension rate by October in years prior, to less than 1 percent since adopting the MOSAIC program. Robert Brower, principal at PS 17, felt that students and teachers were more engaged in productive learning since adopting the MOSAIC program, pointing to the calm, positive energy that filled the school building, and noted that his office sees fewer student referrals. At PS 24, Barnes noted visible changes in individual students. For example, a student who was so disconnected that he often left the classroom and was known for being destructive at school was selected to be an ambassador. As a result of participating in the ambassador project, he not only became more engaged in his classes, but independently took on community service projects in the school, working with the assistant principal or the custodian to make improvements to the school instead of destroying it.[11]

Much of the positive change is attributed to the connections made between teachers and students through the MOSAIC program. Although it is not always possible, students ideally participate in the class daily, and stay with the same MOSAIC teacher for three years, so relationships build consistently and endure. In the class, they discuss topics that are meaningful to students and allow students to share openly with the teacher and each other. Brower said that the teachers at PS 17 were reluctant to have these open-ended discussions at first, and some worried that talking about virtues in the classroom would "open Pandora's box." However, the teachers found that their fears were unfounded. The open format of the class discussions and focus on virtues and purpose allowed them to get to know their students and break through the initial perceptions and assumptions that characterized student-teacher relationships. Where previously interactions between teachers and students were led by negativity and preconceptions, teachers learned to be nonjudgmental when listening to students. In return, students felt trust and connection at school, and learned to talk with teachers about the challenges that affected their behavior and participation in class, rather than acting out.

Principals also noted positive outcomes that they attributed specifically to the purpose development aspects of the MOSAIC program.

They noticed that students more often come to adults with ideas and proposals for improving the school. In response, adults in the school engage with students more openly. They listen to students' ideas and concerns and share feedback that is more authentic to real-world collaborative problem solving and community building, compared to the top-down feedback that can typify student-teacher interactions. Relationships, especially between teachers and student ambassadors, are more collegial—as Brower described it, there is more laughter—because students and teachers work together toward a shared purpose and students are respected for their ideas and abilities. Principal Luce said that the focus on purpose had an important impact on their most disadvantaged students: "It provides training in becoming who they truly want to be so they don't fall into the same patterns in their community, patterns of drug use, early pregnancy, and gangs." She also found that the purpose curriculum is beneficial for all her students because it provides them with language and skills that support their successful transition into high school.

LEARNING FROM PURPOSE EDUCATION PROGRAMS

The work on purpose education programs and interventions is still emerging, and there is little evidence proving which aspects of these programs might be effective for supporting student purpose development. Regardless, they each were developed with careful attention to the existing purpose development research, combined with expertise that comes from working directly with students and teachers, and have evolved through the learning that comes with the experience and data gained along the way. They have been tested in school settings and revised to better fit their particular settings and to be more effective. They offer ideas that educators can use to nurture purpose in their students, in their classrooms, and in their schools with some confidence that they are tried and have shown positive effects. There are at least five elements that emerge again and again in these programs that appear to be key to positive, and even purposeful, outcomes. First, they provide students guided opportunity to explore, clarify, and strengthen positive values, ponder big questions about life, and reflect on what matters most to them. Second, they engage students in future-minded goal setting, asking them to think big and then set smaller, incremental goals to work toward a larger and more distant goal. Third, they ask students to take action steps, often working in collaboration with other students, to make a positive impact in their community or in the lives of others. Fourth, they instill a sense of social responsibility and community connection, showing students that they have a significant role to play in the world and guiding them to develop that role. Finally, they develop students' and teachers' voices, encouraging them to share themselves with each other and demonstrate agency and leadership in shaping their school, community, and world.

These programs are innovative and experimental, with some still in the pilot phase of their implementation. They shared with me what they are learning as they gain experience in schools, not only what is working, but also what has not worked and the changes they have made along the way. Some have learned that younger is better when it comes to purpose education, and high school is too late to start. By high school, students find it challenging to adapt to the open dialogue and vulnerability in the classroom that these programs require. Some program leaders also found that students needed to start in middle school, or even earlier, to develop the skills and mind-sets required to take on a substantial purpose project in high school. Some learned that purpose programs are more effective if they are offered as electives in high school, rather than required, because students are more engaged when the program is optional. However, some also found that it is better to require the program in middle school, so that all students have exposure before going to high school. Also, by requiring it in middle school, the program contributes to transforming the culture of the school into a setting that normalizes school as a place where students and teachers explore values, goals, and purpose together.

Lessons were also learned about who should implement a purpose education program, in terms of teacher selection, but especially in terms of teacher professional development. In most cases, teachers already in the school were selected and trained to teach the program. Teachers might be selected as school leaders given the responsibility of implementing the program, as is the case with Quaglia Institute. Some teachers asked to be involved, while others were grudgingly recruited. In the process of deciding who should teach the class or convey the program to students, some program leaders found that certain teacher qualities were vital to the program's success. They noticed that teachers adapted more easily to the program if they were compassionate and willing to engage students in authentic, open-ended dialogue, and be vulnerable enough to share their own stories with students. Teachers, as some program directors found, must be willing to raise their voice in the school, and encourage students to do the same. The Future Project, which brings in its own team to do projects outside of class time, learned that their Dream Directors should be uniquely dynamic, energetic, creative, and inspirational personalities to be purpose role models and mentors for high school students. Regardless of whether these programs sought teachers with ideal qualities for teaching purpose, they all said that teacher training is vital to program success. Most teachers reported that the curriculum and activities offered by these programs were unfamiliar, and even uncomfortable to do with students without intensive training. Erin Hayes, a Project Wayfinder teacher, said that the three-day summer training made the difference between teachers at her school who took up the program and those who did not: "It helped to wrap your mind in the tools." In most cases, teachers who wrapped their mind in the tools then had the autonomy to adapt them. For example, Hayes selected some but not all Wayfinder tools to integrate into her course. Dream Director Eve King said that the two-week training program, which taught her how to use all of The Future Project tools and course materials, prepared her to select from and adapt the tools according to the projects her students were working on throughout the year. Noble Impact selects teachers who show imagination and social intelligence, trains them in the program learning goals, then encourages them to create activities that will help students reach those goals.

Finally, program leaders learned that purpose can be a central and organizing piece of a purpose-development program, but other components are needed. Most found that purpose works as a primary outcome, but students need a broader set of social and emotional skills to develop purpose. Both Project Wayfinder and the QUESTion Project started as purpose-education programs, but evolved to become comprehensive social-emotional learning programs with the ultimate aim of supporting students to create a purposeful life. Noble Impact learned that social and emotional skills are a necessary foundation for the civic innovation and social entrepreneurship projects they engage students in to develop purpose. MOSAIC started as a more comprehensive social-emotional learning program, established with purpose as an organizing principle and teaching students social-emotional skills and character virtues to provide a foundation for purpose development. Aligning with longstanding philosophy, theory, and research on purpose, these programs converged on the idea that purpose is a multifaceted character strength that requires ongoing attention to many aspects of social and emotional development in an environment that prioritizes students' humanity.

CHAPTER ELEVEN

Creating a Place for Purpose

Throughout this book, I have argued for making purpose the purpose of school and tried to provide educators with the inspiration and encouragement to make purpose a priority in their work with students. I have avoided being prescriptive, because I believe that teachers are the best sources of ideas for giving purpose life in their classrooms. The work that we researchers and theorists do can only get us part of the way there. Real change happens when ideas are put into practice by the people who work with students every day. To that end, I want to close with thoughts for educators and other school personnel, about what you can do to start creating a culture of purpose in your school. We are fortunate that the tide seems to be turning, as teachers, school leaders, and parents are increasingly willing to stand up to a faceless system and say enough is enough. Our children's lives—their humanity, their self-worth, their purpose—are more important than the churning machinery of the system.

Before getting to action steps, here is a quick summary of some of the ideas for supporting purpose development that were discussed in this book. I described purpose as a multidimensional concept, a source of drive and direction in our lives that integrates meaningful and future-minded goal setting, beyond-the-self motivation, and action to accomplish goals. Purpose develops when the capacity for each of these dimensions develops and can emerge as early as late childhood or adolescence. Adults at school can provide the conditions that nurture the development and integration of these dimensions toward purpose, and in doing so, let students know that their life purpose is a priority for their education. Above all, adults can provide students with encouraging and supportive relationships, and show authentic interest in students' values, interests, concerns, and dreams, while also pushing students to explore, expand, and deepen their values, interests, and goals. Students' potential for purpose can be sparked by adults who model compassion and prosocial activity. Purpose can emerge in a school environment where students feel a sense of belonging and community, and where they can safely exercise autonomy and agency. A purpose-supportive school environment will also provide time in learning activities for play, inquiry, and students' intentional engagement with ideas and materials. Project methods, in particular, can provide opportunities for this playful and intentional engagement in the context of purpose-supporting "real world" questions and problems. Teachers can consider ways to help students attach purpose to what they are learning, for example, by having students reflect on how their learning enables them to work toward becoming who they want to be and how they want to contribute to the world; by designing learning activities that are sufficiently open for students to engage with intentionally; or providing learning experiences from which students can draw relevance to their personal values, questions, or goals. Providing opportunities for reflection in various forms is essential for helping students develop purpose at school, such as reflection on the purpose, process, and outcome of learning activities; reflection on big questions about life, and reflection on personal values and goals in the context of learning. Finally, purpose development is supported when students have opportunities to act on their goals and beyond-the-self concerns, which allows for both agency to develop and for the integration of the dimensions of purpose.

The most ambitious goal of this book is to transform our schools from the inside, by encouraging educators to create a culture of purpose in their schools. If you are one of those educators, or are in some other way a member of a school community that could be more purposeful, what action steps can you take now to get started? Following is a list of entry points—actionable ideas to take whether you want to dip a toe into creating a more purposeful school culture or dive in. The first step, which encompasses all the following action ideas, is to *start where you are*. Every educator is coming at this possibility from a different place, with a different existing school culture, and with different limitations and resources. Therefore, I continue to avoid being prescriptive, but hope to inspire educators and other school personnel to connect with and build from the following actions in whatever way make sense for their circumstances. The following steps are written to be specific to teachers, but in most cases, can be adapted by those working in different school roles.

Reflect on Your Purpose

A good starting point for anyone who works with students is to reflect on what gives you a sense of purpose, and what gives you purpose in working with students, by doing the purpose reflection activity in chapter 1. This is not a one-time activity, but something that can be revisited every summer to prepare for the school year. By doing so, you can start each year with a renewed sense of purpose for your work and ready to convey that sense of purpose to your students. You will also be better able to convey the purpose of what you are teaching to your students, and why they should learn it, if you have a deep sense of the purpose of that content yourself.

DO AND REFLECT: If you have not already, do the reflection activity in chapter 1. What connections can you make between your purpose for teaching or in life and your existing teaching goals? How can your purpose or aspirations as a teacher organize and drive your day-to-day teaching goals and tasks? Does it point to any daily goals or tasks that should be given more priority? Or less priority? In what ways does your current practice align with your values and purpose, and in what ways do they diverge? What did you learn from the purpose reflection activity that you can explore to make changes to your practice?

Ask Big, Open Questions

Another starting point, especially in schools where student voice is not already prioritized, is to introduce open-ended questions in the classroom. By asking questions to which you do not know the answer, you open the door to student voice, meaning, and intention in your classroom, and create potential for more positive relationships with your students, all of which will form a foundation for purpose to build on. As we saw in several of the purpose programs described in previous chapters, teachers who started asking their students big, open questions in the classroom found that their students were eager to discuss these big questions at school, to share their ideas, goals, and concerns, and their beliefs about society and the world. Big questions that get students to think and talk about their place in the world beyond themselves, and about the impact on the lives of people other than themselves, will be especially relevant to developing purpose. Discussing big questions at school might be foreign to students at first, but the experience of the purpose programs shows that students warm up to it with practice and soon benefit from improved relationships with teachers, greater sense of relevance to what they are learning, and increased sense of belonging at school. The experiences of the purpose programs also suggest that it is ideal to start having open discussions about big questions earlier than we might expect. Even elementary students can benefit from discussing big questions and exploring their dreams, values, and what they find meaningful in the classroom, and those who start this young will be comfortable doing so by the time they go to middle and high school, when they will have increased capacity for thoughtful, purpose-exploring discussion.

DO AND REFLECT: Revisit the big questions posed in chapters 1 and 4, and in the program profiles in chapters 6, 8, and 10. With these models in mind, what are some big questions that you can pose to your students to initiate open-ended discussion? Can you identify similar questions that relate to your curriculum or that could engage meaningful discussion about a topic in your curriculum? What has been your experience with asking students big, open-ended questions in the classroom? What did you learn about your students when you have done so?

Do Purposeful Projects

Not all schools and teachers are situated to use project-based learning, but the idea of purposeful projects can be applied to make for more purposeful instruction and learning. Whether you are at a fully integrated project-based learning school or have never done projects with students, the elements of purposeful projects can be used to evaluate your own teaching in terms of how it might be supporting student purpose development. As a starting point, remember Kilpatrick's definition of learning projects as "purposeful activity" in chapter 7. Although he was describing the project method, any learning activity that we engage students in should be purposeful. To be purposeful, learning activities should be meaningful to students. Students should have opportunities to reflect—in writing or class discussion—on the meaning and purpose of what they are doing in the classroom, not only at the end of a lesson or unit, but during as well. Learning activities should be authentic and relevant to students' lives outside of the classroom and raise their awareness of issues in their community and in the world that require human solutions. Learning units should sustain attention to a topic or question long enough for students to make a meaningful connection to the topic and gain deep understanding of the material. The project method—especially service projects, social entrepreneurship, and other applied forms of problem-based learning—is sometimes used by educators seeking to foster student purpose, because it is a natural fit for the active, beyond-the-self–oriented, goal-driven engagement with the world that indicates purpose. Although there is yet little evidence that project-based learning increases students' purpose, it is reasonable to conclude that projects—when implemented as purposeful projects—give students practice in the skills and strengths needed for purposeful goal pursuit, such as self-regulation, social agency, and social awareness. If you do not use project-based learning but want to create a more purposeful learning experience for your students, consider exploring the role that purposeful projects can play in your curriculum.

DO AND REFLECT: Reflecting on some of the examples described in chapter 7, what are some takeaway ideas or inspirations that can inform your teaching, whether you do projects or not? If you already use project-based methods, are they purposeful? Do they invite students' questions, meaning, and intentions? Do students reflect throughout to make sense of their activities? Do they reflect to consider the impact their activities are having on others or in the world? If you are not using project-based, inquiry or service-learning methods, what elements of project methods—or purposeful activities—can you adapt to your teaching to make it more purposeful?

Collaborate

Purpose is not an individual pursuit, even if it reflects what is meaningful or central to our unique identity. It is by definition a way of engaging with the world beyond ourselves. It makes sense, then, that collaborating with others is essential if the goal is to create a purposeful school culture. An entry point for creating a culture of purpose is to identify colleagues who share your interest and explore purpose together; explore your purpose as individuals, as a school, and as a community. You can do this using the purpose reflection activity in chapter 1 with a small group of colleagues. By doing so, you will each have the powerful experience of being heard when talking about the things that matter most to you. You will also see the different perspectives of people you work with, which will support you in being more perspective-taking and empathetic in the classroom. Opening a discussion of purpose among colleagues is also a way to generate new ideas for creating a more purposeful school culture. Beyond talking about purpose, you can examine how your school works in teams and whether your teaching teams are structured to support or inhibit purpose. At the high school level, use of grade-level teams is recognized as an important way to build strong relationships between teachers and students, which is essential for supporting student purpose.[1] Grade-level teams can focus their discussion and reflection on individual students, rather than solely on content and instruction, and build a strong network of support for each student. As a result, they can support student purpose because they enable positive and caring relationships that ensure that students feel safe to share their interests and concerns at school. They also allow for more robust interdisciplinary project work, which can lead to more authentic, relevant, and purposeful projects.

DO AND REFLECT: Revisit the purpose reflection in chapter 1 with some of your colleagues, first to share your purpose and values as a teacher with each other, then adapt the questions to your school, grade-level, or other learning community. For example, the questions about what is most important to you and how you spend your time can be adapted to be, "What is most important to our school?" and "How does our school use our students' time?"

Develop Your Social-Emotional Strengths

Teachers are better prepared to support students' social and emotional development when they have taken time to develop their own social and emotional competencies.[2] As described above, teachers can support purpose when they are purposeful themselves, so they can focus classroom activities on what matters, convey a sense of purpose in learning activities, and be role models of purpose for students. Another important social-emotional strength teachers can develop to support student purpose is the capacity to respond compassionately to students. With greater compassion, teachers can have more purpose-supportive relationships with students and establish a classroom climate that is emotionally and psychologically safe for all students. Adults with a strong sense of compassion will also be empowered to prioritize students' humanity over the mechanics of the system. A third social-emotional strength that is essential for teachers who want to create a culture of purpose in their schools, as learned by Quaglia Institute, is self-worth and the related strength of agency.[3] To assert the priority of student purpose in their school, teachers may need to break boundaries, which requires teachers to feel confident that their values and beliefs matter to the school community. With increased self-worth and agency, teachers are better able to recognize their own power and strive to transform the culture of the school. Aside from these purpose-specific strengths and skills, teachers need support to develop the general social and emotional skills that enable them to have positive relationships with students and manage their own stress in the classroom.

DO AND REFLECT: When have your social-emotional strengths been an asset in your teaching? When have you wished you could have handled an interpersonal or emotional situation in the classroom differently? Is your classroom a compassionate space where students feel a sense of community and feel safe to explore purpose? If so, what do you do to make it that way? If not, what can you do to make it more so? There are growing numbers of professional development programs aimed at supporting teachers' development of social and emotional competencies. Seek out and identify resources for educator social-emotional development for yourself and your school. For example, at the time of writing, organizations such as the Greater Good Science Center at UC Berkeley and the Center for Reaching & Teaching the Whole Child, which started at San Jose State University, offer training and other resources for teachers to develop their own social-emotional strengths and learn strategies for teaching social-emotional skills to students.[4]

Claim Your Power

Most educators who want to make changes to their school are quickly faced with obstacles and barriers that can thwart their effort before they have a chance to make progress. The structural and systemic barriers to changing school culture, and even making changes to teaching practice, can be daunting. In chapter 9, you read about Eric Liu's power curriculum, which he developed to provide citizens with the skills and knowledge we need to cause civic change when we do not hold the power. Schools and districts are systems that can be impacted with the same tools. What are the barriers to change in your school or district? Ineffective leadership? Lack of parent support? A culture that does not support innovation? Too many conflicting demands on your time? I hope the programs and examples provided throughout this book show that teaching for purpose is not impossible in today's challenging education policy environment. The schools described in these pages are public, charter, and private. They are high-poverty inner-city schools, middle class suburban schools, and affluent schools. Most of them work within the same policy constraints that all public schools in the US work in today. One of the big differences seen in these schools is leaders who reset their priorities to align with what they know their students need rather than what the system needs. Therefore, if there are barriers preventing you from creating a culture of purpose in your school, you need to find ways to break through them, and you can. Teachers, who often lack the power of school leaders, can learn from Liu's plan for gaining power as described in chapter 9. In short, he suggests becoming aware of where the power is in your community or system, including how and why the current barriers were put into place, then begin participating in the power system by attending meetings, organizing with colleagues, and advocating with those who control the power. He further suggests asking "what if . . . ?" to identify actionable ideas for making change, even small changes, and work with colleagues to implement them. Through small changes, you can make cracks in the barriers to change and gain the momentum that comes with success.

DO AND REFLECT: Identify a barrier that gets in the way of purposeful work with students. Read the power that resulted in those barriers, getting beyond the first and second layers of blame to recognize the way power works to create barriers to change in your school. Write power by participating in committees and attending board meetings that are relevant to your concerns. What are some "what ifs . . . ?" you can identify to effectively get through those barriers? Start small and connect with colleagues who share your interests and concerns.

Rethink Assessment

I did not address assessment in this book, and for good reason. Assessment of social-emotional learning and character strengths development is currently a hot and contested topic, and tools for assessing purpose development are not at a point where they can be recommended for classroom use. There are many efforts underway to figure out how to assess social-emotional learning and character development, including but not limited to purpose, and these efforts must address the serious implications that could arise from giving students a score for aspects of their emotional development and moral character. All of that said, it is true that the content that is assessed gets more attention in the school day, and the demands of state-level accountability can overwhelm efforts to focus on non-academic development. The potential for developing student purpose is diminished by the pervasive emphasis on academic testing and grades in schools today. When the only tools used to assess student growth amount to single score measures—GPAs, quizzes, standardized tests—students are discouraged from exploring what is most meaningful to them, taking time to reflect on their values, developing awareness of the circumstances and experiences of others around them, identifying problems in the world they want to solve, and dreaming in broad and expansive ways about who they want to become. In short, there is no room for purpose in a classroom overwhelmed by academic testing. Yet, as was noted above, teachers and leaders in many public schools, subjected to the same accountability demands as all other public schools, are finding ways to bring purpose into their classrooms. The accountability pressures put on schools by the policy structure will continue to evolve, hopefully in favor of more purpose-friendly assessments. In the meantime, the challenge for teachers and school leaders is to question how you assess students and the role that assessments and other methods of scoring students play in shaping the culture of your school and your students' lives. How are you evaluating your students' worth and potential when you assess them? Do your assessments support their personal growth as a student and their sense of purpose about what they are learning? How does testing effect the social and emotional climate in your classroom?

DO AND REFLECT: Assess your assessments. What do your assessments say about what you prioritize for your students? How do your assessments relate to creating a culture of purpose in your schools? Do your assessments encourage students to be inquisitive, compassionate, and purpose-driven? Or do they only encourage competition and compliance? Are there ways to reconsider how you assess student progress?

We have seen already that creating a culture of purpose at school is not incompatible with academic achievement and can even support students toward academic success. As Quaglia Institute found in surveying thousands of students, those who indicated that they felt school was relevant to their future were eleven times more likely to report feeling academically motivated, and those who said that their teachers were supportive and cared about them as an individual were seven times more likely to report feeling academically motivated, compared to students who reported less caring teacher support.[5] Our challenge is to take the leap and choose to prioritize students' purpose. Though emerging, the research on school climate, student-teacher relationships, deeper learning methods, and brief purpose interventions suggests that we will not sacrifice academic achievement by doing so and may contribute to greater academic motivation, engagement, and performance.

Although teachers are the driving change agents who can provide a more purposeful classroom climate and learning experience for students, the programs investigated throughout this book made clear that principals play an essential role in taking that leap to prioritizing student purpose in their schools. Several school and district leaders I spoke with said that they shifted their priorities to be more student-centered, *human*-centered, compassionate, and purpose-driven, because it was the right thing to do for their students. Their effectiveness as change agents in their schools is evident, and it echoes the framework for principal-led reform described by Michael Fullan in his book *The Principal.* Fullan calls for principals to become "learning leaders" whose first job is to facilitate the collaborative learning of teachers. Principals can become learning leaders, in Fullan's model, by shifting away from prevalent "wrong drivers" of reform to their counterpart "right drivers."[6] The first wrong driver, he argues, is emphasizing accountability to measure teacher effectiveness instead of investing in capacity building, such as resources for teacher learning and professional development. As we saw throughout this book, teaching for purpose requires intensive teacher training, and the school leaders we met believed it was worth the investment. Likewise, Fullan argues that systemic change must be driven by collaborative teacher effort, rather than the wrong driver of individualistic approaches, and instructional decisions should be driven by pedagogy rather than technology. The principles behind both of these wrong drivers—individualism and technology—apply to work with students as well as teachers and explain why I do not examine the trend of *personalized learning* as a strategy for developing student purpose. On the surface, personalized learning seems a good fit for purpose development because it enables students to tailor their learning to their unique needs. In its current form, however, it emphasizes individualism and technology—neither of which should be driving pedagogical change in schools that aim to create a culture of purpose. Instead, the focus should be on shaping a school community and culture characterized by healthy student-teacher relationships, where students can see that they are valued members of something larger than themselves, and where learning is deep, reflective, and meaningful.

Ultimately, Fullan argues for principals to be agents of change in their schools by driving their teams forward and prioritizing teacher development and learning. Principals can, if they choose, establish purpose as the organizing principle for their school, collaborate with their team to develop an institutional purpose for their school, identify an overarching pedagogical approach that provides for deep and purposeful learning, and take the lead in developing teacher capacity in the areas of pedagogical practice and social and emotional competencies (which would include school climate). By reflecting on and identifying institutional purpose for their school, principals can implement strategies for change suggested by Douglas Reeves in his book *Leading Change in Your School.*[7] The first strategy Reeves suggests is "pulling the weeds." With institutional purpose identified, principals can be intentional about eliminating existing reforms and programs that are not aligned with that purpose, then highlight what is working (the "flowers") and shift the emphasis to teacher capacity building in the areas that will support the school's purpose.

Principals, teachers, staff, and students can collaboratively develop an institutional purpose for their school by adapting the purpose reflection activity from chapter 1. Although statements of purpose are standard for schools, the emphasis here is not on the statement that encapsulates the driving values, aspirations, and identity of the program, but the process of creating the driving vision. Ambassadors for different stakeholders in the school community can reflect together on what matters most for school life and education and what their central values are, then identify what they aspire to and the goals they want to accomplish, and finally discuss how the school uses time and other resources. Next, they can assess the alignment between the predominant values, goals, and use of resources. Do the highest priority goals align with the values identified by stakeholders? Does the allotment of student time align with the goals that are most important to teachers and students?

Next comes determining where a school is in terms of development toward fully realized purpose. Does the school dabble in endless reform efforts without any sense of coherence, meaning, purpose, or identity as an institution? Does the school have lofty aspirations that are not being pursued realistically or systematically? Is the school goal driven, but by the wrong vision of success, such as one that serves the interests of bureaucrats, politicians, or profiteers at the expense of students, teachers, families, and the community? Schools with fully realized purpose aspire to make a positive contribution to the world, for example by serving as the heart of a healthy local community, acting as a role model of effective innovation for other schools, setting high expectations for all students and committing to help students meet those expectations, or providing all students with a solid foundation for creating a life of purpose. They can identify specific opportunities for capacity building that will enable them to work toward making that contribution, and they allocate resources in line with that goal.

Demand for the six purpose programs described in this book far outpaces what they can provide, a welcome indicator that the pendulum is finally swinging. School leaders and teachers across the US are taking a stand against a rudderless system driven in all directions by politics, greed, and a dysfunctional cycle of blame. They are seeking a new paradigm for schools that puts students first, both as children and as the creators of society they will soon become. Based on over twenty years of experience in education and youth development research, I argue that nothing less than purpose in life should be the driving paradigm for our schools. What our children need, and what our society needs, are schools where students learn what kind of person they want to be, what values and personal strengths they want to cultivate, how they want to contribute to their world, and how to act on their most aspirational future goals. In other words, we need schools that teach students how to create lives of purpose. I wrote this book to examine the question "What if purpose were the purpose of school?" because I believe that there is a bidirectional effect of making schools purposeful. Students can develop into more purposeful people, but also, schools can become more compassionate, community-oriented, and meaningful, with deeper learning and greater expectations for student achievement. Students become more engaged in their learning because it is relevant and active. They develop social awareness, autonomy, and agency that they can use in the classroom and beyond. They can connect what they are learning to broader and more meaningful future aspirations. Teachers and school staff have a stronger sense of purpose for what they do and more effective collaboration with their colleagues. They do more learning along with students and less direct instruction. They develop their own social and emotional capacities and have healthier relationships with their students. With healthier relationships and more purposeful learning, they spend less time managing behavior problems in the classroom.

Schools that prioritize student purpose as an outcome do not expect children to plow headlong into the future with no sense of what is going on in the world around them, missing out on childhood along the way. Nor does such a school allow children to drift aimlessly, giving up on them for not fitting the narrow demands of the system. Prioritizing purpose means raising expectations for all our children, but not in a narrow band of academic skills. Instead, we expect them to create nothing less than a life of purpose for themselves by developing their personal strengths and values, reflecting on what it means to be a good person, engaging deeply with challenging questions and problems in the world, and envisioning, planning for, and acting on a future that expresses their personal vision of success.

NOTES

CHAPTER 1

1. William Damon, Jenni Menon, and Kendall Cotton Bronk, "The Development of Purpose During Adolescence," *Applied Developmental Science* 7, no. 3 (2003): 119–28. This definition of purpose was first outlined in Damon, Menon, and Bronk, and has been widely used in the research on purpose since then, although it is not universally accepted.
2. The Stanford Youth Purpose Interview was developed for the Youth Purpose Project, which originated in 2005 and was funded by the John Templeton Foundation. Under the leadership of William Damon, the research team at the Stanford Center on Adolescence developed the interview protocol for use with eleven- to twenty-three-year-old study participants. The full interview first developed for use with adolescents can be found in: William Damon, *The Path to Purpose: Helping Our Children Find Their Calling in Life*, (New York: Free Press, 2008), 183–86.
3. Brandy P. Quinn, "Learning from the Wisdom of Practice: Teachers' Educational Purposes as Pathways to Supporting Adolescent Purpose in Secondary Classrooms," *Journal of Education for Teaching* 42, no. 5 (2016): 602–23.
4. Damon, *Path to Purpose*, 59–70; Seana Moran, "Purpose: Giftedness in Intrapersonal Intelligence," *High Ability Studies* 20, no. 2 (2009): 143–59.
5. Anna Vazeou-Nieuwenhuis, Edward Orehek, and Michael F. Scheier, "The Meaning of Action: Do Self-Regulatory Processes Contribute to a Purposeful Life?" *Personality and Individual Differences* 116 (2017): 115–22.
6. Sonja Lyubomirsky, *The How of Happiness: A Practical Approach to Getting the Life You Want* (New York: The Penguin Group, 2007), 205–14.
7. Sara Konrath, Andrea Fuhrel-Forbis, Alina Lou, and Stephanie Brown, "Motives for Volunteering are Associated with Mortality Risk in Older Adults," *Health Psychology* 31, no. 1 (2012); Arthur A. Stukas et al., "Motivations to Volunteer and Their Associations with Volunteers' Well-Being," *Nonprofit and Voluntary Sector Quarterly* 45, no. 1 (2016): 112–32; Omri Gillath et al., "Attachment, Caregiving, and Volunteering: Placing Volunteerism in an Attachment-Theoretical Framework," *Personal Relationships* 12, no. 4 (2005): 425–46.

8. Brandy P. Quinn, "Learning from the Wisdom of Practice: Teachers' Educational Purposes as Pathways to Supporting Adolescent Purpose in Secondary Classrooms," *Journal of Education for Teaching* 42, no. 5 (2016): 602–23.
9. Oxford Dictionaries definition: https://en.oxforddictionaries.com/definition/passion.
10. William Burnett and David J. Evans, *Designing Your Life: How to Build a Well-Lived, Joyful Life* (New York: Alfred A. Knopf, 2017), xxix.
11. Emily Morton et al., "Hiding in Plain Sight: Older U.S. Purpose Exemplars," *Journal of Positive Psychology,* Manuscript under revision (2018).
12. Heather Malin et al., "Adolescent Purpose Development: Exploring Empathy, Discovering Roles, Shifting Priorities, and Creating Pathways," *Journal of Research on Adolescence* 24, no. 1 (2013): 186–99.
13. Kendall Cotton Bronk, *Purpose in Life: A Critical Component of Optimal Youth Development* (New York: Springer, 2016); Matthew J. Bundick et al., "Thriving across the Life Span," in *The Handbook of Life-Span Development*, ed. Willis F. Overton (Hoboken, N.J.: John Wiley & Sons, Inc., 2010), 1–24.
14. The javelin image is a reference to the Ancient Greeks, specifically Aristotle, who laid the philosophical groundwork for our contemporary understanding of purpose in his writing on meaningful happiness, called *eudaimonia*. For contemporary psychologists, eudaimonia distinguishes the well-being found in having a sense of purpose from hedonistic happiness, which is pleasurable but less fulfilling; Aristotle, *Nicomachean Ethics*, Translated by Terrence Irwin, 2nd ed. (Indianapolis, IN: Hackett Publishing Company, Inc., 1999).
15. Seana Moran, "Youth Purpose Worldwide: A Tapestry of Possibilities." *Journal of Moral Education* 46, no. 3 (2017): 231–44; Patrick Cook-Deegan, "Wayfinding Our Purpose," in *Purpose Rising: A Global Movement of Transformation and Meaning*, eds. Emanuel Kuntzelman and Dustin DiPerna (Bright Alliance, 2017), 241–259.

CHAPTER 2

1. Michael W. Casby, "Developmental Assessment of Play," *Communication Disorders Quarterly* 24, no. 4 (2003): 175–83.
2. Walter Mischel and Nancy Baker, "Cognitive Appraisals and Transformations in Delay Behavior," *Journal of Personality and Social Psychology* 31, no. 2 (1975): 254–61; Walter Mischel et al., "'Willpower' Over the Life Span: Decomposing Self-Regulation," *Social Cognitive and Affective Neuroscience* 6, no. 2 (2010): 252–56.
3. A review of research on children's play shows a mixed relationship between sociodramatic play and executive function. Angeline S. Lillard et al., "The

Impact of Pretend Play on Children's Development: A Review of the Evidence," *Psychological Bulletin* 139 no. 1 (2013): 1–34.

Bodrova, Germeroth, and Leong responded by arguing that the theory is strong, especially grounded in Vygotsky's theory of sociocultural development, and some of the research evidence supports this theory. Some research using play curriculum based on Vygotsky's theory have had promising results for supporting self-regulation development. Elena Bodrova, Carrie Germeroth, and Deborah J. Leong, "Play and Self-Regulation," *American Journal of Play* 6 no. 1 (2013): 111–123.

Moreover, theory about positive youth development suggests a relationship between purpose and a more mature form of intentional self-regulation (goal selection, optimization, and compensation, or SOC), which suggests that having a purpose goal can support development of self-regulation skills. Christopher M. Napolitano et al., "The Development of Intentional Self-Regulation in Adolescence," in *Positive Youth Development Advances in Child Development and Behavior,* eds. Richard M. Lerner, Jacqueline V. Lerner and Janette B. Benson, (2011): 19–38.

4. Heather Malin, "Making Meaningful: Intention in Children's Art Making," *International Journal of Art & Design Education* 32, no. 1 (2013): 6–17; Heather Malin, "Creating a Children's Art World: Negotiating Participation, Identity, and Meaning in the Elementary School Art Room," *International Journal of Education and the Arts* 13, no. 6 (2012).
5. Jean Lave and Etienne Wenger, *Situated Learning: Legitimate Peripheral Participation*, (Cambridge: Cambridge University Press, 1991); Etienne Wenger, *Communities of Practice: Learning, Meaning, and Identity*, (Cambridge, UK: Cambridge University Press, 1998).
6. Jonathan David Fineberg, *Discovering Child Art: Essays on Childhood, Primitivism and Modernism.* (Princeton, NJ: Princeton University Press, 2001).
7. Malin, "Children's Art Making," 6–17.
8. Names of all minors interviewed have been changed to pseudonyms throughout the book.
9. Malin, "Children's Art Making," 10–15.
10. Bruno Bettelheim, *The Uses of Enchantment* (New York: Vintage Books, 1989).
11. Gordon Wells, *The Meaning Makers: Children Learning Language and Using Language to Learn*, (Portsmouth, N.H.: Heinemann Educational Books, 1986).
12. This idea was discussed in a series of articles written in *The Atlantic* in 2012. Peg Tyre, "The Writing Revolution," *The Atlantic*, September 25, 2012, https://www.theatlantic.com/magazine/archive/2012/10/the-writing-

revolution/309090/; Robert Pondiscio, "How Self-Expression Damaged My Students," *The Atlantic,* September 25, 2012, https://www.theatlantic.com/national/archive/2012/09/how-self-expression-damaged-my-students/262656/

13. Karen L. DeVogler and Peter Ebersole, "Young Adolescents' Meaning in Life," *Psychological Reports* 52, no. 2 (1983): 427–31.
14. Michael F. Steger, "Meaning in Life," in *Oxford Handbook of Positive Psychology* (2nd ed.) eds. Shane J. Lopez and C. R. Snyder (Oxford, UK: Oxford University Press, 2009), 679–687.
15. Victor E. Frankl, *Man's Search for Meaning: An Introduction to Logo-Therapy* (Boston, MA: Beacon 1959).
16. Roy F. Baumeister, "The Meanings of Life," *Aeon*, September 16, 2013, https://aeon.co/essays/what-is-better-a-happy-life-or-a-meaningful-one; Roy F. Baumeister, *Meanings of Life*, (New York: The Guilford Press, 1991).
17. Jerome S. Bruner, *Acts of Meaning*. (Cambridge, MA: Harvard Univ. Press, 2002), 118.
18. Several theorists have identified purpose, in the sense of being committed to an important life goal, as one of the factors that contributes to meaning in life. Michael J. MacKenzie and Roy F. Baumeister, "Meaning in Life: Nature, Needs, and Myths," in *Meaning in Positive and Existential Psychology*, eds. Alexander Batthyany and Pninit Russo-Netzer (New York: Springer, 2014), 25–38; William Damon, Jenni Menon, and Kendall Cotton Bronk, "The Development of Purpose During Adolescence," *Applied Developmental Science* 7, no. 3 (2003): 119–28; Michael F. Steger, "Meaning in Life," in *Oxford Handbook of Positive Psychology* (2nd ed.) eds. Shane J. Lopez and C. R. Snyder (Oxford, UK: Oxford University Press, 2009), 679–687.
19. Aristotle, *Nicomachean Ethics* Translated by Terrence Irwin, 2nd ed. (Indianapolis, IN: Hackett Publishing Company, Inc., 1999).
20. Richard M. Ryan and Edward L. Deci, "On Happiness and Human Potentials: A Review of Research on Hedonic and Eudaimonic Well-Being," *Annual Review of Psychology* 52 (2001): 141–66; Carol D. Ryff, "Psychological Well-Being Revisited: Advances in the Science and Practice of Eudaimonia," *Psychotherapy and Psychosomatics,* 83 (2014): 10–28; Carol D. Ryff and Burton H. Singer, "Know Thyself and Become What You Are: A Eudaimonic Approach to Psychological Well-Being," *Journal of Happiness Studies* 9, no. 1 (2008): 13–39.
21. Karen L. DeVogler and Peter Ebersole, "Categorization of College Students Meaning of Life," *Psychological Reports* 46, no. 2 (1980): 387–90.
22. Karen L. DeVogler and Peter Ebersole "Young Adolescents' Meaning in Life," *Psychological Reports* 52 (1983): 427–31.

CHAPTER 3

1. Maurice J. Elias, "Social-Emotional and Character Development and Academics as a Dual Focus of Educational Policy," *Education Policy* 23, no. 6 (2009): 831–46; *A Framework for School Success: 11 Principles of Effective Character Education* (Washington, D.C.: Character.org) http://character.org/more-resources/11-principles/.
2. Jeffrey Aaron Snyder, "Teaching Kids 'Grit' is All the Rage. Here's What's Wrong with It," *New Republic*, May 6, 2014, https://newrepublic.com/article/117615/problem-grit-kipp-and-character-based-education.
3. Angela Duckworth, *Grit: The Power of Passion and Perseverance* (New York, NY: Scribner, 2016); Joke Simons, Siegfried Dewitte, and Willy Lens, "The Role of Different Types of Instrumentality in Motivation, Study Strategies, and Performance: Know Why You Learn, So You'll Know What You Learn!" *British Journal of Educational Psychology* 74, no. 3 (2004): 343–60.
4. William Damon, *The Path to Purpose: Helping Our Children Find Their Calling in Life*, (New York: Free Press, 2008), 183–86, 22.
5. Heather Malin, Indrawati Liauw, and William Damon, "Purpose and Character Development in Early Adolescence," *Journal of Youth and Adolescence* 46, no. 6 (2017): 1200–215.
6. Interview with Youth Purpose Project participant, 2006.
7. Malin, Liauw, and Damon, "Purpose and Character Development," 1200–215; David S. Yeager et al., "Boring but Important: A Self-Transcendent Purpose for Learning Fosters Academic Self-Regulation," *Journal of Personality and Social Psychology* 107, no. 4 (2014): 559–80.
8. Kendall Cotton Bronk, *Purpose in Life: A Critical Component of Optimal Youth Development* (New York: Springer, 2016).
9. Anthony L. Burrow, Amanda C. O'Dell, and Patrick L. Hill, "Profiles of a Developmental Asset: Youth Purpose as a Context for Hope and Well-Being," *Journal of Youth and Adolescence* 39, no. 11 (2009): 1265–273.
10. László Brassai, Bettina F. Piko, and Michael F. Steger, "Meaning in Life: Is it a Protective Factor for Adolescents' Psychological Health?" *International Journal of Behavioral Medicine* 18, no. 1 (2011): 44–51; Anthony L. Burrow and Patrick L. Hill, "Purpose as a Form of Identity Capital for Positive Youth Adjustment," *Developmental Psychology* 47, no. 4 (2011): 1196–206; Anthony L. Burrow, Rachel Sumner, and Anthony D. Ong, "Perceived Change in Life Satisfaction and Daily Negative Affect: The Moderating Role of Purpose in Life," *Journal of Happiness Studies* 15, no. 3 (2013): 579–92; Patrick L. Hill and Nicholas A. Turiano, "Purpose in Life as a Predictor of Mortality Across Adulthood," *Psychological Science* 25, no. 7 (2014): 1482–486; Carol D. Ryff et al., "Purposeful Engagement, Healthy Aging, and the

Brain," *Current Behavioral Neuroscience Reports* 3, no. 4 (2016): 318–27.

11. Sonia Issac Koshy and Jenni Menon Mariano, "Promoting Youth Purpose: A Review of the Literature," *New Directions for Youth Development* 2011, no. 132 (2011): 13–29.
12. Matthew J. Bundick, "The Benefits of Reflecting on and Discussing Purpose in Life in Emerging Adulthood," *New Directions for Youth Development* 2011, no. 132 (2011): 89–103.
13. Todd B. Kashdan and Patrick E. McKnight, "Commitment to a Purpose in Life: An Antidote to the Suffering by Individuals with Social Anxiety Disorder," *Emotion* 13, no. 6 (2013): 1150–159.
14. Jane Elizabeth Pizzolato, Elizabeth Levine Brown, and Mary Allison Kanny, "Purpose Plus: Supporting Youth Purpose, Control, and Academic Achievement," *New Directions for Youth Development* 2011, no. 132 (2011): 75–88.
15. University of Pennsylvania and Stanford Center on Adolescence, *Character Development in Adolescence Project*, Unpublished survey data, November, 2011.
16. Nancy Eisenberg, Sarah K. VanSchyndel, and Tracy L. Spinrad, "Prosocial Motivation: Inferences from an Opaque Body of Work," *Child Development* 87, no. 6 (2016): 1668–678; Netta Weinstein and Richard M. Ryan, "When Helping Helps: Autonomous Motivation for Prosocial Behavior and its Influence on Well-Being for the Helper and Recipient," *Journal of Personality and Social Psychology* 98, no. 2 (2010): 222–44.
17. Sam A. Hardy and Gustavo Carlo, "Identity as a Source of Moral Motivation," *Human Development* 48, no. 4 (2005): 232–56; Heather Malin, Parissa J. Ballard, and William Damon, "Civic Purpose: An Integrated Construct for Understanding Civic Development in Adolescence," *Human Development* 58, no. 2 (2015): 103–30; Larry P. Nucci, *Education in the Moral Domain* (Cambridge: Cambridge University Press, 2004).
18. Interview with Youth Purpose Project participant, 2006.
19. Interview with Youth Purpose Project participant, 2006.
20. Nancy Eisenberg and Paul A. Miller, "The Relation of Empathy to Prosocial and Related Behaviors," *Psychological Bulletin* 101, no. 1 (1987): 91–119; Eisenberg, VanSchyndel, and Spinrad, "Prosocial Motivation": 1670; Martin L. Hoffman, *Empathy and Moral Development* (Cambridge, UK: Cambridge University Press, 2000); Martin L. Hoffman, "Empathy and Prosocial Behavior," in *Handbook of Emotions*, eds. Michael Lewis, Jeannette M. Haviland-Jones, and Lisa Feldman Barrett (New York: The Guilford Press, 2008), 440–55.
21. Interview with Civic Purpose Project participant, 2011.
22. Robert Atkins and Daniel Hart, "Neighborhoods, Adults, and the Development of Civic Identity in Urban Youth," *Applied Developmental Science* 7, no. 3 (2003): 156–64.

23. Hoffman, *Empathy*, 221–49.
24. Eisenberg, VanSchyndel, and Spinrad, "Prosocial Motivation": 1671.
25. Sam Hardy and Gustavo Carlo, "Moral Identity: What Is It, How Does It Develop, and Is It Linked to Moral Action?" *Child Development Perspectives* 5, no. 3 (2011): 212–18.
26. Hardy and Carlo, "Identity," 234–36; David Moshman, *Adolescent rationality and development: cognition, morality, and identity*, (New York: Psychology Press, 2011), 179.
27. Michael W. Pratt, Bruce Hunsberger, S. Mark Pancer, and Susan Alisat, "A Longitudinal Analysis of Personal Values Socialization: Correlates of a Moral Self-Ideal in Late Adolescence," *Social Development* 12, no. 4 (2003): 563–85; James Youniss and Miranda Yates, *Community Service and Social Responsibility in Youth* (Chicago: University of Chicago Press, 1997).
28. Heather Malin, Indrawati Liauw, and Kathleen Remington, "Early Adolescent Purpose Development and Perceived Supports for Purpose at School" (manuscript under review, 2018).
29. Interview with Civic Purpose Project participant, 2011.
30. William Damon and Heather Malin, "Purpose as a Particular Character Strength: Conceptual, Methodological, and Developmental Implications" (Invited presentation, PRYDE Conference on Purpose and Health Across the Lifespan, Half Moon Bay, CA, October, 2016).
31. Stacey M. Schaefer et al., "Purpose in Life Predicts Better Emotional Recovery from Negative Stimuli," *PLoS ONE* 8, no. 11 (2013).
32. Adriana Feder et al., "Coping and PTSD symptoms in Pakistani Earthquake Survivors: Purpose in Life, Religious Coping and Social Support," *Journal of Affective Disorders* 147, no. 1–3 (2013): 156–63.
33. Richard G. Tedeschi and Lawrence G. Calhoun, "TARGET ARTICLE: 'Posttraumatic Growth: Conceptual Foundations and Empirical Evidence,'" *Psychological Inquiry* 15, no. 1 (2004): 1–18.
34. James W. Pennebaker and Janel D. Seagal. "Forming a Story: The Health Benefits of Narrative," *Journal of Clinical Psychology* 55, no. 10 (1999): 1243–254.
35. David Finkelhor et al., "Prevalence of Childhood Exposure to Violence, Crime, and Abuse," *JAMA Pediatrics* 169, no. 8 (2015): 746; Michelle M. Perfect et al., "School-Related Outcomes of Traumatic Event Exposure and Traumatic Stress Symptoms in Students: A Systematic Review of Research from 1990 to 2015," *School Mental Health* 8, no. 1 (2016): 7–43; Michelle V. Porche, Darcé M. Costello, and Myra Rosen-Reynoso, "Adverse Family Experiences, Child Mental Health, and Educational Outcomes for a National Sample of Students," *School Mental Health* 8, no. 1 (2016): 44–60;

Trina R. Williams Shanks and Christine Robinson, "Assets, Economic Opportunity and Toxic Stress: A Framework for Understanding Child and Educational Outcomes," *Economics of Education Review* 33 (2013): 154–70.

36. Jerusha Conner, Denise Pope, and Mollie Galloway, "Success with Less Stress," *Educational Leadership* 67, no. 4 (2009): 54–58; Jerusha O. Conner, Sarah B. Miles, and Denise C. Pope, "How Many Teachers Does It Take to Support a Student?: Examining the Relationship between Teacher Support and Adverse Health Outcomes in High-Performing, Pressure-Cooker High Schools," *The High School Journal* 98, no. 1 (2014): 22–42.; Suniya S. Luthar, Samuel H. Barkin, and Elizabeth J. Crossman. "'I Can, Therefore I Must': Fragility in the Upper-Middle Classes," *Development and Psychopathology* 25, no. 4 pt2 (2013): 1529–549.
37. Heather Malin, Hyemin Han, and Indrawati Liauw, "Civic Purpose in Late Adolescence: Factors that Prevent Decline in Civic Engagement After High School," *Developmental Psychology* 53, no. 7 (2017): 1384–397.
38. Gustavo Carlo et al., "The Roles of Parental Inductions, Moral Emotions, and Moral Cognitions in Prosocial Tendencies Among Mexican American and European American Early Adolescents," *The Journal of Early Adolescence* 31, no. 6 (2010): 757–81.
39. Lisa Kiang and Andrew J. Fuligni, "Meaning in Life as a Mediator of Ethnic Identity and Adjustment Among Adolescents from Latin, Asian, and European American Backgrounds," *Journal of Youth and Adolescence* 39, no. 11 (2009): 1253–264.
40. Margaret B. Spencer, Suzanne G. Fegley, and Vinay Harpalani, "A Theoretical and Empirical Examination of Identity as Coping: Linking Coping Resources to the Self Processes of African American Youth," *Applied Developmental Science* 7, no. 3 (2003): 181–88.
41. Brent W. Roberts and Richard W. Robins, "Broad Dispositions, Broad Aspirations: The Intersection of Personality Traits and Major Life Goals," *Personality and Social Psychology Bulletin* 26, no. 10 (2000): 1284–296.
42. Interview with Character Development in Adolescence participant, 2015.
43. Interview with Youth Purpose Project participant, 2006.
44. Find more information about community and civic purpose among adolescents in Malin, Ballard, and Damon, "Civic Purpose."
45. Interview with Civic Purpose Project participant, 2011.
46. Ulisses F. Araujo et al., "Principles and Methods to Guide Education for Purpose: A Brazilian Experience," *Journal of Education for Teaching* 42, no. 5 (2016): 556–64.
47. Interview with Character Development in Adolescence Project participant, 2015.

48. Heather Malin, "Arts Participation as a Context for Youth Purpose," *Studies in Art Education* 56, no. 3 (2015): 268–80; Seana Moran, "Changing the World: Tolerance and Creativity Aspirations Among American Youth," *High Ability Studies* 21, no. 2 (2010): 117–32.
49. Jenni Menon Mariano and William Damon, "The Role of Spirituality and Religious Faith in the Development of Purpose in Adolescence," in *Positive Youth Development and Spirituality: From Theory to Research,* eds. Richard M. Lerner, Robert W. Roeser, and Erin Phelps (West Conshohocken, PA: Templeton Foundation Press, 2008), 210–230; Kirsi Tirri and Brandy Quinn, "Exploring the Role of Religion and Spirituality in the Development of Purpose: Case Studies of Purposeful Youth," *British Journal of Religious Education* 32, no. 3 (2010): 201–14.
50. Interview with Civic Purpose Project participant, 2011.
51. Paul Tough, "How Kids Learn Resilience," *The Atlantic*, June, 2016, https://www.theatlantic.com/magazine/archive/2016/06/how-kids-really-succeed/480744/, C. Kirabo Jackson, "Non-Cognitive Ability, Test Scores, and Teacher Quality: Evidence from 9th Grade Teachers in North Carolina," (working paper 18624, National Bureau of Economic Research, Cambridge, MA, 2012); C. Kirabo Jackson, Jonah E. Rockoff, and Douglas O. Staiger, "Teacher Effects and Teacher-Related Policies," *Annual Review of Economics* 6, no. 1 (2014): 801–25.

CHAPTER 4

1. William Damon, *The Path to Purpose: Helping Our Children Find Their Calling in Life*, (New York: Free Press, 2008); Patrick E. Mcknight and Todd B. Kashdan, "Purpose in Life as a System that Creates and Sustains Health and Well-Being: An Integrative, Testable Theory," *Review of General Psychology* 13, no. 3 (2009): 242–51; Seana Moran, "Youth Purpose Worldwide: A Tapestry of Possibilities." *Journal of Moral Education* 46, no. 3 (2017): 231–44.
2. Todd Rose, *The End of Average: How We Succeed in a World that Values Sameness*, (London: Penguin Books, 2017).
3. Daphna Oyserman, Kathy Terry, and Deborah Bybee, "A Possible Selves Intervention to Enhance School Involvement," *Journal of Adolescence* 25, no. 3 (2002): 313–26.
4. http://www.nbcbayarea.com/news/local/Los-Altos-School-Children-Work-To-Save-Beloved-Redwoods-Suffering-In-Drought-304672591.html
5. Larry Nucci and Elliot Turiel, "Capturing the Complexity of Moral Development and Education," *Mind, Brain, and Education* 3, no. 151–159; Laura Wray-Lake and Amy K. Syvertsen, "The Developmental Roots of Social

Responsibility in Childhood and Adolescence," *New Directions for Child and Adolescent Development* 2011, no. 134 (2011): 11–25.

6. Sam A. Hardy and Gustavo Carlo, "Moral Identity," in *Handbook of Identity Theory and Research*, eds. Seth J. Schwartz, Koen Luyckx, and Vivian L. Vignoles (New York: Springer, 2011), 495–513.
7. David Moshman, *Adolescent Rationality and Development: Cognition, Morality, and Identity*, (New York: Psychology Press, 2011), 176.
8. Anna Vazeou-Nieuwenhuis, Edward Orehek, and Michael F. Scheier. "The Meaning of Action: Do Self-Regulatory Processes Contribute to a Purposeful Life?" *Personality and Individual Differences* 116 (2017): 115–22.
9. Interview with Youth Purpose Project participant, 2006.
10. Patrick L. Hill, Anthony L. Burrow, and Rachel Sumner, "Sense of Purpose and Parent–Child Relationships in Emerging Adulthood," *Emerging Adulthood* 4, no. 6 (2016): 436–39.
11. Liang, Belle et al., "Adolescent Girls Finding Purpose: The Role of Parents and Prosociality," *Youth & Society* (2017), doi:10.1177/0044118x17697850.
12. Seana Moran et al., "How Supportive of Their Specific Purposes Do Youth Believe Their Family and Friends Are?" *Journal of Adolescent Research* 28, no. 3 (2012): 348–77.
13. Liang, Belle et al., "The Four P's of Purpose Among College Bound Students: People, Propensity, Passion, Prosocial Benefits," *The Journal of Positive Psychology* 12, no. 3 (2017): 281–94.
14. Heather Malin, Parissa J. Ballard, and William Damon. "Civic Purpose: An Integrated Construct for Understanding Civic Development in Adolescence," *Human Development* 58, no. 2 (2015): 103–30.
15. Interview with Civic Purpose Project participant, 2011.
16. Interview with Youth Purpose Project participant, 2006.
17. Moran et al., "Supportive," 363–64.
18. Malin, Ballard, and Damon, "Civic Purpose," 124–25.
19. Moran et al., "Supportive," 365–66.
20. Heather Malin, Timothy S. Reilly, Brandy Quinn, and Seana Moran, "Adolescent Purpose Development: Exploring Empathy, Discovering Roles, Shifting Priorities, and Creating Pathways," *Journal of Research on Adolescence* 24, no. 1 (2013): 186–99.

CHAPTER 5

1. Megan M. McClelland, Alan C. Acock, and Frederick J. Morrison. "The Impact of Kindergarten Learning-Related Skills on Academic Trajectories at the End of Elementary School," *Early Childhood Research Quarterly* 21, no. 4 (2006): 471–90; Michelle V. Porche, Darcé M. Costello, and Myra

Rosen-Reynoso, "Adverse Family Experiences, Child Mental Health, and Educational Outcomes for a National Sample of Students," *School Mental Health* 8, no. 1 (2016): 44–60; Sara E. Rimm-Kaufman, Robert C. Pianta, and Martha J. Cox, "Teachers' Judgments of Problems in the Transition to Kindergarten," *Early Childhood Research Quarterly* 15, no. 2 (2000): 147–66.

2. Joseph Berryhill, Jean Ann Linney, and Jill Fromewick, "The Effects of Educational Accountability on Teachers: Are Policies Too Stress Provoking for Their Own Good?" *International Journal of Education Policy and Leadership* [Online] 4, no. 5 (2009); Elisa S. Shernoff et al., "A Qualitative Study of the Sources and Impact of Stress Among Urban Teachers," *School Mental Health* 3, no. 2 (2011): 59–69.
3. Jonathan C. Erwin, *The School Climate Solution: Creating a Culture of Excellence from the Classroom to the Staff Room* (Golden Valley, MN: Free Spirit Publishing Inc., 2016); Patricia A. Jennings and Mark T. Greenberg, "The Prosocial Classroom: Teacher Social and Emotional Competence in Relation to Student and Classroom Outcomes," *Review of Educational Research* 79, no. 1 (2009): 491–525.
4. Ibid., 492.
5. Jonathan Cohen, Elizabeth M. McCabe, Nicholas M. Michelli, and Terry Pickeral, "School Climate: Research, Policy, Practice, and Teacher Education," *Teachers College Record* 111, no. 1 (2009), 180–213.
6. Ibid., 185–86; Deborah L. Roorda, Helma M. Y. Koomen, Jantine L. Spilt, and Frans J. Oort. "The Influence of Affective Teacher–Student Relationships on Students' School Engagement and Achievement," *Review of Educational Research* 81, no. 4 (2011): 493–529; Dorothy M. Steele and Becki Cohn-Vargas, *Identity Safe Classrooms: Places to Belong and Learn* (Thousand Oaks, CA: Corwin, 2013); Gregory M. Walton and Geoffrey L. Cohen, "A Question of Belonging: Race, Social Fit, and Achievement," *Journal of Personality and Social Psychology* 92, no. 1 (2007): 82–96.
7. Heather Malin, Indrawati Liauw, and William Damon, "Purpose and Character Development in Early Adolescence," *Journal of Youth and Adolescence* 46, no. 6 (2017): 1200–215.
8. Thupten Jinpa, *A Fearless Heart: How the Courage to be Compassionate Can Transform our Lives* (New York: Avery, 2016).
9. Hooria Jazaieri et al., "Enhancing Compassion: A Randomized Controlled Trial of a Compassion Cultivation Training Program," *Journal of Happiness Studies* 14, no. 4 (2012): 1113–126.
10. Lisa Flook et al., "Promoting Prosocial Behavior and Self-Regulatory Skills in Preschool Children Through a Mindfulness-Based Kindness Curriculum," *Developmental Psychology* 51, no. 1 (2015): 44–51; Lisa Flook et al.,

"Effects of Mindful Awareness Practices on Executive Functions in Elementary School Children," *Journal of Applied School Psychology* 26, no. 1 (2010): 70–95; Melanie Viglas and Michal Perlman, "Effects of a Mindfulness-Based Program on Young Children's Self-Regulation, Prosocial Behavior and Hyperactivity," *Journal of Child and Family Studies* (2017). https://doi.org/10.1007/s10826-017-0971-6; Dianna Quach, Kristen E. Jastrowski Mano, and Kristi Alexander, "A Randomized Controlled Trial Examining the Effect of Mindfulness Meditation on Working Memory Capacity in Adolescents," *Journal of Adolescent Health* 58, no. 5 (2016): 489–96.

11. Mark T. Greenberg and Alexis R. Harris, "Nurturing Mindfulness in Children and Youth: Current State of Research," *Child Development Perspectives* 6, no. 2 (2011): 161–66. Research more clearly shows that mindfulness practices can have beneficial impacts for children with particular challenges, such as ADHD, anxiety, or PTSD.
12. https://www.edutopia.org/blog/creating-more-compassionate-classrooms-joshua-block
13. Karen F. Osterman, "Students Need for Belonging in the School Community," *Review of Educational Research* 70, no. 3 (2000): 323–367; Nathaniel M. Lambert et al., "To Belong Is to Matter: Sense of Belonging Enhances Meaning in Life," *Personality and Social Psychology Bulletin* 39, no. 11 (2013): 1418–427.
14. Jennifer A. Fredricks, Phyllis C. Blumenfeld, and Alison H. Paris, "School Engagement: Potential of the Concept, State of the Evidence," *Review of Educational Research* 74, no. 1 (2004): 59–109; Osterman, "Need for Belonging," 336–38.
15. Osterman, "Need for Belonging," 338–41.
16. Osterman, "Need for Belonging," 331–34.
17. Jonathan E. Cook et al., "Chronic Threat and Contingent Belonging: Protective Benefits of Values Affirmation on Identity Development," *Journal of Personality and Social Psychology* 102, no. 3 (2012): 479–96.
18. Gregory M. Walton and Geoffrey L. Cohen, "A Brief Social-Belonging Intervention Improves Academic and Health Outcomes of Minority Students," *Science* 331, no. 6023 (2011): 1447–451.
19. Walton and Cohen, "A Brief Social-Belonging Intervention," 1448; Cook et al., "Chronic Threat," 489; Walton and Cohen, "A question of belonging," 82–96.
20. Osterman, "Need for Belonging," 338.
21. Osterman, "Need for Belonging," 329.
22. Lambert et al., "To Belong Is to Matter," 1418–427.
23. Edward L. Deci and Richard M. Ryan, "The Support of Autonomy and the

Control of Behavior," *Journal of Personality and Social Psychology* 53, no. 6 (1987): 1024–037; Richard M. Ryan and Cynthia L. Powelson, "Autonomy and Relatedness as Fundamental to Motivation and Education," *The Journal of Experimental Education* 60, no. 1 (1991): 49–66.

24. Avi Assor, Haya Kaplan, and Guy Roth, "Choice Is Good, but Relevance Is Excellent: Autonomy-Enhancing and Suppressing Teacher Behaviours Predicting Students' Engagement in Schoolwork," *British Journal of Educational Psychology* 72, no. 2 (2002): 261–78.
25. Christopher P. Niemiec and Richard M. Ryan, "Autonomy, Competence, and Relatedness in the Classroom," *School Field* 7, no. 2 (2009): 133–44.
26. Ryan and Powelson, "Autonomy and Relatedness," 54–55.
27. Cohen et al., "School Climate," 180–213; Kathryn R. Wentzel, "Social Competence at School: Relation between Social Responsibility and Academic Achievement," *Review of Educational Research* 61, no. 1 (1991): 1–24.
28. Laura Wray-Lake and Amy K. Syvertsen, "The Developmental Roots of Social Responsibility in Childhood and Adolescence," *New Directions for Child and Adolescent Development* 134 (2011): 11–25; Laura Wray-Lake, Amy K. Syvertsen, and Constance A. Flanagan, "Developmental Change in Social Responsibility During dolescence: An Ecological Perspective," *Developmental Psychology* 52, no. 1 (2016): 130–42.
29. Marjorie Lindner Gunnoe, E. Mavis Hetherington, and David Reiss, "Parental Religiosity, Parenting Style, and Adolescent Social Responsibility," *The Journal of Early Adolescence* 19, no. 2 (1999): 199–225.
30. Wray-Lake, Syvertsen, and Flanagan, "Social Responsibility," 30–42.
31. Jean Lave and Etienne Wenger, *Situated Learning: Legitimate Peripheral Participation* (Cambridge: Cambridge University Press, 1991).
32. "Introduction to Communities of Practice: A Brief Overview of the Concept and its Uses," Etienne and Beverly Wenger-Trayner, 2015, http://wenger-trayner.com/introduction-to-communities-of-practice/
33. Interview with Civic Purpose Project participant, 2011.
34. Interview with Civic Purpose Project participant, 2013.
35. Jennings and Greenberg, "The Prosocial Classroom," 493–94; Richard Weissbourd, Suzanne M. Bouffard, and Stephanie M. Jones, "School Climate and Moral and Social Development," in *School Climate Practices for Implementation and Sustainability,* ed. Teri Daly and Terry Pickeral (New York: National School Climate Center, 2013), 30–34; Jones, Stephanie M. and Suzanne M. Bouffard, "Social and Emotional Learning in Schools: From Programs to Strategies," *Social Policy Report* 26, no. 4 (2012).
36. Seana Moran, Matthew J. Bundick, Heather Malin, and Timothy S. Reilly, "How Supportive of Their Specific Purposes Do Youth Believe Their Family

and Friends Are?" *Journal of Adolescent Research* 28, no. 3 (2012): 348–77.
37. Interview with Youth Purpose Project participant, 2006.
38. Interview with Youth Purpose Project participant, 2008.
39. Interview with Character Development in Adolescence Project participant, 2014.

CHAPTER 6

1. Russ Quaglia, "Students Hopes and Dreams" (talk presented at Schools Students and Teachers Network National Conference, 2015), https://www.youtube.com/watch?v=DJEwzGHgY3Y.
2. *The Aspirations Framework*, Aspirations Briefs (Portland, ME: The Quaglia Institute for School Voice and Aspirations, 2016), http://quagliainstitute.org/qisa/library/view.do?id=145.
3. *The Aspirations Framework*.
4. *School Voice Report*, (Portland, ME: Quaglia Institute for School Voice and Aspirations, 2016).
5. Russell J. Quaglia and Michael J. Corso, *Student Voice: Instrument of Change* (Thousand Oaks, CA: Corwin, 2014).
6. Interview with Kristine Fox (senior field specialist and research associate at QISA, January 12, 2017).
7. Interview with Melissa Morse (director of instruction and innovative practice at Cobb County School District, September 25, 2017).
8. Interview with Kerri Waller (art teacher and Teacher Leader at Cobb County School District, October 24, 2017).

CHAPTER 7

1. William Heard Kilpatrick, *The Project Method: The Use of the Purposeful Act in the Educative Process* (New York: Teachers College, Columbia University, 1918).
2. Kilpatrick, *The Project Method*, 3.
3. Kilpatrick, *The Project Method*, 5–6.
4. Ulisses F. Araújo et al., "Principles and Methods to Guide Education for Purpose: A Brazilian Experience," *Journal of Education for Teaching* 42, no. 5 (2016): 556–64. Jongho Shin, Myung-Seop Kim, Hyeyoung Hwang, Byung-Yoon Lee, "Effects of Motivation and Feedback in Service- Learning Programs on the Development of College Students' Life Purpose," *Journal of Moral Education* 48, no. 3 (2018).
5. A description of this study and links to publications and resources are available at learning4purpose.org.
6. Design thinking is an approach to design and innovation that begins with

an empathic process of gathering experiences and inspiration from future users of the end-product, then prototyping ideas and solutions to test with users; https://www.ideou.com/pages/design-thinking.

7. Araújo et al., "Brazilian Experience," p. 3–4.
8. Daniel T. Willingham, *Why Don't Students Like School?: A Cognitive Scientist Answers Questions About How the Mind Works and What It Means for the Classroom* (San Francisco: Jossey-Bass, 2009), 64.
9. http://www.learningpersonalized.com/using-essential-questions-engage-student-inquiry/
10. David S. Yeager et al., "Boring but Important: A Self-Transcendent Purpose for Learning Fosters Academic Self-Regulation," *Journal of Personality and Social Psychology* 107, no. 4 (2014): 559–80.
11. https://www.edutopia.org/blog/high-quality-student-work-pbl-john-larmer
12. These two principles are supported by several other key Reggio principles, such as the environment as teacher, documentation, and the hundred languages of children.
13. The Episcopal Identity provides a framework for Episcopalian schools, and includes values such as open-minded learning about diverse beliefs and perspectives, equity, inclusiveness, social justice, and a sense of interconnectedness in society that drives service. http://www.episcopalschools.org
14. The most often cited resource for understanding the Reggio Emilia philosophy and how it is applied in a collection of interviews and essays by the original founders and early practitioners: Carolyn Edwards, Lella Gandini, and George Forman. *The Hundred Languages of Children: The Reggio Emilia Approach to Early Childhood Education*. (Norwood, NJ: Ablex Publishing Corporation, 1993).
15. My daughter is a student at Ventana School. Notes about the ocean project were collected from teacher documentation that was sent home to parents in weekly reports.
16. Core curriculum standards used in this lesson include: (Common Core ELA-Literacy.RL.3.3), (Common Core ELA-Literacy.RL.3.2), and (Common Core ELA-L.3.1.A); http://www.corestandards.org/ELA-Literacy/.
17. Description of Dragonology project comes from password-protected classroom blog at ventanaschool.org.
18. Interview with Harfijah Oliver, October 17, 2017.
19. Interview with Amanda Stewart, October 17, 2017.
20. Buck Institute for Education is a nonprofit organization that provides project-based learning resources for teachers, schools and districts. http://www.bie.org.
21. http://www.bie.org/blog/gold_standard_pbl_essential_project_design_elements.

22. https://newtechnetwork.org.
23. *Evidence of Deeper Learning Outcomes* (Washington D.C.: American Institutes for Research, 2014).
24. *2017 Impact Report: New Tech Network Schools* (Napa, CA: New Tech Network, 2017).
25. For example, see the following webinar on creating inquiry-driven service-learning projects that build on a foundation of core content standards and inspire student interest and engagement: *Investigation: Creating Inquiry-based Service Learning Projects* (National Youth Leadership Council, 2015), https://gsn.nylc.org/topics/350/videos/280.
26. Seana Moran, "Youth Purpose Worldwide: A Tapestry of Possibilities," *Journal of Moral Education* 46, no. 3 (2017): 231–44.
27. My comments about students' developing and sharing their gifts and knowing their value were inspired by a conversation with Josclyn Wiley and Bobby Hart in the Hope School District in Arkansas, whom we will meet in the profile of Noble Impact in chapter 8.
28. Heather Malin et al., "Adolescent Purpose Development: Exploring Empathy, Discovering Roles, Shifting Priorities, and Creating Pathways," *Journal of Research on Adolescence* 24, no. 1 (2013): 186–99.
29. Shelley H. Billig and Wokie Weah, "K-12 Service-Learning Standards for Quality Practice," summary of *Growing to* Greatness (National Youth Leadership Council, 2008).
30. Araújo et al., "Brazilian Experience," 559–60; Shelley Goldman and Zaza Kabayadondo, *Taking Design Thinking to School: How the Technology of Design Can Transform Teachers, Learners, and Classrooms* (New York: Routledge, 2017).
31. Billig and Weah, "K-12 Service-Learning," 11; Stacy K. Dymond, Adelle Renzaglia, and Eul Jung Chun, "Elements of High School Service Learning Programs," *Career Development for Exceptional Individuals* 31, no. 1 (2008): 37–47.
32. Dymond, Renzaglia, and Chun, "Service Learning Programs," 40–41.
33. Interview with Civic Purpose Project participant, 2011.
34. Billig and Weah, "K-12 Service-Learning," 11; Dymond, Renzaglia, and Chun, "Service Learning Programs," 37–47.
35. Dymond, Renzaglia, and Chun, "Service Learning Programs," 40, citing the following: Martha Burns, Keith Storey, and Nicholas J. Certo, "Effect of Service Learning on Attitudes Towards Students with Severe Disabilities," *Education and Training in Mental Retardation and Developmental Disabilities* 34, (1999): 58–65; Kim Patrick Moore and Judith Haymore Sandholtz, "Designing Successful Service Learning Projects for Urban Schools," *Urban Education* 34, (1999): 480–498.

36. Billig and Weah, "K-12 Service-Learning," 11.
37. Moran, "Youth Purpose Worldwide," 235–37.
38. Jongho Shin, Myung-Seop Kim, Hyeyoung Hwang, Byung-Yoon Lee, "Effects of Motivation and Feedback in Service- Learning Programs on the Development of College Students' Life Purpose," *Journal of Moral Education* 48, no. 3 (2018).
39. Matthew Bundick and Kirsi Tirri, "Student Perceptions of Teacher Support and Competencies for Fostering Youth Purpose and Positive Youth Development: Perspectives from Two Countries," *Applied Developmental Science* 18, no. 3 (2014): 148–162.
40. Examples are Linked Learning (https://www.linkedlearning.org), Big Picture Schools (https://www.bigpicture.org), and Center for Advanced Professional Studies (https://yourcapsnetwork.org).
41. https://www.bigpicture.org.
42. Bundick and Tirri, "Student Perceptions," 28; Malin et al., "Adolescent Purpose Development," 192–193.

CHAPTER 8

1. D.school refers to the Hasso Plattner Institute of Design at Stanford University, which includes the K12 Lab Network where Project Wayfinder originated.
2. Patrick Cook-Deegan, "Seven Ways to Help High Schoolers Find Purpose," *Greater Good Magazine* (January 11, 2016), https://greatergood.berkeley.edu/article/item/seven_ways_to_help_high_schoolers_find_purpose.

CHAPTER 9

1. There is ongoing debate in philosophy and psychology about the definition of empathy, in terms of distinguishing it from sympathy, compassion, perspective taking, and other related concepts, and about the relevance of empathy to morality. Some define empathy specifically and only as having the same feeling that another person is feeling in reaction to the other person's pain. This specific form of empathy may not be relevant to moral development, because morality is not inherently born out of our own pain or distress. However, the term empathy is usually discussed and used more broadly, encompassing sympathy, compassion, and perspective taking, all of which can follow from empathy and which might form a bridge between empathy and moral development. I use empathy here in that broader sense, because that is how it is used in the education literature and practice that is relevant to this discussion. For more on the empathy debate, see: Paul Bloom. *Against Empathy: The Case for Rational Compassion*. (New York:

HarperCollins Publishers, 2018); Nancy Eisenberg, Tracy L. Spinrad, and Amanda Morris, "Empathy-Related Responding in Children," in *Handbook of Moral Development*, eds. Melanie Killen and Judith G. Smetana (New York: Psychology Press, 2014).

2. See Bloom, *Against Empathy* for a counterargument that empathy is a poor foundation for moral development
3. Sam A. Hardy and Gustavo Carlo, "Moral Identity," in *Handbook of Identity Theory and Research*, eds. Seth J. Schwartz, Koen Luyckx, and Vivian L. Vignoles (New York: Springer, 2011), 495–513; Martin L. Hoffman, *Empathy and Moral Development* (Cambridge, UK: Cambridge University Press, 2000).
4. Eisenberg, Spinrad, and Morris, "Empathy-Related Responding," 194–99.
5. Scott Seider, Madora Soutter, and Shelby Clark, "The Role of Character and Character Education in Fostering Student Success at School," in *Handbook of Social Influences in School Contexts: Social-Emotional, Motivation, and Cognitive Outcomes*, eds. Kathryn R. Wentzel and Geetha B. Ramani (New York: Routledge, 2016), 296.
6. Nancy Eisenberg, Natalie D. Eggum, and Laura Di Giunta, "Empathy-related Responding: Associations with Prosocial Behavior, Aggression, and Intergroup Relations," *Social Issues Policy Review* 4, no. 1 (2010): 143–80.
7. Douglas A. Gentile et al., "The Effects of Prosocial Video Games on Prosocial Behaviors: International Evidence from Correlational, Longitudinal, and Experimental Studies," *Personality and Social Psychology Bulletin* 35, no. 6 (2009): 752–63; Tobias Greitemeyer, Silvia Osswald, and Markus Brauer, "Playing Prosocial Video Games Increases Empathy and Decreases Schadenfreude," *Emotion* 10, no. 6 (2010): 796–802; David Comer Kidd and Emanuele Castano, "Reading Literary Fiction Improves Theory of Mind," *Science* 342 (2013): 377–80; Anita D. Misra-Hebert et al., "Improving Empathy of Physicians Through Guided Reflective Writing," *International Journal of Medical Education* 3 (2012): 71–77; Loris Vezzali et al., "The Greatest Magic of Harry Potter: Reducing Prejudice," *Journal of Applied Social Psychology* 45, no. 2 (2015): 105–21.
8. http://www.changemakerschools.org
9. Interview with Christina Ballantyne (principal at San Miguel Elementary School), November 6, 2017.
10. The Center for Inspired Teaching was started by an Ashoka social entrepreneurship fellow.
11. https://startempathy.org/resources/a-second-new-resource/
12. Robert Thornberg, "The Lack of Professional Knowledge in Values Education," *Teaching and Teacher Education* 24 (2008), 1791–98.

13. This is a longstanding debate that was captured in an exchange in the *Phi Delta Kappan* in 1998: Alfie Kohn, "How Not to Teach Values," *Phi Delta Kappan* 78, no. 6 (1997), 428–39; Jacques S. Benninga and Edward A. Wynne, "Keeping in Character: A Time-Tested Solution," *Phi Delta Kappan* 79, no. 6 (1998): 435–48; Thomas Lickona, "A More Complex Analysis is Needed," *Phi Delta Kappan* 79, no. 6 (1998): 449–54.
14. Anne Colby and William Damon, *Some Do Care* (New York: The Free Press, 1992).
15. Peggy Veljkovic and Arthur J. Schwartz, eds., *Writing from the Heart: Young People Share Their Wisdom* (Radnor, PA: Templeton Foundation Press, 2000); Maurice J. Elias et al., eds., *Urban Dreams: Stories of Hope, Resilience, and Character* (Lanham, MD: University Press of America, 2008).
16. Seana Moran et al., "How Supportive of Their Specific Purposes Do Youth Believe Their Family and Friends Are?" *Journal of Adolescent Research* 28, no. 3 (2012): 348–77.
17. Marc J. Stern et al., "What Difference Do Role Models Make? Investigating Outcomes at a Residential Environmental Education Center," *Environmental Education Research* 39, no. 4 (2017): 31–43.
18. Hyemin Han et al., "Attainable and Relevant Moral Exemplars are More Effective than Extraordinary Exemplars in Promoting Voluntary Service Engagement," *Frontiers in Psychology* 8, Article 283 (2017).
19. Stacie Molnar-Main, *Deliberation in the Classroom: Fostering Critical Thinking, Community, and Citizenship in Schools* (Dayton, OH: Kettering Foundation Press, 2017); Paula McAvoy and Diana Hess, "Classroom Deliberation in an Era of Political Polarization," *Curriculum Inquiry* 43, no. 1 (2013): 14–47.
20. Albert Bandura, *Social Foundations of Thought and Action: A Social Cognitive Theory* (Englewood Cliffs, NJ: Prentice-Hall, 1986); Raymond B. Miller and Stephanie J. Brickman, "A Model of Future-Oriented Motivation and Self-Regulation," *Educational Psychology Review* 16, no. 1 (2004): 9–33.
21. Kristina L. Schmid, Erin Phelps, and Richard M. Lerner, "Constructing Positive Futures: Modeling the Relationship Between Adolescents' Hopeful Future Expectations and Intentional Self-Regulation in Predicting Positive Youth Development," *Journal of Adolescence* 34, no. 6 (2011): 1127–35; Jean S. Phinney, Kathleen Baumann, and Shanika Blanton, "Life Goals and Attributions for Expected Outcomes Among Adolescents from Five Ethnic Groups," *Hispanic Journal of Behavioral Sciences* 23, no. 4 (2001): 363–77.
22. Phinney, Baumann, and Blanton, "Life Goals," 370.
23. Phinney, Baumann, and Blanton, "Life Goals," 364.
24. Phinney, Baumann, and Blanton, "Life Goals," 364.

25. Christopher P. Niemiec, Richard M. Ryan, and Edward L. Deci, "The Path Taken: Consequences of Attaining Intrinsic and Extrinsic Aspirations in Post-College Life," *Journal of Research in Personality* 43 (2009): 291–306.
26. Arthur A. Stukas, "Motivations to Volunteer and Their Associations with Volunteers' Well-Being," *Nonprofit and Voluntary Sector Quarterly* 45, no. 1 (2009): 112–132.
27. Daphna Oyserman, Kathy Terry, and Deborah Bybee, "A Possible Selves Intervention to Enhance School Involvement," *Journal of Adolescence* 25, no. 3 (2002): 313–26.
28. https://yale.app.box.com/v/hums411.
29. http://lifedesignlab.stanford.edu/dyl; William Burnett and David J. Evans, *Designing Your Life: How to Build a Well-Lived, Joyful Life* (New York: Alfred A. Knopf, 2017).
30. Summit Public Schools is a network of charter middle and high schools in California and Washington that emphasizes preparing students to be successful in college, contribute to society, and lead a fulfilled life. Summit uses a personalized approach to teaching and learning and project-based methods to develop students into self-directed learners. http://www.summitps.org.
31. Interview with Amy Sandoz (director of diploma at Summit Public Schools), January 26, 2018.
32. https://en.oxforddictionaries.com/definition/power.
33. http://www.gettingsmart.com/2015/12/201512tips-for-developing-student-agency; Ronald F. Ferguson et al., *The Influence of Teaching, Beyond Standardized Test Scores: Engagement, Mindsets, and Agency* (Cambridge, MA: The Achievement Gap Initiative at Harvard University, 2015), http://www.agi.harvard.edu/projects/TeachingandAgency.pdf
34. https://www.ted.com/talks/eric_liu_why_ordinary_people_need_to_understand_power.
35. https://www.facinghistory.org/resource-library/citizen-power-makes-democracy-work.
36. https://ed.ted.com/lessons/how-to-turn-protest-into-powerful-change-eric-liu#review. Eric Liu, *You're More Powerful than You Think: A Citizen's Guide to Making Change Happen* (Philadelphia: PublicAffairs, 2017).
37. Matthew J. Bundick, "The Benefits of Reflecting on and Discussing Purpose in Life in Emerging Adulthood," *New Directions for Youth Development* 132 (2011): 89–103.
38. The Claremont purpose intervention was launched as a challenge for high school students in 2017 at https://purposechallenge.org. The purpose toolkits for teachers and students are available at https://www.fosterpurpose.org.
39. Kendall Cotton Bronk et al., "Fostering Purpose among Adolescents:

Effective Online Interventions," (manuscript under review, 2018).

40. David S. Yeager et al., "Boring but Important: A Self-Transcendent Purpose for Learning Fosters Academic Self-Regulation," *Journal of Personality and Social Psychology* 107, no. 4 (2014): 559–80.

CHAPTER 10

1. Interview with Gerard Senehi (president of Open Future Institute, October 13, 2017).
2. See more about the five pillars at www.openfutureinstitute.org.
3. Soulpancake "Share a Cup of Success" video https://www.youtube.com/watch?v=_JrIuHVAn70.
4. Interview with Lola Osoria (English teacher at Bronx High School for Law & Community Service, October 13, 2017).
5. Interview with Novelette Foote (teacher at Belmont Preparatory Academy, October 13, 2017).
6. Danielle Hatchimonji, Arielle Linsky, and Maurice Elias, "Cultivating Noble Purpose in Urban Middle Schools: A Missing Piece in School Transformation," *Education* 138, no. 2 (2017), 162–178.
7. The MOSAIC program was initially piloted in New Brunswick Middle School, with funding from Rutgers. John Templeton Foundation funded the Jersey City program in six middle schools.
8. Maurice Elias, "Why All Schools Must Be Schools of Social-Emotional Competence and Character" (keynote address presented at the New Jersey School Board Association Conference, 2017), https://www.njsba.org/wp-content/uploads/2017/10/NJSBA-Conference-2017-Keynote-Elias.pdf.
9. SMART goals are specific, measurable, achievable, relevant, and time-bound.
10. MOSAIC Project, June 2017 Ambassador Showcase, https://www.youtube.com/channel/UClDCPKxBjK6e0BVi1I0_Baw/videos.
11. Data and information provided by principals was reported in interviews, October 16, 2017.

CHAPTER 11

1. Brandy P. Quinn, *International School of the Americas: Social emotional learning and social justice education for the 21st Century* (Stanford, CA: Stanford Center for Opportunity Policy in Education, 2015), 31.
2. Patricia A. Jennings and Mark T. Greenberg, "The Prosocial Classroom: Teacher Social and Emotional Competence in Relation to Student and Classroom Outcomes," *Review of Educational Research* 79, no. 1 (2009): 491–525.

3. *The Aspirations Framework*, Aspirations Briefs (Maine: The Quaglia Institute for School Voice and Aspirations, 2016), http://quagliainstitute.org/qisa/library/view.do?id=145
4. https://ggsc.berkeley.edu/who_we_serve/educators; http://crtwc.org.
5. *School Voice Report*, (Portland, ME: Quaglia Institute for School Voice and Aspirations, 2016).
6. Michael Fullan, *The Principal: Three Keys to Maximizing Impact* (Hoboken, NJ: Wiley, 2014).
7. Douglas B. Reeves, *Leading Change in Your School: How to Conquer Myths, Build Commitment, and Get Results* (Alexandria, VA: Association for Supervision and Curriculum Development, 2009).

ACKNOWLEDGMENTS

Perhaps the most meaningful aspect of writing this book, for me, has been the opportunity it provided to meet the people who are doing the most vital and inspiring work in schools today. Since I'm a few years out of the classroom, I started this project by asking teachers, principals, and other school staff to talk with me about their work with students and experiences in schools. I appreciate the discussions I had with Carlee Adamson, Charlene Brock, Vito Chiala, Ken Kleinman, Aurora Moore, Katie Remington, Lori Rhodes, and Sara Stillman, who were all candid and constructive about the realities of school life today and helped me see where my vision of purposeful schools did and did not fit with that reality. I also appreciate the equally candid and constructive feedback some of them provided on these chapters as they were in progress.

The heart of this book is the teachers, principals, school staff, and program teams who invited me into their classrooms and generously shared their work with me. John Bacon and the staff at eStem Charter School in Little Rock; the teachers and principals at Bronx Center for Science and Mathematics, Belmont Preparatory High School, Theatre Arts Production Company School, and Bronx High School for Law and Community Service in New York; PS 17, PS 24, and MS 40 in Jersey City; and in California, David Porter at James Lick High School, Christina Ballantyne at San Miguel Elementary School, Reem Bilbeisi at Averroes High School, Eve King at Academy San Francisco, and the teachers at Ventana School, all opened their classroom doors and invited me in, and proved to me that this work is necessary and can be done with great success. I'm also grateful to the staff in Cobb County School District in Georgia, Blue Valley School District in Kansas, and Hope School District in Arkansas, who took time to talk with me even though I wasn't able to visit their schools, and to Rhonda Hill at the Buck Institute for Education and Amy Sandoz at Summit Public Schools for sharing their work with me.

I am especially indebted to the leaders and teams of the purpose education programs that were profiled in this book. Patrick Cook-Deegan and Kelly Schmutte at Project Wayfinder; Kanya Balakrishna, Andrew Mangino, Jessica Koehler, Matt Skibinski, Kat Evasco, and Maria Tranquilli at The Future Project; Gerard Senehi at Open Futures Institute; Kris Fox at Quaglia Insitute; Danielle Hatchimonji, Arielle Linsky, Sam Nayman, Kellie McClain, and Karen Colello at MOSAIC; and Chad Williamson, Eric Wilson, and Chris Forster at Noble Impact, all took time to talk with me about their work, connected me with their partner schools, generously prepared school visits for me, and let me see with my own eyes the impact that their programs were having on students. In addition to my gratitude for the generosity they showed me, I appreciate the ongoing dialogue we share about the need for purpose in our schools and how it can be done.

To these dedicated educators and youth development professionals, I'm grateful for your contributions to this book and to my education, but I'm especially grateful that you are doing the essential work you do with students. So many of you told me that you do this work, despite the obstacles, because it's the right thing to do. Thank you.

My interest in purpose development was sparked when Bill Damon at the Stanford Center on Adolescence (COA) hired me to do research on the Youth Purpose Project. I thank Bill for giving me the opportunity to work on many purpose development projects since then, and for his mentorship along the way. At COA, I have been lucky to work with a wonderful team of researchers and support staff over the past fifteen years. Matt Andrews, Parissa Ballard, Robby Borah, Kendall Bronk, Matt Bundick, Anne Colby, Hyemin Han, Elissa Hirsh, Indra Liauw, Jenni Mariano, Seana Moran, Tenelle Porter, Brandy Quinn, Tim Reilly, Jim Sirianni, Lisa Staton, and David Yeager all made significant contributions to the COA research projects shared throughout this book, and each has helped me grow in my thinking about purpose and education. Each of our research projects benefits from the thoughtful participation of the children and teens we interview. Their words, such as those shared throughout this book, have shaped our understanding of how, when, and under what circumstances purpose emerges for different people. I am also grateful to the John Templeton Foundation and the Spencer Foundation for the generous funding that made this work possible.

This book has been playing in my mind for years, but it only became a reality because Nancy Walser at Harvard Education Press gave me the opportunity to write it. I'm grateful to Nancy for her encouragement and guiding insight. I also want to acknowledge and express my gratitude to Katharine Atwood, who created the visual representation of purpose development in chapter 4.

My deepest gratitude goes to my husband Shawn, daughter Kaia, and my mom and dad for encouraging, supporting, and tolerating my pursuit of purpose.

ABOUT THE AUTHOR

HEATHER MALIN is the director of research at the Stanford University Center on Adolescence, where she conducts research on diverse aspects of purpose development. She has published articles in academic journals on adolescent purpose development, youth civic engagement, artistic development, and purpose among young entrepreneurs. Her career in developmental psychology and education spans over twenty years, during which she taught elementary school, taught art to children through community-based programs, provided professional development programs for teachers, evaluated art education in Alameda County and academic programs provided by nonprofit organizations, and was an instructor for the Stanford Teacher Education Program (STEP), where she taught art education to preservice teachers and served as a new teacher mentor. She holds a PhD from Stanford Graduate School of Education and an MA from Teachers College Columbia University, and she received her BA from Sarah Lawrence College.

ABOUT THE AUTHOR

INDEX